Hockey
Is a
Battle

1.

Graphic Artists

2.

3.

4.

5.   6.

8.

7.

9.

10. Alexandra Studio (Turofsky)

11. Alexandra Studio (Turofsky)

13.

14.

15.

The Globe and Mail, Toronto

The Globe and Mail, Toronto

18.   Michael Burns

19.   Graphic Artists

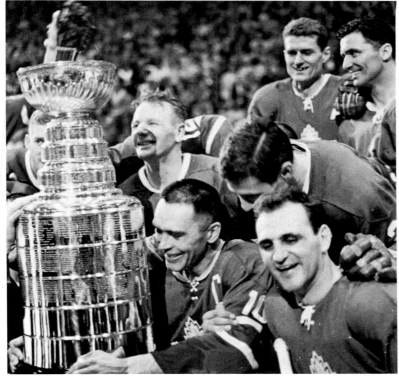

20.

Michael Burns

21.

Graphic Artists

22.

Michael Burns

23.

Graphic Artists

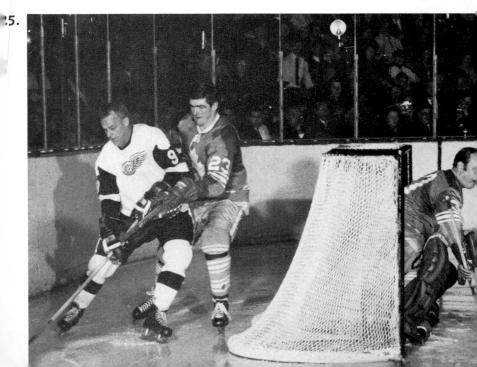

26.

Graphic Artists

List of Photographs

HOCKEY IS A BATTLE

Punch Imlach's own story
with Scott Young

Macmillan of Canada / Toronto / 1969

Printed in Canada by
McCorquodale & Blades Printers Ltd.
for The Macmillan Company of Canada Limited
70 Bond Street, Toronto

To Dodo, Marlene, Brent,
and all the other great hockey fans

Contents

Hockey
Is a
Battle

Life in the Pressure Cooker

One day in the summer of 1968 I received a letter from Stafford Smythe, who is a millionaire and at that time was president of Toronto Maple Leafs. It had been dispatched all the way from his office, two doors down the hall from mine in the executive part of Maple Leaf Gardens. One line in his letter said something to the effect that he, or he and the other directors, wanted to get a few things straightened out with me '. . . before you are hired for next year'.

I jumped fifteen feet when I read that bit. Then I sat down and wrote a reply to Stafford. I pointed out that my contract as general manager and coach did not expire until the end of the 1969-70 season. Therefore it was rather academic to be talking about hiring me for next year. I was already hired. But discussions have to get started one way or another – and maybe this was as good a way as any, in the circumstances, because it put my guard up a little.

A day or two later we met to talk it over. This wasn't exactly a friendly meeting. Stafford's father, Conn Smythe, had founded the Maple Leaf Hockey Club, had built Maple Leaf Gardens, and had managed the Maple Leafs to six Stanley Cups. I always had the feeling that Stafford wanted to match his father any way he could and a first step, in a hockey way, would be to run the hockey club himself so that when he spoke everybody jumped. But under the terms of my contract, I had operational control. I had it in Conn Smythe's last years at the Gardens and I had it after Stafford and two associates, Harold Ballard and John Bassett, bought out Mr. Smythe in 1961. The subject of the discussion was whether I should keep on coaching the Leafs. Now this was something that we must have discussed one way or another a hundred times in the previous ten years. When I took over the team from Bill Reay late in November 1958, it was supposed to be just for the time being. Even doing the job of Leafs' general manager was new to me then and I didn't really want the double load. But I'd taken on the coaching that year. The team had played for me. They played well enough to get to the Stanley Cup finals that season and the next, to finish second by a whisker the third year, and then to go on and win three Stanley Cups in a row – the only time this had ever been done in the National Hockey League with one guy acting as both manager and coach. We won another Stanley Cup three years after that string, too – a real upset in 1967 just when our team had seemed on the downgrade.

But I'd always said that I'd coach only as long as the team wanted me. I mean, as long as they'd play for me. They didn't have to like me. I'm not an easy guy to get along with, and I'm the first to admit it. Tim Horton, one of my best defencemen all the years I'd been with Leafs, once told a writer, 'He preaches a strange gospel, but he gets results.' I wouldn't argue with either of those propositions.

But determining whether a team still wants to play for me isn't simply a matter that if they lose a few games, I take it as being final and quit as coach. They lost ten in a row in the spring of 1967. I wound up in the hospital partly from worry. But we came back and upset Montreal to win the Stanley Cup. So you don't just have a bad week or two and throw everything up and say, well, that's it, I'm through as a coach. If people did things that way, there isn't a coach in hockey who'd last a season.

Anyway, I'd started to coach Leafs as well as manage them in 1958. Here it was ten years later, and Stafford and I had this talk. Didn't I think that the double job was too much work for one guy to handle, he asked.

'Maybe it is,' I said. 'But I'm not going to drop it now.' I don't remember whether I set out my reasons in so many words. One thing about working with a guy for ten years, there's a lot you don't have to put into words. But maybe I repeated it: that I had been out of the playoffs in the spring of 1968 for the first time since I started to coach. I had been a winner and I didn't want to leave coaching a loser. But it wasn't just a matter of stupid pride, or vanity, with me. Ever since the end of the previous season, and even before, I'd been working at deals and so on, trying to change the club. We'd finished fifth out of the six teams in the East division of the NHL and I'd been trying to root out what was wrong. I had added several rookies on defence and made other changes. I wanted to take these guys through the seventy-six games we would play in the two Canadian and ten United States cities that make up our League, and finish high enough to make the Stanley Cup playoffs, the World Series of hockey. I thought I could do it, but I knew it would be a tight fit. If they didn't make it, I wanted to be the guy responsible for that too. I didn't want to turn over a marginal hockey team to the guy I had in mind as coach; I'd rather turn over to him a team that had proved itself.

But hockey is a multi-million-dollar business as well as a sport. The business side has to count too. Stafford made the point that what I said was all very well, but suppose the club just went into a nose-dive at the start of the year and never stopped – what then? In other words, he wanted some sort of performance yardstick. I agreed he had a right to that, and I agreed that if we were more than two points out of a playoff position – fourth place – by December 1, I would make a statement that the pressure of the two jobs had become too much and I would hire a new coach. We decided also that the next meeting of Leafs' hockey committee (a group of directors with a special interest in the game, sometimes called the 'Silver Seven') would be informed of this arrangement.

Early in September, just before the team left for training camp in Peterborough, the hockey committee met in a private apartment not far from the Gardens. With the kind of attention we got from sports writers and broadcasters, especially in our home town, having meetings in out-of-the-way places sometimes helped.

Some of the hockey committee once played the game pretty well. Others aren't that expert but are successful and well-heeled businessmen. These meetings weren't really formal. Sometimes we had a drink or two, but minutes were kept and one of the standard procedures was that I reported on the state of the hockey team, answered any questions they had, and generally was what I was – the general manager reporting to the directors.

One of the original members of the hockey committee was John Bassett, president and publisher of the Toronto *Telegram* and also head of CFTO television. But some time during 1968 he resigned from the hockey committee, although remaining one of the three principal owners of the Gardens, along with Stafford and Harold Ballard. The other members were George Gardiner, a broker and thoroughbred breeder and owner; George Mara, an importer; Bill Hatch, an industrialist; Paul McNamara, a restaurateur; and Jack Amell, a diamond merchant.

So there they were, sitting around the apartment when I arrived. We went back over the same ground. I told them I wanted to coach the Leafs for the 1968-69 season, and why. But they were also told of my agreement with Stafford that if I didn't have the club within two points of fourth place, or better, by the first of December, I'd step down as coach and call in Johnny McLellan from our farm club in Tulsa. I'd have about seven weeks in October and November and then the whole matter would come up again. Meanwhile, this was all supposed to be strictly between us. No use upsetting the team by letting it get around that the coach had a deadline for producing, or else.

The season began. We had our good nights and our bad nights. About the middle of November, Paul Dulmage, one of the two reporters who cover the Leafs for the Toronto *Telegram,* called me on the phone. I had been warned by Harold Ballard, whose office as executive vice-president of the Gardens was between mine and Smythe's. 'He's looking for you, Punch,' he said. 'He tried to get me to comment on a report he had that you'd be relieved of the coaching if you aren't in a playoff spot by December 1.' Ballard knew what the real story was because he'd been at the meeting. He'd told Dulmage, 'No comment.' A little later that day Dulmage got to me.

The way he put it was: 'I hear that if you're not in the playoffs by December 1 you're out.'

'Is that so?' I said.

'That's what I hear.'

'Who told you?'

He said he couldn't reveal that. Of course, I wouldn't say anything one way or another. Lots of times sportswriters ask questions as if they know, when they're really just fishing. I sometimes thought the *Telegram* reporters were extra well-informed. Perhaps this was a natural suspicion on my part because for so many years their publisher had been on the hockey committee. But also Stafford had a way of letting secrets get out.

We sparred for a little while longer and then Dulmage said, 'Well, what do I do?'

I told him to print it or not print it, that was up to him. But if he couldn't quote whoever his informant was, he wasn't going to get corroboration from me.

When I hung up the phone I was mad. Our arrangement had been for secrecy until December 1 and then an announcement from me about a new coach. That put the decision in my hands, instead of making it look as if I was a dumb-bell who had to be relieved of a job on a deadline imposed by management. That might be a fine distinction, but those are the terms I'd agreed to.

I went down and had a pot of tea while I simmered down. But then on my way back to my office I dropped in at Leafs' dressing room. Ballard was there in the steam bath. He is a big, hearty guy and has been a good friend to me in many ways. I told him I was sore at the rumour getting out the way it had, sounding as if I wasn't good enough, that after four Stanley Cups and ten years I still had to prove myself a few weeks at a time.

'I'm going up to see Stafford right now. We're going to get this settled one way or the other. Now.'

Ballard said slowly, 'If I was you, I wouldn't do it.'

That kind of advice is like a red flag to me. Up I went and into Smythe's office. I told him about the phone call. 'What kind of (censored) is this?' I asked him. 'The deal was that if I wasn't contending for a playoff position by December 1, I'd bring in a coach from Tulsa. You'd better make up your mind right now – do you want me to be the coach, or don't you want me to be the coach? Because if this report is in the paper tomorrow, that's the decision you're going to have to make right then.'

'Is this an ultimatum?' Stafford asked.

'It's no ultimatum,' I said. 'It's just a statement of fact.'

'If I can get it squelched, will that solve the problem?'

I said, 'If it hadn't got to the papers in the first place, there'd be no problem. You do what you want, but this has to be settled today.'

He called me a little later and said he had talked to someone at the *Telegram* and had the story killed. That got us over that particular crisis, on the surface at least. But I kept getting reports back, second or third hand, that Stafford was telling his friends I wouldn't be coaching after December 1. One day about the middle of November, Dave Keon, a fine player who normally never says much, came to my office. Apparently there'd been some talk around the dressing room that bothered him; perhaps coming from a young player named Mike Walton, who was sort of on the family pipeline for news and views because he had married Stafford's niece. It bothered Davy enough that he asked me, 'Look, are you the boss of this club or aren't you? Or is somebody else the boss, like I keep hearing?'

I said, 'Davy, I run the club.' But I didn't give him any details of what had been going on, because I still didn't want the team knowing about this deadline idea.

We went on about our business for the rest of November, never far from the spot that would put us in the playoffs if we were still there when the season ended in March: the spot that would mean, December 1, whether I coached the Leafs any more.

On December 1 we played in New York. We lost to them 3–1. We were in the game all the way. They got their third goal late in the third period, leaving us tied for fourth place with Chicago. That meant I had lived up to my end of the deal and would stay on as coach for the rest of the season anyway.

We couldn't get out of New York that Sunday night because of bad flying weather. We were supposed to leave in the morning, early. But something else happened that night that had some bearing on what went on in the next day or so. The previous week I'd had another talk with George Armstrong, the Leaf captain who had retired before the season started. He was thirty-eight but I'd always thought that he could play one more year and help the club with his leadership as well as his play. I hadn't appointed another captain, always hoping he'd come back.

Some people thought I was nuts to hold the job open, but I never thought so. Conn Smythe once said that Armstrong was the best captain, as a captain, that the Leafs ever had. I didn't know other captains, but I do know that George Armstrong did more for the Maple Leafs than any other hockey player who played for me. He felt always that he had a responsibility to the game, that it gave him a lot, and he was always trying to put some of it back. That made him a wonderful guy for a coach to have around.

Anyway, we'd had this long talk about the Leafs a few days

before and I'd also told him that the owners were trying to get me to quit as coach.

'If I can do anything for you, I will,' he said.

'Well,' I told him, 'I think you can make the difference if you'll come back and play.'

He said he'd think it over.

So in New York I was in the hotel room some time after midnight when the phone rang. Army had been at home in Toronto listening to the radio broadcast of the game, and he'd been thinking a lot about my invitation for him to come back. He'd also talked to some of his friends to get their opinion. He'd called, he said, to tell me that if I really thought he could help the Leafs he would come back and give it a try. I was delighted. I told him to go to the Gardens that morning and be ready to practise with the Leafs. I'd see him when we got back, and we'd announce his return.

It must have been nearly three when I was finally ready to go to sleep. The team had been told they'd be called at six-thirty to fly home. Then I just got to sleep and the airline called me and said the flight would be later than that, not leaving until almost noon. So I called the players – one guy wasn't in, incidentally; he had some plausible story later that I didn't really believe, but stood for it anyway – and I told them the new departure time. It meant waking them up, but that seemed better than telling them at 6.30 to try to go back to sleep again. In the airport that morning I had a feeling that something was happening back in Toronto. I mentioned it to King Clancy, who in addition to helping me run the club as assistant manager and assistant coach was about the best friend I had. 'Something is up,' I said. It was just a hunch but it was right.

We got back to Toronto around one or so. I drove the two Toronto afternoon paper hockey writers, George Gross of the *Telegram* and Red Burnett of the *Star,* in from the airport. Told them I had a story for them. On the way I told them about Army coming back. They came to the Gardens with me to see Army for this story so they could phone their papers and get it in that afternoon. Well, they called their offices. It didn't seem their offices were interested in that story at all. Gross and Burnett came back from the phone and Burnett said, 'You're fired.'

'What do you mean?' I asked. He said that, as he understood it, Stafford had told the newspapers that under a deal we made in September, if I wasn't in a contending position for *first or second place* by December 1, I was out as coach. By then this report had been carried on the radio. A press conference had been called for later in the day. A meeting of the hockey committee was to be held late in the afternoon. Even then photographers and television crews were converging on the Gardens looking for me.

I went upstairs to my office. Gross and Burnett followed. I guess that was quite an afternoon around our offices for secretaries and other people who were more or less innocent bystanders. George Gross followed me right into my office and as I sat down he said, 'Well, *are* you fired?'

I said, 'For God's sake, why ask me? Go ask Ballard.'

He went next door and asked Ballard. Ballard said, 'No comment,' which really enraged Gross, with all this nonsense going on and his paper demanding a story. He told Ballard, 'If that's what you want, I'll quote you as saying, "No comment".'

Then Smythe came out of his office, two along from mine. Maybe the noise had smoked him out. He said to me, 'I want to see you.' I just pointed to Gross and said, 'He wants to see you first.' Stafford has a rasping voice, not unlike his father's. He growled at Gross, 'Can't we do any business around here without you newspapermen around?' Then he went back into his office and I followed him, along with Clancy and Ballard.

We sat and faced him. He brought up again that he wanted me to give up the coaching. I said I'd lived up to my commitments and that I thought this team was good enough to be in the playoffs. He said our deal had been that the team was to be in first or second place. I said, 'What kind of a jerk do you take me for, to make that kind of a commitment on a team that finished fifth last spring?' I told him he'd made a deal and he'd have to live up to it. Then I got out of there for a while. I knew this was a showdown. I had to know what I was going to do. About 4 p.m. I called a lawyer friend, Tom O'Neill. He played with me in Quebec City and he'd played for Leafs before that.

'I just want to know one thing,' I said. 'You know my contract. If they fire me as coach when the contract provides that I am hired as coach and general manager, do they have to pay me to the end of the contract?' That was a year and a half away, in the spring of 1970.

He said, 'If they don't have to pay you, I'll take down my shingle as a lawyer.'

That's all I wanted to know. I got Gross and Burnett and told them what had happened in Stafford's office and that as far as I was concerned they would have to honour my contract. It was all or nothing: both coach and general manager, or nothing at all. I was going to put that to them at the hockey committee meeting.

About 5.30 Clancy went to the apartment where the hockey committee was meeting, and told them I'd be along soon. I followed in about twenty minutes. Those present were Smythe, Ballard, George Mara, Bill Hatch, Jack Amell, and Paul McNamara. I told them I had fulfilled my end of the bargain we made in September, but if they want to get rid of me, 'Pay me my contract in full and I'll go.'

After a lot of discussion they decided, instead, to give me a vote of confidence! Meanwhile, there must have been a hundred guys waiting around in the Hot Stove Lounge for this press conference where my demise was supposed to be announced. Only now the script had been changed.

Stafford came down to the Lounge with other members of the committee. King, Windy, and I joined them. Paul McNamara, who seemed to have been one of my best supporters in any discussions they had, had written out a brief announcement saying that I had presented my recommendations as to the operation of the hockey club, and that they had been accepted, in full and unanimously.

In the papers the next day, Red Burnett and George Gross called it a power struggle that I had won. Well, I like winning but I don't mind saying the whole thing left a very bad taste in my mouth. All my life I have believed in honouring agreements. Suddenly I found Stafford trying to change the one we had made. That's when I got mad. But Stafford could have been acting on a genuine misunderstanding. He's the only one who knows everything about his side. And he did do his best to patch it up when he got to a face-to-face situation in the press conference.

'Bring those blankety-blanks in here,' he said, meaning the press. It didn't help any that some of the blankety-blanks heard him say it. But that was his last harsh statement, for that night anyway.

He admitted that he was a needler, and I quickly admitted that I was a stubborn bastard who rises to the needle. I sometimes wonder why I took him off the hook that way when he would have had to keep on explaining. But we tried to put the stress positively, that we were now going to go out and make the playoffs with me as coach and manager. All the television and radio stations and newspapers that had had me dead on the Monday covered my resurrection very well on Tuesday, but I'll just quote one as an example.

This was written by Gordon Walker in the *Globe and Mail*: 'Last night honey would have tasted sour compared to the sweet nectar that poured forth at a press conference . . . in the Hot Stove Lounge.

'With extremely clever verbal stick-handling Smythe dazzled the assemblage. . . . Punch Imlach's job is not in jeopardy, now, won't be in jeopardy next year and may never be in jeopardy. That was the message. . . .'

The next day when I came down to the Gardens for the practice I had a funny feeling about going into the dressing room. It was all out in the open now – that the club had wanted to fire me as coach, the December 1 deadline, all my troubles. I was nervous for the first time in years. I kept trying to think what the players would say, and what I would say back. I actually didn't want to go in.

The players were dressing, some standing, some sitting. They all read the papers and watch television and listen to radios. They looked at me. Then one of them said, half-grinning, 'I hear you had a little fight on your hands last night, eh, coach?' And things like that, kidding. And Keon looked up from where he was, with quite a smile. 'Well, I asked you who was the boss,' he said. 'But you didn't have to go to all that trouble to prove it.'

It was nearly three months before the next time my job was in jeopardy. But I went into this one incident in detail for a specific reason. The life of a coach is a battle. He always fights the opposition. Some years he also has to fight his own players and some years he has to fight his owners. Is there anybody I've missed? Oh, yeah – Alan Eagleson, the players' lawyer. But you get the idea. My life is not exactly a peaceful one. And it hasn't been for as long as I've been in hockey.

2

A Big Man and a Skinny Kid

In my years with the Toronto Maple Leafs, that big building at the corner of Church and Carlton was sort of a second home to me. I've been there when the cheering was so loud that a guy literally couldn't hear his own voice down around our bench. 'Go Leafs Go' would be rolling down from the top of the greys, the highest and cheapest seats, as if it could go on forever. Those were the heights, always when I was winning.

I've been in the depths there too; times when I was sick or disgusted or frustrated. I've had the fights with the owners, not all of them publicized. Serious disagreements with individual players – sometimes my fault and sometimes theirs, or sometimes both. Worry over slumps. Nights when we'd be playing with guys with broken wrists or ribs and I had to keep the dressing room door locked an extra long time after a game to keep press people from finding out about the injuries. There's no use letting the other guys know who to hit first, and where. You know a guy has a broken wrist, you hammer him there a few times and you don't have much trouble with him for the rest of the night. It's nothing personal. I'd do it myself. So I'd keep the door locked and nobody would find out. But some of the reporters might get a little, let us say, impatient, waiting outside while we got bandages off, or covered, or anyway not too visible.

11

In that building, Maple Leaf Gardens, I've fired people, and fined people, and given bonuses, and torn up contracts to give a guy a new one when he was playing so well he deserved it. I've also opened a few letters from League headquarters telling me I'd be fined – like when I would wax poetic about some referee in a way the League president didn't like much. In Maple Leaf Gardens I've been through just about everything that can happen to a man in big-time professional hockey, including, eventually, being fired.

In all that time, millions of words were written criticizing or praising me for doing this or that, telling people that I'm a great coach or that I'm a lousy coach. The fact that I sometimes use profanity got a lot more mileage in the press than the fact that I don't use profanity when women or kids are around. I've sometimes responded pretty hotly to criticism, but sometimes I've just sat and taken it – like times when some of those open-line radio shows would spend a day devoted to the question: 'Should Imlach be fired?' But one thing that isn't on the record to any great extent is this: Many of my attitudes towards coaching, towards hockey, and towards life were learned one way or another right in that rink in the first place, when I was a kid.

In the years I worked there I'd walk in, sometimes up or sometimes down, depending on the standings and how we'd been going lately. But at least the doormen knew me. I'll never forget the first time I walked in there. In February of 1935 I was a sixteen-year-old kid and I weighed 120 pounds. I remember walking through those big front doors that first morning with my equipment in a brown duffel bag slung over my shoulder, dangling from my stick. The cold winter morning behind me outside was black dark without even a hint of light in the east. There was a distant clank and rattle. That was the old wooden streetcar I'd just got off. After the stop, it kept going south down Church Street, downtown. I had caught the first one out of the barns that morning, the Bloor car at Danforth and Coxwell. Then I'd transferred to the one going south on Church. As I came into the Gardens, I looked up at the clock that's still there near the front door. It was 5.25 a.m. and I was more excited than I'd ever been in my life.

What led up to that morning was that I'd been playing minor hockey around Toronto while I went to high school at Riverdale Collegiate. A fellow named Red Hughes had seen me play. He recommended me for a tryout with Ed Wildey's Young Rangers, a junior team. In fact, Red Hughes did better than recommend – he arranged for me to go down to the Gardens and have a practice with the Young Rangers. I'll never forget him coming around to the house and telling me. He could have phoned, but maybe he wanted to see my face when I got the news. 'You be there tomorrow morning no later than 5.30,' he said.

The excitement around our house that night was something. The Scottish burrs of my Dad and Mother got even more pronounced when they were excited and that was one of those nights. They'd been married in Scotland and had come to Canada before the First World War, but there was still no mistaking where they were from. I was born in 1918 after my dad, Private George Alexander Imlach, got home wounded from the war. He'd been in the First Division with the famous Toronto regiment, the 48th Highlanders. I was the only child, so maybe that made the excitement more intense. But anyway here you have this 200-pound Scot and his tiny wife (my mother's name was Isabelle) trying to get their only son to get to bed so he'd be rested for this big deal. As if I could sleep! With all the things that go on in the world today some people might not believe that a kid can get so excited over something like a game. You just have to realize that then this was one of the biggest things that could happen in a kid's life. To play in Maple Leaf Gardens! Even to get a chance to practise in Maple Leaf Gardens! Even to skate there! Maybe at the time it was a much greater thrill than it is now, I don't know. The Gardens had only been open for about four years then, but every kid in Canada knew about Charlie Conacher and Busher Jackson and Joe Primeau – King Clancy, Red Horner, all the Leafs of those days. I knew that to be on time I had to catch that streetcar at 5 a.m. I couldn't think of anything else all night. I finally got up about 4. My mother got up with me. And my dad. He limped, partly from his war disability and partly from an accident that had crippled one leg. My dad worked for the Toronto Transit Commission as a property inspector, but his real love was sport, especially soccer, which he'd played before the 1914-18 war. The soccer club he managed, Ulster United, had won the Canadian championship, so we were a family that had sport bred right into it, you might say.

Anyway, my mother made me a good breakfast. I ate it and I was out there in the dark shivering at the car stop and looking up the tracks and wondering where the heck that streetcar was, probably even before the conductor cranked her up. I got to know those first cars out of the barns pretty well in the next few years. A lot of mornings they'd be awfully cold. We did have some new streetcars around Toronto then, but not on that run. The cars I took were high and sort of square looking, the whole body built of wood. You got in the front and dropped a ticket in the box, then headed back towards the stove. I think they used coal or coke in the stove. The conductor would light up just before he left the barns, but that wasn't soon enough to do us any good. We could flap our arms and shiver and that's about all. Not many other people were on it at that time of morning. The ones that were there would look at me with my hockey stuff as if I was nuts or something.

When I came into the Gardens that first morning, I didn't even know where to go. Another kid came by and I followed him. The Young Rangers' dressing room in those days was right where the Gardens directors' room is today, on the west side of the rink. Now it's all quietly lighted and full of deep chairs. You can get a drink or watch colour television. But in those days it was strictly on the other side of the tracks. I mean, the Leafs and their own junior club, the Marlboros, were on the other side. Among the juniors, Marlies and West Toronto had the edge: a little money, sticks, tape, and equipment all first class. Over on our side were guys like myself who were supposed to be not really bad, but just good enough for the Young Rangers, if you get what I mean.

So I went around there. That was the first time I met Ed Wildey. He was a famous man in Toronto sport then; an old boxer, big, muscular, honest, and very tough. He didn't say two or three words to me, just pointed to the bench where I was to change. I sat down and got dressed and out on the ice and into the workout. I was a centre. And naturally I went too hard out there, trying to do too much, trying to prove myself to Ed Wildey all in the first fifteen minutes. He was standing by the boards watching. And, well — suddenly I set a world record getting to the side boards, well away from him, and threw my head over. Up came my breakfast. I learned one lesson that first morning — not to eat before I went to practice. From then on I ate only after I'd finished, and before I went to school. But that was the first time. And throwing up or not, in all my life up to that time the greatest thing that had happened to me was getting the chance to practise in Maple Leaf Gardens.

I was the same as now in one thing I guess — with all my awe, I never doubted for a minute that I was going to make it. I heard later that Ed Wildey had plenty of doubt. In fact he told a guy that I wasn't going to make it. They had a bit of an argument as to whether I should be allowed to come back or not. But I didn't know that at the time. I was there every morning. Sometimes I'd be a little late getting up and I'd have to hitch a ride on one of the horse-drawn milk wagons that hit the streets early in those days. But I always made it. After the first time I knew exactly what I had to do and it was straight routine. At 5.25 there'd be the clock looking me in the face. At 5.35 I'd be on the ice. I'd be there until Bill James, the icemaker in those days, kicked us off. Sometimes I'd be there until eight o'clock. Then I'd catch another streetcar and go straight to school. With no breakfast. My mother packed me big lunches. I'd eat some on the way from the practice.

I never played a game that first winter. I just practised with the Young Rangers. I'd been playing midget, and under the rules of that time Wildey couldn't have played me even if he'd wanted to. I don't think he was really overpowered by the prospect anyway. I had this little bit of a, you might say, strike on me because I was so skinny and small.

I practised with them for about two months, every morning, never really feeling I belonged. But finally it just seemed that one practice made the difference. Suddenly the other guys couldn't get to me. I've seen this happen to other fellows too. Boom, all of a sudden they've arrived. It just happens from one practice to another. I guess if you go often enough and keep working at it, as we were doing with the Young Rangers, something has to give, somewhere down the line.

Wildey saw it, right away, when I did suddenly become good enough to play on his team. I mentioned he was strong. Massive in the shoulders. And I was so puny – shoulders and everywhere else. One of the first things he did with me after he'd made up his mind was to come out to our house and give me a pair of dumb-bells. Little dumb-bells.

'Whirl these a little bit,' he said. 'It'll make you a little bit handier. Try to build yourself up a little.'

That was one of his favourite expressions – to do this or that, because it would make you 'a little handier'.

He was an amazing man. A lot of him rubbed off on me in the three years that I played junior hockey for him. A lot of things that

I learned from him, his principles, I still believe in. Sometimes now I think time is passing me by, and that the things he taught me – like the fact that you have to work hard for everything you get – some people just don't believe in any more. This is the attitude I sometimes get thrown at me today – 'Why work so hard? Why the hell should I work like that?'

Ed Wildey's attitude was that if you don't work, you don't accomplish. The attitude that some people have today is different.

Okay, some do accomplish, all right, without working. But that's natural enough. Most of them are in the same class. If nobody works, somebody still has to win, right? But if other things are equal (or even sometimes less than equal) the guy who works, or the team that works, is *most likely* going to win. That's what Ed Wildey believed, and that's what I believe and always will.

With him, it was truly a labour of love. He had some kind of a job but he used to get up every morning all winter long and go down to that rink. He must have been about sixty when I first met him. He had no car. Somebody with a car would have to go and pick him up and bring him down. There was no money at all in it for him or anyone else. I was lucky if I got two new sticks a year. He would take the broken ones and save the tape off them, to tape up some not so badly broken – and that's sometimes what we used. Compared to the equipment Marlboros or West Torontos had over on the other side of the Gardens, the good side of the tracks, what we got was just tragic.

But this was his life, you might say. And ours. He wanted to do it and so did we. And the guys he got were not the ones with a lot of money themselves, or anything like that. We were always the gashouse gang types, the ones who wouldn't have got a chance at all if it wasn't for this one guy. There is really nothing I can say about Ed Wildey that is good enough for him.

Incidentally, he never got on the ice with us at any time. He would just tell us how he wanted us to play the game, and his ideas are just as good today as they were then. It was, 'Move the puck – click, click, click.' That deal. 'Get that puck from there to there,' he'd say, pointing, 'and see that it gets in the net.' Naturally, he wanted you to skate a lot, use the ice every minute you could.

And he was tough, a really tough man. He had a lot of equipment that went with his boxing background. For instance, we always had a fast bag in our dressing room – that's the little one, like a ball, that hangs from the ceiling. We also had a big bag, the heavy one that boxers use in the gym. If you were hanging around doing nothing you'd take the gloves and hit the bag for two or three minutes. It was there, and on the fast bag especially you came to enjoy the timing. I got so I could just about make the thing talk. I'd have been tempted to put one in the Leafs' dressing room but I knew there'd be a lot of commotion about it: 'Leafs practising to be fighters instead of hockey players' – all that bullfeathers. What the fast bag does besides help timing is give a guy a certain amount of confidence in himself. And it certainly gives you an idea how to hit – whack it, hit your elbow on it, play it off the back of your hand, all very fast. 'It gets you handy,' Ed used to say. 'Everything you do like that gets you a little more handy.'

Sometimes we'd put on the gloves and go two or three rounds in the dressing room. We couldn't hit in the face, just in the body. Half the time a guy would get a good one in the solar plexus and down he'd go. Ed would pick him up. And he'd talk to us. I remember lots of times what he said about hitting people on the ice – not with the fists, I mean body checking. He'd say, 'Hit 'em good, but don't forget to help him up and tell him you're sorry. And the next time he comes down, knock him down again.' I can remember him saying that as if it were yesterday.

Of course, these are things I feel the same way about myself. I don't particularly say to help the other guy up and say you're sorry, though. With me it's more like just look at him and say, 'Too bad, and if you get up I'll knock you down again.' I've maybe gone a step or two further than Ed Wildey in this.

And a lot of this wasn't only in the winter. In the summer when the Gardens was open we'd often come down after school or after work, half a dozen of us, maybe ten. I'd come down when I wasn't playing soccer or baseball. Ed would be there two or three times a week. It was something like an athletic club. We'd go a few rounds with the bag. We'd walk around the floor in walking races. Then we'd get a puck and our sticks out on the floor. We'd have the puck all shined up with wax so it would come off the floor pretty well and we would shoot it off towards the net. And, of course, these are the things that make a guy a little handier, make his reflexes a little better and his conditioning a little better because he is working at it. You shoot the puck all the time, it makes you handier around the net. As simple as that.

One way or another, I would spend two or three hours three times a week in summer working basically on things that would help me in hockey. When the Gardens was closed up, we'd go out to Ed's place in the west end. In the garage he had a fast bag and a big bag, the same sort of thing. And his wife was always giving us something to eat, or whatever.

I think all this had a lot to do with my development, physically and otherwise, as I got good enough to play. We got a physical conditioning, and a mental outlook that went with it. Because of Ed Wildey I saw a lot of physical training equipment for the first time. My parents couldn't afford things like that. Which reminds me of the first pair of new skates I'd ever owned, when I was a kid of eight or so. The day they were delivered from Eaton's I put them right on and went down to the rink in a park near our place. I went down around four o'clock and stayed until, I guess, almost eight. When I came home, were my feet ever sore! So I'm sitting there in the kitchen rubbing my feet and looking at the skates — and I find they are both for the left foot! They'd made a mistake in packaging. Some other person had two for the right foot. We both complained to Eaton's and they remedied the situation. I was against sending them back. I was afraid they'd never be replaced. I don't know whether that was a tipoff to me later in life, but anyway the first skates I had were for two left feet and I hated to let them go, I was just so happy to have the darn skates.

It was sometime after that first few months with Ed Wildey that I opted for hockey over the other sports I played. I didn't seem to get a chance to put on any weight because I was always playing some kind of sports: baseball, soccer, lacrosse, whatever — I just kept on playing all the time. There was no such thing as a season when there wasn't a sport going on.

That first summer after coming to Young Rangers I was playing soccer. I can remember it was during a real heat wave. The temperature was about a hundred. I knew I had to put on weight to play hockey and here I was going to play soccer in that kind of heat — which would have taken it off rather than put it on. It was a hard decision because I was on a good soccer team, the best team in its class in Ontario. We had won the provincial championship. But I went to the manager and told him, 'I gotta put on weight to play hockey, so I'm pulling out, calling it a day.'

When I told my father he was a little disappointed, because of his own connection with Ulster United. But he only said, 'Hockey must look pretty good to you to give up soccer.'

From then on I devoted all the time I had to hockey. Maybe it is also one of the reasons why I have some attitudes I have today. I know what I had to give up, and how much I had to work, to try to be a better hockey player. The most important thing is that it seemed to work. I started putting on a little weight. Not much, but I did get up to about 135 by the time I had finished my three years of junior hockey. And I was scoring, usually one of the top scorers on the team. Billy Taylor from Oshawa was the ace junior around here at the time I was playing, in the late thirties. We ran up against him in the playoffs in my final junior year. Before that, near the end of the season, I'd got a bad knee. I was also playing for the Dominion Bank in a bank league, and I hurt it badly on a Friday night. We had a junior game against St. Michael's on the Tuesday and I couldn't even get out of bed over that weekend. I finally got out of bed on the Tuesday and went down to the Gardens. This junior double-header was the last one of the season, and then we would open the playoffs against Oshawa on the Saturday.

When I got to the rink, I remember, the University of Toronto had the dressing room next to us. Ed Wildey went in and came back with a doctor who I think was one of the head guys in medicine at the University.

'Take a look at this knee,' I said.

He gets the knee in his hands, and I'll always remember how he did it – held it with one hand and gave it a push with the other, putting pressure on the inside of the knee. Holy cripes, I nearly went straight out through the roof. I guess the ligaments on the inside of the knee were gone.

So I sit there as pale as a ghost, almost sick, looking at the knee, with the others grouped around.

'Well, can he play?' Ed Wildey asked the doctor.

The doctor said, 'Oh, he might be able to if we put a little plaster around it.'

I'll never forget this. He took some adhesive plaster about an inch wide and put two strips up the inside of my leg and a couple around the calf to hold the first two in place. That was it. He said, 'Go ahead.'

I didn't know any different – I was only a kid. I thought, well, he's the best doctor there is, he must know. So out I go. Well, geez, every time I fell down I couldn't get up, it was so sore. I just couldn't play that night.

Later in the week there was the problem of trying to get me ready for Saturday, the opening of the playoffs against Oshawa and Billy Taylor. There was this guy around Toronto then, a famous trainer, old Archie Campbell, and they took me to him. He was sort of assistant trainer at the Gardens at that time, but he had all of his equipment down at his home in the Boulton-Queen district. He was all crippled up with arthritis or something, and was an extremely fine person. (I didn't know it at the time, but some of Archie's best friends were people named Simons, with a good-looking daughter named Dorothy who later became my wife.) He worked on my knee for a couple of days, putting heat on it. He said, 'Come down here before the game and I'll put a walking cast on it.' Of course, I was young. I mean, it could have meant ligaments ripped away from the bone, but what did I know about things like that? So he put this little cast on my knee and I went out and played. We beat them 7–6. I got four goals, including the winner in a solo rush in the last thirty seconds of play. Billy Taylor got one. Then we went out to Oshawa for the rest of the series and they beat us, not by much, in the next two games, and went on to win the Memorial Cup, the Canadian junior championship.

To go back a little. I mentioned the bank league, where I got that knee hurt in the first place. That was another case where Ed Wildey had an effect on my life. One day the previous fall he'd said, 'Would you like to work in a bank?' It seems he'd been asked to run a team for Dominion Bank. He needed players – but the great thing was that he could line up some jobs for us.

I mentioned it to my dad. He said, 'The bank will do you a lot of good.' So I said okay. Ed Wildey sent me down to see the right guy at the bank and they hired me as a junior, at $400 a year, less than eight bucks a week. But of course the story was the same at the bank as everywhere else in 1938. You weren't getting much but you were pointed at something, you were learning. I wasn't getting a nickel from junior hockey; Ed Wildey didn't have it to give. But this was a way he could steer me towards a little money. And what the heck, eight bucks a week, that was a big deal at that time.

So I started working for the Dominion Bank, Queen and Broadview branch. And I really liked banking. It just seemed to be something I could do. I had my high school and a business course at Eastern Commerce; I hadn't been any great shakes, but it did help some at the bank. And in these two ways Ed Wildey affected my life: he gave me the hockey background that I needed, and he got me started in the bank. And I was pretty good at the bank. I was given three raises, I think, in the first year and a half. I sometimes think if the money had been right, and a few other things, I would still be with the bank. After the war, when I went to Quebec to play hockey, I needed a job. Because of my banking experience I got into the accounting department at Anglo-Canadian Pulp and Paper, the company that was supporting the hockey team, the Quebec Aces. I did all right there too. Anyway, I'm still technically on leave of absence from their accounting department, although somehow it looks more and more as if I'm not going to go back.

That year we got knocked out by Oshawa was my last season of junior hockey. My knee got a little better and I started right in playing with Toronto Goodyears, a senior team.

I'd always been just plain George Imlach up until then. But there was this game in Windsor. I was going along the boards and this fellow took me into the boards hard and gave me the elbow and foot thing at the same time. Up I went in the air and down I came and hit my head on the ice. I was knocked cold. When I came to, I guess the only thing I knew was that someone had done this to me, so I came up swinging. And who was I swinging at but Bill Smith, our trainer.

They got me quieted down and into the dressing room. I don't remember a thing from then on, really, but other people told me what happened later. The manager of the team said, 'Here, take this – this will fix you up.' I didn't know what the heck it was at the time, but it was a good shot of Scotch. I'd never had a drink of any kind until then. Apparently this shot sort of fixed me up. Anyway, I'm told I got up and went back out on the ice.

They asked me on the bench, 'Are you all right?' I said, 'Sure, I'm all right.' I'd do anything to play hockey at that time. I do recall, hazily, that I couldn't see the end of the rink. I realize now that I had a concussion and shouldn't have been anywhere near the ice right then. But they didn't know that my vision was gone and I wasn't telling them. We were in the third period and I went around out there hardly knowing where I was, although when anybody got close enough to me I could see him all right.

After the game, I was still in that state. They told me later that we got back to the hotel and some of the older guys said, 'Come on, we're going over to Detroit.' So I went along with them and we wound up in a place called the Cork Town Tavern. I didn't know whether I was in Detroit or on the moon. We had some pretty good beer drinkers on our team and I was sitting with them. And what happened to bring me out of it I don't think ever has been told before. I was sitting at a table right beside the stage. There was a couple up there dancing pretty close together. I guess the guy had had too much to drink. Anyway, he was holding her so close he lost his balance and fell down right on top of our table.

Bingo, it was the crash, or something – suddenly I knew what was going on. I didn't remember anything about how we got there, or what had happened since I got hit, but suddenly I remembered some of it and asked questions to fill in the rest. Bunny Morganson wrote it up in the Toronto *Telegram*, saying I had been punch drunk. That stuck. Then Bunny kept on referring to me as 'Punchy Imlach' in the paper until some kindly old typesetter got fed up with putting the last letter on and just left it at 'Punch', which it has been ever since.

I guess there are one or two other things from those days that had some bearing on the direction I took. One is that after the first full year I played for Goodyears, a fellow came over here from Glasgow. There was a league in Scotland then. He was looking for players and got in touch with me. He was staying at the Westminster Hotel in Toronto. I went down there and talked to him around the first of August. He said if I'd come with their club they would put me through Glasgow University in a course that would help with what I was already doing, banking.

I said, 'That sounds pretty good – I'll take it.' But before I could get over there the war started.

The next year, that's 1939-40, I played with Goodyears again. After that season, Goodyears had their name changed to Toronto Marlboros. I was still with the bank, making about sixteen dollars a week by then, and I was getting offers to play senior hockey from all over Canada. One of them was from Jimmy McCaffrey in Ottawa. With Goodyears I'd got $180 the first season and $150

he second. It was $50 when I signed, $50 at Christmas, and a
plit at the end – one year $80 and the other $50. McCaffrey said
hey were paying $60, $70, $80 a week.

Naturally, it was attractive. I told him I was working in the
ank and didn't want to leave my job but I'd ask the bank to
ransfer me to Ottawa. So I went down to head office and saw the
uy. I told him I liked the bank and wanted to stay, but could he
ransfer me to Ottawa so I could play hockey there? He said they
ould, and might even transfer me to Montreal later if I wanted
hat too. Players were getting lots of dough in both Ottawa and
Montreal, more than in Toronto.

Notice of my transfer came through to the bank okay. I had
otified McCaffrey when I would be arriving in Ottawa. But one
ittle thing I hadn't reckoned on was how much Marlboros wanted
o keep me. I had been so sure of the process – that if I was trans-
erred by my employer, the hockey club couldn't refuse my release
- that I hardly had bothered with Marlboros. But suddenly I was
otified by the bank that my transfer had been revoked. They didn't
ive me any reason at all. It looked as if a little pressure had been
pplied. It was a coincidence, maybe, but the president of the bank
nd the president of the Goodyears hockey club were the same
erson. He wasn't directly connected with the club since it had
hanged over to being Marlboros, but the link was there, all right.

When I found out that my transfer wasn't going through after
ll, I went home and talked to my father. All he said was, 'If you
till want to go and play hockey in Ottawa, just go to the bank and
ell them you're finished.'

I said, 'You're not supposed to just quit. You're supposed to give
otice.'

He said, 'They didn't give you any notice about calling off your
ransfer, did they? Or any reason? You give them the same treat-
nent. You go in there tomorrow morning and tell them that's the
ast time you're coming in, and why. If they don't want to pay you,
on't bother with them.'

I walked down and told the bank manager that if that was the
vay they wanted to operate, I quit. And I walked out.

I was still intending to go to Ottawa. Harold Ballard was on the
xecutive of the Marlboros then and Frank Selke, Sr., was working
t the Gardens under Conn Smythe. When I mentioned release to
allard, he said that I should go and see Mr. Selke. I did. He told me

that they weren't going to give me any release to play in Ottawa anywhere else. Finally he said to me, 'How much were they goir to pay you in Ottawa?'

I said, 'Sixteen hundred dollars.'

He said, 'We'll give you that, if you'll stay.'

I looked at him and thought, heck, if you're going to pay me tl same money I might as well stay. Without the bank job, there ju didn't seem any sense in me leaving home. So I took it.

Pressure of this kind is, of course, something that still goes c in sports. Nothing has changed. But sometimes I think everythir happens for the best. Heck, if I'd gone to Ottawa then I might sti be there, doing some kind of a job or other − and not winning ar Stanley Cups from Ottawa, you can be darn sure of that.

There is still a little more to that story, however. I got hurt ear in the season, a bad knee again, a heck of a bad knee. When I w ready to play they were crabbing about me being hurt, and I ha to do another three or four weeks training to get in shape. I nev really started playing until the season was more than half over. got quite a few goals in the playoffs but eventually we got knocke out and that was that.

Naturally I came up at the end of the year wanting my money.

And Frank Selke said, 'You didn't play for us.' Meaning, n enough to get the money we'd agreed on. He offered me a litt less. I argued, but I was still just a kid, and finally took it. I kno now that he was just doing his job, working for the Garden getting a guy as cheap as he could.

He didn't say, 'You have to take it.' He offered me the settl ment and I was stupid enough to take it.

But I have to admit that that incident always was tucked in tl back of my mind any time I had anything to do with Frank Selk After the war, when I was playing and coaching in Quebec Cit he was running Montreal Canadiens. Quebec played in the san league with his Montreal senior club, the Royals. I used to cau him plenty of trouble both on the ice and in the committee room

'Why should we fight?' he would say. 'Here we are two fellov from Ontario, in Quebec − we should be friends.' But I fougl anyway, and he was a hard guy to fight, having the big team ar the Montreal Forum behind him.

As I say, I understand what he was doing. But what happene to me that winter is one of the reasons that I am very emphat about honouring contracts. I expect that people I have contracts with will live up to them and I expect to live up to my end of the bargain. I think this way because of what happened to me that time.

Talking of Quebec, every time I came back from there I used to go to see Ed Wildey. I'd go to say hello to him and his wife and ask him who was a good hockey player around here that I might grab for Quebec.

One of the times I was at his place I said, 'Do you still have that stuff out in the back?'

By then he was nearly eighty years old.

'Yeah,' he said. 'Come on out.'

He didn't have the little fast bag there any more but he still had the big one. He pulled out some gloves and put them on, and hauled off and hit that heavy bag and drove it back a yard. Imagine, eighty years old and he could still drive that heavy bag back a good way. He was marvellous.

'I never backed away.'

One day in the autumn of 1941 a car drew up in front of our house out on Coxwell Avenue and the horn honked. The driver was a big guy named Lex Cook. He was coaching a senior team in Cornwall that winter and wanted me. He'd got my transfer from Marlboros without any trouble. Maybe Selke was a little browned off with me over the money matter of the previous season, or maybe he figured with my bum knee I wasn't much use to him anyway. Whatever it was, I'd agreed to go to Cornwall and play hockey but I wasn't all that enthusiastic. If Lex hadn't come around and picked me up I don't think I would have gone. He had a couple of other hockey players with him in the car and away we went, east to Cornwall, near the Quebec border. I was going to spend most of the next two years around Cornwall, but I didn't know it then.

That winter, the winter of Pearl Harbor and the beginning of the Pacific war, recruiting had been stepped up for the Canadian armed forces. I'd been thinking about it a lot. Everybody was. Some of our airmen were in action over Britain and Europe. Our Navy was on convoy duty in the North Atlantic. The Army hadn't seen much action yet, but was building up strength both at home and in England. That winter all the services had good hockey teams. The Air Force won the Allan Cup, with the whole Kraut

26

line from Boston playing for them – Milt Schmidt, Porky Dumart, and Bobby Bauer. The Army training base at Cornwall had a lot of good hockey players and made a deal with Lex Cook, as a civilian, to run an Army team out of Cornwall the following winter. Army training and discipline came first, of course, but like any coach Lex Cook wanted the best he could get. If he had to persuade them into the Army to get them, that was all right with him. He approached a lot of players like me who he knew would be enlisting in one of the services soon. He'd say, 'What the hell? If you're going to join up, join the Army.' I thought, what the heck, I'm going in anyway. So in April of 1942 I joined up. At Cornwall that spring, when I was getting my rifle, the guy who gave it to me said, 'Well, this isn't a hockey stick you've got there now. This is a rifle and you're going to have to learn how to use it.'

Of course, we started to train right away. Some of us became officers and some didn't, but there were a lot of guys I met then who are my friends today, in hockey and outside it. Jack Riley was there, in the same hut with me. Baz Bastien. Bud Poile. Frankie Mario. Jack Shewchuk. Bobby Laurent. Jimmy Conacher was in C Company. Jack Church was in C Company. Tommy Ivan was in well ahead of me. All of them were to become good pro players or executives later. Sometimes both. And there were a lot of others.

All the hockey players were mixed in with different platoons and different companies, yet we pretty well knew that, barring some big action overseas that would call for more men to be shipped over East, we'd be in Cornwall that next winter playing hockey as well as being trained for action when it did come. After a few months I guess they thought I showed leadership qualities, which pleased me, and I got my commission as a provisional second lieutenant, on December 8, 1942. All along I took every course I could, and later instructed on six-pounders, gas, and about five or six other things. I also tried to win every competition or exercise that pitted one platoon or company against another.

I remember once, I guess in 1943, I had my platoon out for what was supposed to be a three-mile walk. Well, I decided we'd run it, with full pack. I had a big Ottawa cop, I forget his name, as my marker. I'll always remember we were puffing along this street under full pack when all of a sudden he turned to me and said, Jesus Christ! *We* don't have to get in shape for hockey!' I looked right back at him. He'd read my mind but I wasn't going to let on.

'Lookit,' I said. 'I don't want any Germans catching up to you whe
you're running, either way.'

You can tell a lot about people the way they react in competitior
any competition. I remember one time Jack Riley – he's the guy wh
later helped put the Pittsburgh franchise together in the expande
NHL – anyway, Jack Riley got beaten in some kind of platoo
competition. He almost had it won but he made some mistake, an
just missed by a whisker. I've never seen him so mad. He was goin
to tear the mess apart that night just because he blew a little thin
like a platoon competition. I know how he felt because I feel th
same way myself when I lose. Later, when he was running th
Leafs' Rochester farm team and I was in Toronto, I never had an
doubts about Riley. I knew he wouldn't be quitting any job befor
it was done. I'd seen him lose and I knew how hard he took i
That's something valuable to know about a guy.

Anyway, I was no hero in the Army. I did everything they aske
me to do and tried to do it better than anyone else, but they seeme
to think I fitted best staying right where I was, so I never did g
overseas. In January of 1943 I got married. Back when I was wit
the Goodyears sometimes I used to skate at the Royal Rink o
Broadview. When I was there I started skating quite a lot with
good-looking girl named Dorothy Simons. She was pretty good
sports herself, track and field and softball, and she was a hocke
fan. At first she didn't believe that I was a hockey player. I was sti
pretty small in those days, and I'd started to lose my hair. Bu
anyway we went around together more and more, and when w
got married I got, as well as a good wife, the most loyal fan an
supporter a man ever had. People learned pretty early not to criticiz
Imlach out loud while they were sitting near her, and she hasn
changed a bit.

In the Army at Cornwall I took every course I could, got t
know the orderly room inside out, heard punishment cases for
while when the major was sick, and played hockey. I played tw
years, then broke my wrist badly in the first game of the thir
season, against the Provost Corps in Camp Borden. I had it in a cas
and under therapy for about a year. That made me a coach for th
first time. When I broke my wrist and couldn't play, they said, wha
the hell, coach the team.

When the war ended in 1945 some people thought that I wa
good enough to make the NHL. When I'd been playing, I'd don

lot of scoring – more than some other guys who later made the
NHL. And I was fast enough. But during the year I was out with
the bad wrist I put on a lot of weight. I'd been playing at around
150 or 155, and I went up to 180. Detroit invited me to their
camp. My Army buddy Tommy Ivan organized that. He was going
with them as coach of their farm team at Omaha. But I was very
badly out of shape. I practised twice the first day and I couldn't get
out of bed the next day.

Almost from the start I could see the writing on the wall. Ivan
wanted me to go down with him to Omaha, play myself into shape,
and help him coach. But I just couldn't see professional hockey, at
that time, for me. I guess I was depressed a little by the way I figured
I'd slipped. Also, I was getting into my late twenties and in those
days not many pros played much past thirty. Anyway, I decided I
would look for a job, settle down, and get started towards some kind
of solid future. Just about that time Lex Cook phoned me and asked
me to come and play for him at Quebec City. I said I would go only
if he could guarantee me a job outside hockey. Next thing I got a
letter from the personnel manager of the sales company for Anglo-
Canadian Pulp and Paper, the company sponsoring the Quebec
Aces then. The name came from the first letter of Anglo-Canadian
Employees – ACE. My bank training helped me out there and I got
a job in the accounting department at $135 a month, which was
good enough money at the time; and there would be hockey money
besides.

I was still not in good shape after that year's layoff. I remember
a fellow in Quebec City who was a real hockey fan, an insurance
man. We got to be friends, and I remember him telling me two
months later how I looked to him when I first got to Quebec.

'The first time you played, you were lousy,' he said. 'The next
week you were a little better. The next week you were a little better
again. Now, you know, you are a real good hockey player.' As he
said, it took me about two months. It was tough, but I just kept on
getting up, like everybody has to do.

People ask me sometimes if I used to do much fighting when I
was a player. Well, at my weight I didn't exactly go out looking for
fights, but I never backed away from any either. Even if it would
have been the smart thing to do. But the one I can remember in
most detail wasn't in hockey, but in lacrosse. I'd played the game
as a kid in Toronto, but then quit until I hit Cornwall. That's a

great lacrosse town. We didn't go into it very seriously but a lot of us wanted to be playing some kind of sport all the time and you couldn't play hockey in the summer. And the second year I was in Quebec City, lacrosse arrived there. They brought in some pretty good players, but they wanted a little local talent too. I wound up playing on the front line with Bobby Thorpe and we had a hell of a year.

I'll always remember the very last game of lacrosse I ever played. There was a great big guy on the other team, called Windy Debank. He's got to be six feet six, a very tough guy to check. Probably because I was a hockey player, I was put on him. I'm about 165 or 170 at the time, and he is about 220 and so tall that when he got the ball and held it up there was no way you could get the ball away from him – so all you could do was get in his road. So I was told check, check, check, because this guy could beat a team all by himself.

So here I am checking him in front of the net. He's reaching for the ball to take a pass, he's backing up, and I put my foot out and bang, down he goes. I didn't pay any more attention to him, but it was a good thing I was wearing a helmet, as I always did in lacrosse. As soon as he got up he hit me right on the top of the head. Down I go. I'm trying to get up, and I can't do it – the whole place is going around and around. Down I went again. By that time everybody was grouped around. And finally I did get up and went after him. Well, I couldn't do much, I was still dazed, but I was trying.

The penalties were five minutes to him and two to me. So we're sitting in the penalty box, right beside one another, and I'm telling him, you so and so, you gave it to me good, I'm going to get you.

He looked at me and laughed. He said, 'You just think you're smart, because you got that job coaching hockey.'

'That's right,' I said. 'And I want to tell you something else. I don't care if I ever play lacrosse again. You're going to get yours as soon as I get on that floor.'

He was beginning to pay attention.

'I'm going to tell you exactly what I'm going to do,' I said. 'When I get back on the floor I'm going to tell our guys that when you get back, they are to check every other man and leave you open so that the ball has got to go to you. And when you've got the ball, I'm going to come around and knock your (censored) head off.'

He sat looking at me. 'You're crazy,' he said.

I got out of the penalty box. He still had three minutes, so I got it all fixed with our guys. Just when he came out there was a stoppage of play. Windy was standing there looking at me. Play started and he got the ball. But as soon as he saw me coming he threw the ball at me and tried to avoid me. It must have looked pretty funny, a little guy trying to beat the tar out of a giant. I'm chasing him, throwing my gloves at him, and finally I do get to him. The only trouble is, he reaches out one hand and pins me against the wire. I'm flailing away but I can't even reach him. I'm screaming at him. And then he's got me pinned there and all I can see is his other big fist coming over, looking like a ham coming at me. And I'm trying to duck and saying to myself, 'How the hell did I ever get here?' He hit me and I was out again. Also, I got a game penalty. I never played again. But that big guy was a terrific lacrosse player. Not many like him. He could kill me, wrap me up, and throw me in the canal, and he'd never even know he'd been in a fight.

Hockey began taking more and more of my time from then on. When Lex Cook had been offered a job in Dallas and had taken it, I'd got the job of coaching the Aces more or less by default. Playing coach. This was the first time I started getting into the argument that has been with me more or less ever since – splitting duties. Even that first year there were arguments about whether I should be playing or coaching. Later on when I went to the Leafs the argument was always whether I should be both general manager and coach.

When I first started coaching the Aces in 1947 I didn't have any idea of how a hockey team was put together. That first year Jack Adams at Detroit helped me a lot, with both advice and players. I can't say it was a great year, but Adams let me have three players, Gordie Heale, Larry Zeidel, and Rags Raglan. We were fighting all year to make the playoffs – and a so-so team like that just wasn't good enough for Quebec City. The management figured one of the troubles was that I shouldn't be both playing and coaching. But then we did scrape into the playoffs. Montreal Royals had the great team in our league that year. The year before they'd won the Allan Cup. But this year we knocked them off in the playoffs. That made that year. There was no way Aces could fire me as coach after that. Not until the next year, anyway.

And the next year we were doing all right. I was still playing and coaching, doing things my way. But the playoffs the following spring were supposed to start on a Tuesday. Our rink burned down on the Monday. We had to buy all new equipment — skates, everything. And with no rink of our own, we had to play the whole series in Sherbrooke. I'll never forget the sound of all that new leather squeaking when the team walked down the hall to go on the ice for that first playoff game. The combination of away ice, new equipment, and everything else was too much. We got whacked the first game, did a little better the second, and took them into overtime the third — but we lost.

Well, in coaching you don't get many reprieves. When the Aces were being organized for the next season the management laid down the ultimatum. 'You're either going to play or coach,' they told me. 'If you play we'll bring in a coach, and if you coach you are not going to play.'

I was only thirty-one at the time. But I think I made the right move. If I'd kept on playing, who knows what might have happened to me? I didn't really figure I was through as a player, but I said all right, I'd coach.

That started some interesting years, including one of the biggest deals I'd ever been involved in. Jean Beliveau had been playing in Quebec City as a junior, pulling such big crowds into the rink that the senior team, the Aces, was overshadowed. But now he was going to be twenty in August 1951, and Montreal Canadiens — and my old buddy Frank Selke — badly wanted him to help fill the Montreal Forum. There was a lot more to it than that. I don't know how much of it is relevant to this but I guess a little is. There was this big new rink, the Coliseum, in Quebec City. There were people financially involved in it with a lot of political power who wanted to get their money back. Bob Hesketh once wrote a column in the Toronto *Telegram* saying that the power struggle over Beliveau even that first year involved, at one time, either an open or a veiled threat that if Canadiens didn't ease off on trying to get Beliveau out of Quebec City, the Montreal Forum would lose its licence to sell beer.

I don't know for sure about that, but I do know that from the very first year I was in Quebec City there was a connection between politics and sport that I stayed away from. I didn't think they mix and still don't. Because of that I made a lifelong enemy out of a very powerful guy in the Union Nationale party, Gerald Martineau. Next to the party leader, Premier Maurice Duplessis, he was about the most powerful man in Quebec. Martineau is dead now, but when Duplessis was alive and running Quebec, Martineau was a very hard guy to buck.

Anyway, against this background, in the summer of 1951 we wanted Beliveau to play for the Quebec Aces. I signed him. His dad worked for Shawinigan Water and Power at Victoriaville, and the Beliveaus were a close-knit family, with father the boss. There were some preliminary discussions on both sides about money and so on, but this day I went and saw the branch manager in Victoriaville. After a little talk, he called in Jean Beliveau's father. We discussed the matter and came to an agreement. I made out the papers and Mr. Beliveau signed on Jean's behalf. As soon as the paper was signed, my friend behind the desk opened a drawer and brought out a big forty-ounce bottle of whisky and put it on the table.

'Now we seal it,' he said. We had a drink and that was it. For the next two years Big Jean – or le Gros Bill, as they called him in Quebec – played for me. I couldn't even tell you exactly how much he got. He had a job at a dairy, and his pay came from various sources, but it was big enough the first year. In the second I think it was something over twenty thousand dollars. Not bad for so-called amateur hockey.

But Martineau had a junior team in Quebec City, the Frontenacs, with Phil Watson coaching. Martineau had benefited when Jean was playing junior hockey, but now that he was playing with the Aces we were murdering them at the gate. Martineau wanted to knock the Aces down somehow, and Montreal wanted Beliveau as badly as ever, or more so. He had signed a form that gave Montreal his professional rights. But as long as I could keep him amateur, at twenty thousand dollars a year, he had to play for us. He wanted to stay in Quebec City, there was no doubt about that. But by this time, with all the forces in play around him, he really didn't have all that much to do with it.

Remember I said that if he turned pro, he had to go to Canadiens? What Canadiens did was to make that whole Quebec league professional so that they could get Beliveau. How could they do that? Well, they had their farm team, the Montreal Royals in our league. The Royals were run by Frank Selke of Canadiens. There was a fair amount of power there. And there was also Martineau, with plenty of power all through the province, and knowing that as long as the Aces had Beliveau, his junior team was going to run second to the Aces at the Quebec box office.

There was a league meeting in Montreal in the summer of 1953. I was there. All the other clubs, well prompted by Canadiens, said they wanted to turn professional. If the league turned pro it meant that Beliveau would go to Montreal, which Montreal wanted, and Martineau's club in Quebec City would be rid of him as a counterattraction. Of course, I didn't want to turn the league pro – for exactly the opposite reasons; I wanted to keep Beliveau. Losing him would weaken not only us but the whole league.

I remember asking the other guys, 'Doesn't Beliveau draw in your building? Isn't it worth something to keep him in the league?'

I remember Forrest Keene from Sherbrooke telling me, 'Nah, he doesn't draw a thing in my building.'

And Tommy Gorman from Ottawa – I asked him, 'What's wrong with you?' And he said, 'Well, I'm losing money and I think if I can own my own players I'll be better off.' I later find out that Montreal had offered to play an exhibition game in Chicoutimi, and another in Sherbrooke. Needless to say, these games would do very well financially for the home clubs. But anyway I was outvoted. The league turned pro. The Aces, and the league, lost Beliveau. Before we even started the season that year Sherbrooke dropped out of the league – and that had been one of the votes to turn pro. And before Christmas Ottawa dropped out; that was another of the turn-pro votes.

One funny thing was that after the vote to go pro, a column was written in Quebec City demanding that I be fired from the Aces! The reason given was that I had cost the people of Quebec City their great star Beliveau, by helping to turn the league pro, the very thing I had fought against.

However, that's nothing new. A coach's life from that standpoint is never very pleasant. I mean, the coach is the handiest target. Every year of my life, somebody is going to fire me. With the Leafs, one year I'm going to be fired because the team plays badly. Another year I'm going to be fired because I trade away their favourite hockey player. There's always something to fire a coach for.

But Martineau was one of the toughest I ever faced. I never bothered with him, really; never had much to do with him. But that was the main trouble. It started in 1945, the first year I was in Quebec as a player. I'd been there only a few weeks when Martineau had a New Year's cocktail party for the players and their wives. My wife had just arrived in time to see a game we played that afternoon. She was tired. I said there was this party. She said she didn't feel very well, after the trip. So I said, 'Well, we don't go.' Of course, I was supposed to have snubbed Martineau by not going, and he was a guy nobody was supposed to snub.

Then later, as I said, I wouldn't do things he wanted because I didn't think politics had anything to do with hockey. Hockey is hockey, and that's it. Maybe that's one of the things that makes me the way I am now. Nothing is allowed to interfere with hockey. There is no other consideration when you are making a decision. And if I was making those kinds of decisions twenty years ago, refusing to let anything interfere with hockey, that's the same way I am now.

To understand the Quebec situation you have to understand that politics, then at least, reached into everything in Quebec. Like one time there was a political fight going on about the mayor. In the middle of it I got called in by one of Martineau's hatchet men.

'Just keep the hell out of the mayoralty race,' he said.

I looked at him and said, 'You have no right to tell me that. As far as I'm concerned you can take politics and shove it.'

It seems silly to me even now, but they were scared that I would get into it somehow, just enough to give the other guy a few votes, or say something that wouldn't be to their advantage. In power politics they don't miss a trick. And just about everybody went along with Martineau. I remember one programme his junior Frontenacs put out, a one-shot affair. You should have seen it. Anybody who had anything to do with the government or got any patronage took an ad. It must have been worth twenty thousand dollars to his club, the Frontenacs.

Martineau made more direct attempts to get me too. Or to harry me. One year in the playoffs the Montreal *Star* came out with a story that after the playoffs I was through and Frank Carlin would get my job. This was a headline right across the top of the sports page in the *Star*. As soon as the paper came out, the main owner of the Aces came to the apartment my wife and I had. He told me that there was no truth to the story, that someone had planted it. As far as I could learn, Martineau had had it planted.

Also, one day I came into the office and one of the owners of the Aces was on the phone, listening. As I came in, he looked at me and motioned to me to come close. Then he said into the phone, 'What did you say? Will you repeat that?'

He handed me the phone. I listened. It was Martineau. He repeated what he had just said: 'I want to buy the hockey club just for one day, so I can fire Imlach.'

I handed back the phone to my boss, who said into the phone: 'You can't buy the hockey club for that.' It took a lot of guts for the man to refuse Martineau. It would have been easy to knuckle under. After all, I was a nothing, compared to Martineau — and the Aces were just a plaything for the company officials who owned the club then. Not a plaything for me, but for them.

The only thing I ever had in writing from Martineau, though, was a very friendly and complimentary note that he wrote to me at Christmas that first year — just before the business of us not turning up at his New Year's party. I have kept a lot of things and this is one of them. A long time later when he said something nasty about me to someone else, who told me, I pulled out this enthusiastic note from the Christmas card and said, 'Well, he didn't always think that of me. Take a look.' Martineau went to jail eventually over patronage. One of the pieces of evidence they brought against him was about a sportswriter being on the payroll of a paint company he never did anything for at all. This writer was one of the guys who was always knocking the Aces and praising the Frontenacs in the press. You figure it out — it doesn't take much figuring.

Prelude to the Big Time

In hockey there are characters and there are characters, but no one I have run into in the NHL comes up to a player I had in Quebec City. I'm going to have to tell about him without naming him, because for all I know he might be president of a big company by now and I wouldn't want to get him kicked upstairs to be chairman of the board.

He was about the average height, but very well developed. Dark hair. He played defence and he could handle the puck just like Doug Harvey. But this guy of mine could do some things not normally counted as athletic feats. Like he'd be in a tavern, out of money, and he'd bet whoever was at the table that he could drink a quart bottle of beer in ten seconds.

'There's no way,' the guys would say.

'Put your money on the table,' he'd reply. And he'd take a bottle and tip it up and down it would go. As far as I could see it would just go straight down without even touching the sides of his throat. He'd win, and that would give him the money for another few quarts.

Also, he could chin himself with the tips of his fingers. Again it would be in a tavern. He'd be out of money. He'd point maybe to the little ledge over the door, not more than an inch thick at the most.

'I can chin myself on that thing,' he'd say.

'Ah, you can't.'

'Put up your money,' he'd say. And when he had all the suckers in he'd go over, put the tips of his fingers on the top of the doorjamb, and up he'd go. Strong! He had to be, to punish his body the way he did and still play hockey.

But you couldn't keep track of him without an awful lot of effort. I had a couple of other players who were difficult, but none like him. The only way I could ever be sure where they were was to keep on talking to them. I got to have a reputation for being quite a night-clubber myself, but it was just because if I didn't know every place in Quebec City that some of my characters might go, I'd never be able to ice a hockey team some days. I'd go around and flush them out. Some of them eventually would get so discouraged at moving all the time that they might even go home and get some sleep, which was the general idea.

I remember one night I was on my way to this fellow's place, our hero, to make sure he was in. I'm just going up Grande-Allée and I see him coming out of a house with another guy and a girl. I pull my car up beside his. He's parked and I pull my car up so he can't get out. I could see him and he was going to get out and give it to me. Then he saw who I was. So I look at him.

'Where you going at this time of night?' I said.

'I'm just going to take these people home,' he said.

I said, 'Okay, go ahead. I'll follow you to make sure you come right back.'

He said okay so I back up and let him out. So down the street we go. He's got an old car and I've got an Oldsmobile. He starts to speed up, so boom I put my foot down on the gas and get right up behind him, knowing that the so-and-so hero now wants to play games. So he speeds up some more and comes to John Street, which is a thoroughfare, and he doesn't stop at the stop sign, he goes right through the corner as if there was no stop street. I stopped, of course, then started after him. But the first street down was a one-way street. It didn't matter a damn to him. He goes down it against the traffic. I had to go past this street to the next street where I could go in the same direction as he was, except legally.

Anyway, he lost me. So I went back to the place where he was staying. I walked in and told the landlady I wanted to see his room.

She said she wouldn't show it to me. I looked at her and said, 'You do a little business with the hockey team, don't you?'

She said yes.

'Well,' I said, 'if you don't let me check that room you won't get any more hockey players.'

She looked at me and then took me to the room and opened the door. No one there. I thanked her and told her there was a good chance I would be back about three o'clock in the morning. The clubs closed at three. Maybe that would send him home.

I went to a club and sat there and had a drink or two and watched the show. At three o'clock I'm in that club with a friend of mine, a scout for Boston. I said to him, 'Come on, I need a witness. This is the last chance I'm giving this guy. If he's not there in bed, he's through.'

So the two of us went to his room and opened the door. Nobody there. Next day I called him into the office and told him he was through. Well, the story he gave me you wouldn't believe, and I didn't either, but – well, I let it go that time. We were an independent operation and it wasn't all that easy to get players. In that situation, in the minors, a coach has to put up with a lot.

Another time, this was a weekend, we had a practice at home and then were supposed to play the next afternoon, Sunday, in Shawinigan Falls. Saturday night he got into the Montcalm Hotel and got drinking. The next morning the bus was supposed to leave for Shawinigan at eleven o'clock. The time came and went and he was nowhere to be seen, so we had to go without him.

Now what happened I found out later. When he was drinking on the Saturday night, he got plastered and was thrown out of the place. He'd parked his car somewhere around there but couldn't find it, so he got home somehow. The way I found out about this was that when he was on his way downtown on one of the city buses the next morning, a local radio guy was on the same bus. The radio man looked at our hero and said, 'What the hell are you doing here? You're supposed to be on your way to Shawinigan Falls.'

Our hero told him he couldn't make the bus because he couldn't find his car; he figured it was downtown somewhere and he had to go to find it.

Anyway, halfway through the second period in Shawinigan, my trainer nudged me. The game was on but I turned away for a minute to see what he wanted. And there was our hero, looking at me, pleading. I told him to get away from me. After the game he came to the dressing room. From there we were going on up north for another game. He wanted to come with us. I told him he knew he was through, that I'd told him the next time he goofed up he was off the team. Well, he talked about his wife and kids and was very broken up. He never thought of them much, as far as I knew, when he was getting himself stiff. That sort of guy never does. But that doesn't stop him worrying about them after. Anyway, he was pleading. 'I'll promise you I'll never drink again,' he said.

I told him I'd heard that before too many times.

'Honest, honest,' he said. 'I'll never have another drink.'

So what the hell. I told him, 'Come along.'

There's plenty of tragedy in a guy like that, of course, but in a hockey team you look at it differently. A guy just has to pull his weight, or everybody else is carrying him one way or another. I'm just telling the way it happened. Some guys laughed at him and some didn't, but this is how it went.

I guess the most sensational thing he ever did was one time when we had been playing an exhibition game in Cornwall and were going to take a bus to Montreal and then a train for Rouyn to play. So there we were this morning in Cornwall, the bus parked and ready to go, and we're all sitting around waiting for him.

I sit in the bus for about ten minutes and then I say, 'Okay, I know where he is,' and I get out of the bus and go into the beer parlour. And there he is. He's got a quart of beer in front of him. I stand there and look at him and finally he looks at me.

'Out,' I said. 'Right now. We've been waiting twenty minutes for you.'

'Okay,' he said. And out he went and got on the bus. He'd had about four quarts of beer by then and he's feeling no pain – the beer is just starting to hit him. He went to the back of the bus and he was in the craziest mood. He wouldn't shut up, telling everybody how good he was. He's the best this and the best that. He's the greatest tennis player on the team, he said. He's the best at doing feats of strength. Which he was. So he kept on going – and it goes on for an hour or so. By then we're driving that long stretch of old No. 2 highway beside the Soulanges Canal. And he gets on to swimming and how good he is at that.

Well, it was only a matter of minutes before somebody – Joe Crozier, in fact – piped up: 'You couldn't even swim that canal.'

'Oh, I can't, eh?'

'You can't.'

'I bet I can. Who is going to bet against me?'

Remember, it's November and bloody cold. Somebody said, 'I got five that says you can't.' And others chip in until there is about a fifty-dollar bet. Of course, he didn't have any money. He never had. But he said he'd take the bet. I could hear all this from the front of the bus, but the next time I looked back he had all his clothes off except his underwear shorts and he's yelling, 'Stop the bus.'

Well, I was sick and tired of listening to him anyway. The driver was looking at me. I said, 'Stop it at the first bridge.' We needed a bridge. If he's going to swim it, he has to get back again somehow.

So we stopped at the first bridge and everybody got out. This was No. 2 highway, the big highway at the time, and cars were going by, everybody wondering what was going on, I guess. Out he got in his shorts. And I was wondering what the heck the guy was going to do – go down and put his toe in the water or what? But mainly I was thinking, I sure fooled him with all his big talk. Called his bluff. I got back on the bus, but I was watching. Now I could see that there was a little skim of ice along the shore.

Well, he went down toward the canal and he didn't bother with any toe in the water or anything else. He dived right in. Danny Nixon was there, he was a lifeguard in the summer. So I told him quick to get up on the ruddy bridge and, I said, if he goes down and doesn't come up, you go in after him.

But by that time our hero was up from his dive and was really going fast towards the other side. He got there, climbed up, and he'd lost his underwear on the way over! I guess when he hit the water everything went. He was stark naked. All the guys were coming up the bank on our side. I told them, 'Get his pants and get across the bridge.' I always remember the guy who runs the drawbridge. He was standing there in his little shack looking out of the window and shaking his head. Couldn't believe it, you know.

Anyway, we got our hero back on the bus. He was shaking like a leaf by then. So I told the driver to stop at the first tavern we came to. I got him into the tavern and told the guy I wanted hot water, as hot as I could get it, and I got some rum. When he must have had about six ounces of rum in him, I said, okay, let's get back on the bus. But even with all that in him he was still shivering and yelling that he was cold. I was thinking I might wind up with pneumonia on my hands, so when we got to Montreal I said to the rest of them, okay, the train north leaves at such and such a time, be on it. And I got him into a hotel and took all the blankets off one bed and put them on the other and got him in. Then I sent somebody out for a bottle of rum and I kept him in that bed sweating for two hours, until he was warm.

By this time the other guys had gone up the street and found a place where you could get headlines printed on what looked like regular newspapers. They came back to the hotel and they had five or six of these papers and they said to our hero, 'Boy, you really made the headlines.' And they showed him these papers with the big front page headlines saying, '. . . SWIMS CANAL!' He believed it for a minute or two anyway, and he really whooped and hollered. Up in Rouyn the next night he played a great game. None the worse for wear at all.

However, I suppose in the eyes of some people in Quebec City at the time I wasn't exactly an ideal character myself. Like, there was one time I got suspended. It was the last game of the season and we were playing in Montreal against the Royals. Ernie Mundy was the referee. He made some boo-boos and I started giving him a rough time. One thing led to another. I told him a few choice things and finally I went too far.

'Out!' he said. 'You're out of the game!'

I just happened to have two tickets in my pocket for seats right behind the bench. I went and sat in them. Ernie saw me there, still running the team, but now from the seats.

He came over and said, 'You can't sit there.'

I said, 'Who the hell says I can't? Here's the two tickets for these two seats.'

He looked at me. He should have had a cop come and throw me out, you know. But he didn't. The league executive had a meeting in Montreal the next afternoon and sent me a telegram saying that I was suspended for one game, for defying the referee's order to leave the bench. I argued that I *had* left the bench, but what the hell. As a result of that they changed the rule, made it read that, when ordered to leave, a coach had to go to the dressing room.

Meanwhile, this one game I was suspended for was the first game of a playoff series against Chicoutimi, in Quebec City. Well, that's our home rink, eh? I could get just about anything done there. So I got a walkie-talkie hookup to a seat right behind the bench, where Kilby Macdonald was sitting. Pete Martin was behind the bench running the team. But all the time I'm up there in the crowd on the phone, telling Kilby who to play and who not to play. He'd pass it on to Martin. I also had a hookup right into the dressing room so I could talk to the team by phone on an amplifier between periods. After the second period we were ahead 5–1. I'd stayed up in my seat at the end of the first period. At the end of the second I went down and walked around the corridors so that all the Quebec Amateur Hockey Association people who'd suspended me could see me wandering around and figure I was staying away from the club as ordered. We did have a picture taken showing me in action on the set, but I didn't let it out to any of the papers.

One thing I learned in Quebec City was how much the human body can take as long as the mind in that body won't give up. I had some great hockey players in Quebec City, besides Beliveau. Gaye Stewart was there. Orv Tessier, Joe Crozier, Marcel Bonin, Bob Beckett, Armand Gaudreault. Maybe they weren't all what you'd call great players, in comparison with Bobby Hull and Frank Mahovlich and some of those, but they were good hockey players and there were some great characters. Skip Teal. Willie O'Ree, Jack LeClair, Herbie Carnegie, Dick Gamble, Larry Regan – dozens of them. But some of the guys I remember just as well weren't much known outside Quebec. Like there was one big strong kid who's a cop in Montreal right now, Claude Robert. One night we were in Grand'Mère, Quebec, playing an exhibition game against Providence, and Claude was coming out of our end with the puck when – did he get it! A real tough check. He went up and he came down wrong, hurting his leg. He limped off the ice and went into the dressing room.

I went in after him and he told me, 'Geez, I don't think I can play.'

Well, we really needed him out there and I felt a little psychology wouldn't do any harm. I said to the trainer, 'Did you bring that needle with you?'

There wasn't any needle, of course, but the trainer looked at me and said, 'Yeah, it's in the trunk.'

And I said, 'Well, get it and get the freezing. We'll freeze the leg and it'll be all right.'

As soon as I said needle, and freeze, Claude was up. 'There's nothing wrong with me,' he said.

'Are you sure?' I asked. 'We can just stick a little needle in and give you the freezing, you know.'

'No, no,' he said. 'I'm all right.'

He went out and played. Next day he practised and then played. He played for several weeks after that but he kept complaining about the leg. This went on until finally I said, 'Go down to the hospital and see the doctor.'

When he came back he took the precaution of bringing the X-ray pictures with him. His leg was broken. He'd been playing on the thing – he was so scared of the needle he played hockey on a broken leg. It happened before and has happened since – Bert Olmstead and Bob Baun both played on broken legs at one time or another, and others have played with other bones broken, like wrists – but that was the first time I'd run into it.

'What are you going to do about it?' he asked me.

Asking me what you can do about a broken leg! I said, 'What can you do? Better take ten days off and then start to skate.' He said, 'Only ten days?' And I said, 'Well, after all, you have been playing on it for about a month already, haven't you?'

Another time we were playing in Quebec City on Sunday afternoon. This was the first year I was in at Quebec, and I was rooming with Eddy Emberg. And that afternoon he got hit by a shot. The next day we were due at a practice. I got up and said to Eddy, 'Get up. Come on.'

He said, 'I can't. My leg is too sore.'

I said, 'The hell with the leg. If you can walk on it, come on, let's get going.'

So away we go down to the Coliseum on the streetcar. He hobbled into the rink, put his skates on, and out we go to work out. After that we went for supper. Next day, we got up and went to work. He went to see the plant doctor. When I got home, who do I see coming down the street towards me but Eddy, on crutches.

'What's wrong with you?' I asked.

'My ankle is broken,' he said. 'I'm going home for six weeks. See you later.'

I said, 'What are you talking about? You practised on that yesterday! What are you using crutches for now?'

He was a little offended. He said, 'It's broken, now.'

I'll always remember that: it's broken now. It had been broken yesterday, too, but he'd been practising on it.

There were other things about playing in Quebec that weren't strictly hockey, but that a guy remembers. One of the funniest was a time when I was still just a player and we were in New York with the Aces, playing the New York Rovers. I got three goals in Madison Square Garden one night when the Rovers were in our league, but this was a different time – must have been, because we didn't score three this night I'm thinking of.

We had Roy Heximer and Sid Smith with our club then. Lex Cook was coaching. Smitty was playing wing for me.

The game was on a Sunday. On Saturday afternoon when we got in I ran into Johnny Mitchell. He was scouting for the Maple Leafs then and was down to watch Smitty play. So I knew this. Anyway, that night Smitty and I were out for a walk and there didn't seem much to do. You've got to remember I was a player then. Maybe things like this are why I think I understand players pretty well today. One thing led to another and we did a little celebrating. To tell the truth it lasted until about four in the morning. There were four or five of us in one room. And by that time I had decided I wasn't going back to my room, because I roomed with the trainer and he would already know I was out, so there was no use going back and letting him know what time I did get to bed. I thought I'd just bunk in with Heximer and Bill Boorman from Winnipeg. Then when Cook started checking up in the morning at least he wouldn't know what time any of us got to bed. We pushed the two beds together and went to sleep.

Well, the next morning Lex Cook starts checking around and found I hadn't been in my bed the night before. He started knocking on doors. When he came to where I was with Heximer and Boorman he started in to call us everything. I told him to shut up and let a guy sleep; that I'd just bunked in here so I wouldn't disturb the trainer. He went out without another word, but he had a pretty good idea what had happened. And it really affected us that afternoon. We always figured we must have got a bad batch of mix. Some of the guys fell flat on their faces. I don't think Smitty played a worse game in his life. We got beaten, I think it was 9–0 or 9–1 or something.

Then we went to the dressing room. Montmorency Paper, the sales company for Anglo-Canadian, had offices in New York. Several company officials had brought friends to the game telling them how great we were, and we'd got shellacked. And were they mad. A lot of them came to the dressing room after, too, just in time to hear Lex Cook chewing us out – which we richly deserved.

Before the game, one of the players had picked up a couple of loaded cigars at a novelty place and had given them to our publicity man – Bobby Martineau, who hadn't smoked them. When Lex started in on us he got so mad that Bobby thought he was going to have a heart attack or something.

Finally Bobby stepped in and said, 'Take it easy, Lex. Here, smoke a cigar."

Well, Lex took the cigar and he's lighting it up and still calling us a lot of rotten so-and-sos between puffs when . . . BOOM!

The whole room just burst out laughing, couldn't help it, even the guys who had been maddest. Everybody but Cook. He threw the cigar to the floor and snarled, 'There's one sure thing, there is no scout going to pick up any of you rotten so-and-sos the way you played today.' But he was wrong. Toronto signed Smitty the next night. He went on to play for their farm club at Pittsburgh and later for the Leafs, and scored a lot of goals in the NHL.

I never made much money out of hockey in Quebec City. I figured it out once. There was only one year out of the eleven I was in Quebec City that I made more than six thousand dollars – and that was one of the early years when I was working full time in the office, and also getting hockey pay. I'd gone there in the first place figuring to settle down and raise the family, get some roots down, put the job ahead of hockey. Well, we did get started on it.

When my wife arrived there just after Christmas of 1945 we hunted around for an apartment, which was very tough to get in those days. The first one that came up was a three-bedroom, a lot too big for us, but in those days you didn't turn down any apartment. But it was walking distance from the rink and we soon filled up the rooms. Our son Brent was born during the hockey season of 1946. I remember I was home getting over an injury when he was born, so I got my wife to the Jeffrey Hale Hospital in Quebec City and saw her a little after. But the next morning I had to leave to rejoin the team. Five years later I was also home when our daughter Marlene was born in the same hospital, so we were lucky both times. Hockey wives can't count on their husbands being there at those times.

Anyway, hockey now really had taken over my life. When I was only a player it was a cinch. Player-coach, and I was in a little deeper. Then there were the years when they argued that I shouldn't be both a coach and a player, and finally I went along with that. I wasn't coach long before I was handling the manager's job, too, and pretty soon they were arguing that I shouldn't be both of those at the same time either. They said I should take one or the other. So I said, okay, I'll take general manager. So I hired a coach. But it didn't work out and the next year I had to go back and do both jobs again. I think this happened three times – hiring a coach and then taking the job back. This was in my mind sometimes when I was resisting hiring a coach during the 1968-69 season. Also, both Wren Blair in Minnesota and Emile Francis in New York had hired coaches – and wound up dropping them to do the job again themselves. Anyway, I didn't find these two jobs heavy at all. In 1952, after I was voted minor league executive of the year, the company guys who owned the club began to get promoted, or retired. I began to take over more of their jobs too. At one time I was coach, general manager, and vice-president.

Things weren't going so well financially after Beliveau went to Montreal. Attendance was down and the whole league was shaky. Our owners wanted to get out. I guess they figured they owed me something so they said they'd sell the club to me. It was a very nominal price. I interested the doctor and the dentist and Joe Crozier, who'd been playing for me. And we took it over and we owned it. But the big profit years had been the ones when Beliveau was playing, and after that I could see the writing on the wall. I tried to get us into the American Hockey League, but of course I had no money. I was a guy in the business and knew it well by then, but I didn't have any money and you know, money talks. I turned down a few coaching offers, including one from the Soo, and then came the one I took.

In the spring of 1957 the Aces won the Edinburgh Trophy – that was the trophy that was put up for minor pro teams in Canada, falling somewhere between the Allan Cup and the Stanley Cup. Lynn Patrick was in the Boston club then. He came to Quebec City for the playoffs against Brandon, Manitoba.

He got talking and looking and I guess he must have figured I'd been doing a good job in Quebec City. Boston was going to go into Springfield, Massachusetts, in the American Hockey League that year, with Eddie Shore still owning the club but Boston operating it. Lynn told me they were looking for someone to manage Springfield. 'We want you to do it,' he said. I like Lynn. He was always fair about everything, and I was ready to move. I went in to see my boss at Anglo. He said they'd give me a leave of absence.

I said all right and went down to Boston and told Lynn I'd take the Springfield job. With the leave of absence, I thought, well, if I don't like it I can always come back. Anglo has never cancelled my leave of absence. I'm still on the roll as far as group insurance is concerned and I'm in the pension plan. I think I'll get about forty dollars a month when I'm sixty-five, so I won't be broke.

I thought I was going to be the general manager at Springfield. But when I got down there things had changed and I was going to be the coach too. Now, Eddie Shore and I are good friends. Socially, he's the finest guy you'd want to meet. But to work for him – wow! It was a tough year; the only good thing about it was that I got my money from Boston. Even at that, Shore was on the phone trying to get me fired two or three times. He had a big office in the rink, which he owned, along with some players and the league franchise. And he had some very loyal good guys, like Jack Butterfield, working for him. But I guess after all Shore's years in hockey, and doing things his way, it was hard for him to sit by and let somebody else like me run his club. He owned some players and Boston owned some. I had to sign them all, though, and it was pitiful what he wanted me to sign some of his players for. I did manage to get some of them a little more, but it was tough all around. Just to give you a hint: Shore and I never spoke a word to each other from November 15 that season, until we'd been put out in the league finals the following April.

Yet in another way I had the best job in hockey. We used to have a practice at eleven o'clock. I'd leave the house about half past ten and I'd be there in fifteen minutes, and on the ice by eleven. The practice would be over about 12.15 or 12.30. I'd go over to the little desk I had in the place – it wasn't even an office, but a working area that newspapermen used too. I'd see Butterfield and tell him I'd need X number of dollars to go away for the next game. I'd be home in early afternoon. I guess I knew by then that I wasn't likely to go back to Quebec, because I'd bought a house in a place called Long Meadow, near Springfield. It was the first my wife and I ever owned. That year she was spoiled all to the devil, for a hockey wife. I'd be home every afternoon we were in town, working around the house or yard. I hardly knew anybody in Long Meadow, so I was around all the time, playing the home-owning husband. But that was partly because Boston had intimated to me at the start that this was a long-term thing in Springfield. I wasn't the kind of guy, then or now, to figure on going somewhere for a year and then moving on. But it wasn't long after we'd bought the house that I knew I wasn't going to be around Springfield forever.

When Eddie and I stopped speaking to one another was an example. He had a goal tender that he owned named Claude Evans, and we also had Al Millar who I'd brought with me from Quebec City. He'd been in goal for me the previous season when we won the Edinburgh Trophy, and he'd won the best goalie award in the league. Shore called me into his office on a Thursday in November and said, 'Who are you gonna play in goal on Saturday?'

I wasn't feeling well. I was just coming down with the flu. I knew who he wanted me to play, Evans. But I said, 'I'm gonna play Millar.'

'You're not,' he said.

'What do you mean, I'm not?'

He said, 'I'm telling you, you're going to play the other guy.'

'Let's get this straight,' I said. 'Is this an ultimatum?'

He looked at me. I must have stood there five minutes in front of his desk while he looked at me, waiting for me to fold. I had a pretty good idea what he was thinking: he'd been pushing me a bit, and now I suddenly had picked the time to stand up to him, and that put him on the spot.

So he sat there. I didn't say anything. Finally he said, 'Yes.' Meaning it was an ultimatum.

'Thank you very much,' I said. 'I'm going home.' And I walked out.

I played Millar on that Saturday night. Shore called me a god-damned something or other, but I played Millar and that was all there was to it. We never spoke again all season. But he wasn't an easy guy to beat in a fight like that any more than he was in hockey. He managed to get Millar traded out of there. In fact, Millar played with five clubs that year at least partly as a result of that battle between me and Shore. He was with Boston a few games, then with Buffalo after he left Springfield, and then with Chicoutimi, and finally wound up back in Quebec City. Actually, it worked out well for both Millar and Evans. Millar spent considerable time with Boston as a backup goalie and Evans played well enough to get us into the American Hockey League finals.

But it wasn't a workable deal. Eddie had leased the hockey club to Boston; I don't know the terms, except that you can be pretty sure they were good financially for Shore. Anyway, we did get to the finals of the American Hockey League. Nobody expected us to. After we got knocked out in the finals I was walking along the hallways of the rink to the press room and Eddie was coming towards me, going somewhere else. And he stopped. A big, hard man. One of hockey's alltime great defencemen when he was playing for Boston.

'I guess you had yourself a pretty good year, son,' he said.

'I guess so,' I said.

'Will you play hockey for me?'

As sometimes happens, I didn't really recognize the opening moves in what was to be the most important change in my life. In the spring of 1958 I knew only one thing for sure: that there was no more job with Springfield for me. Eddie Shore wasn't wasting any time taking his club back from that one-year agreement with Boston. I remember thinking, that's what I get for buying a house. Of course, I could have lived in Long Meadow and worked in Boston, but a hockey man spends enough time away from home without adding that kind of trip to work. I was frankly up in the air. Lynn Patrick wanted me to be a trouble-shooter in their organization, including taking charge of their farm system. But somehow I didn't want that job.

I'd been around hockey long enough to be able to smell something out. I had an idea there was going to be trouble in the Boston club. If there was, and I was supposed to be the trouble-shooter, I was going to be in the middle of it. I didn't want Coach Milt Schmidt's job. I didn't want anybody's job on that club. And I didn't want to be standing around in a position where I might be called on to fill in, if there were changes, looking as if I'd just been waiting to grab somebody else's job. Maybe that was screwy, for a guy who is supposed to be ruthless sometimes, but that's the way I felt, although naturally I didn't confide this to anybody at the time.

This was still the situation when the annual hockey meetings came up in June in Montreal. I'd always gone to the meetings when I was in Quebec. That's where everybody in hockey meets once a year. If you want to do hockey business and keep up contacts that's where to do it. Lynn asked me if I wanted to go to the meetings. I said, sure, if he thought I could be of any help.

So I went. I was having a great time because I really didn't have any responsibilities. The job with Boston had been offered, but I still hadn't taken it. And I was standing around in the hall one day when Harold Ballard came along. I knew him from back 'in my playing days in Toronto. Now he was on the Toronto club's hockey committee in the first stage of Conn Smythe's passing on his control of the club to others, including his son Stafford.

He pulled me aside and said, 'Mr. Smythe would like to talk to you.'

'Conn Smythe?' I said.

'No,' he said. 'Stafford. He'd like to talk to you up in his room.' He gave me the number. 'Why don't you go on up?'

'Okay,' I said.

Something happened right then. I forget what. Anyway, I forgot all about going up to see Stafford. An hour and a half later I ran into Ballard again.

'Have you seen Stafford?' he asked.

I said, 'Oh, geez, I forgot all about it.' But then I did go up to see him. He was alone. He talked about me coming to work for him in Toronto, but he was rather hazy about exactly what he wanted me to do. Anyway, I told him that I was still working for Boston. Under league rules he had to get Boston's permission before he could really talk to me about a job. So he approached Walter Brown, Boston president at the time, and got permission. Then, of course, Toronto could talk to me as much as they liked. I didn't particularly like what they were offering me, though. It was roughly the same kind of trouble-shooting, farm-system job that Boston was offering me. But I had in the back of my mind the personal reservations I had about taking the Boston job. I told Stafford that I'd come to Toronto to see them.

A few weeks later I did. I had two things in mind on that trip. One was to get more details of the job. The other was to talk to a lot of other people I knew, and learn what I could about the lay of the land. I wanted to hear how the inner working of the Toronto club looked to people who were watching it every day. I talked to Ed Wildey, for instance, and Red Burnett of the *Star*. Red suggested I talk to his sports editor, Milt Dunnell. I did. Also I talked to Bobby Laurent, who runs a hotel in West Toronto, and Tommy O'Neill, the lawyer. They were friends of mine from the Quebec days when they played with me. And also I phoned Tommy Ivan, my old Army buddy. He was general manager in Chicago by then, after coaching for many successful years in Detroit. Of course, I heard both the good and the bad — the opportunity as well as the dragons.

About this time, also, Lynn Patrick became ill, and Walter Brown asked Conn Smythe to cease negotiating with me because they'd need me, Lynn being ill. Mr. Smythe wrote back to say that negotiations had gone too far to quit now. But I didn't know that until later. I went back to Springfield and talked the Toronto job over with my wife. I hadn't given Toronto a decision. I had told them I'd think it over and come back and see them pretty soon. A couple of weeks later I drove up again. This time I was in earnest. I met Stafford at his office in the Conn Smythe sand pit, up on Jane Street, headquarters of the building industry part of the Smythe holdings. This time I talked turkey. Being in charge of the farm clubs, I said, the hell with that, I've got the same job offered in Boston. I don't owe Toronto anything, I said. I do owe Boston something. If I'm going to run a farm system I'd do it in Boston.

Then we got down to cases. 'As far as I'm concerned,' I told Stafford, 'you have no general manager. I want that job, or at least the opportunity of getting it.'

I was talking to Stafford alone when Conn Smythe walked into the office. His manner is rasping and direct. 'How you doing with this fellow, Stafford?' he asked. Stafford said something to the effect that we hadn't got anything settled yet.

Conn Smythe turned to me and said, 'What's wrong with you, are you scared of the job?'

I said, 'I'm not scared at all. It's just a case of not being offered what I want.'

He left after a few more words. I asked Stafford if they had promised the general manager's job to anybody else. He said they hadn't. Apparently they had offered it to Bill Reay, but he'd told them he wanted another year to prove himself as coach. Leafs had finished last the year before, his first as their coach, and that

rankled with him, as it would with any guy with pride. Staffo
finally said they'd give me, not the general manager's job, but th
'opportunity' – that was his word – of getting it. The way he p
it, I'd have the same chance as anybody else. They'd make n
assistant general manager; I'd be responsible for the club. Fro
there I could prove myself or not. He also said they'd have to as
King Clancy, who also was listed as assistant general manager,
he had any objection to me coming in with the same title as he ha

I hardly knew King at the time. I'd been introduced to him
couple of times at hockey gatherings and spent a little time wit
him, always with others around, but that was all. He'd been
great player with the Leafs, and had coached them in the midd
fifties. There was no obstacle from him. I think he said somethir
like, 'Hell, no. Hire the guy if you want.'

There was no difficulty about money. Money has never been
problem with me in a job. I believe that if you give a service, th
money follows. I haven't been proven wrong on that at any tim
Maybe there have been times when I could have made a better de
than I did. I mean, when I could have forced the money issu
further. But I feel that if I'm satisfied with a deal I make, that's i
And once I've made a deal money doesn't mean anything to me
Maybe this is the cause of some of the trouble I have had since i
hockey. Some people, players and others, don't believe the way
do, that when you make a deal you make a deal, and come hell o
high water you live up to it.

After the talks with Stafford the whole hockey committee go
into it. One thing they asked me was, could I get along with Bill
Reay? Billy had been hired by Conn Smythe, who was very loya
to him as he always is to people who work for him. I said I wouldn
have any trouble with Reay. I didn't want anything to do wit
coaching the hockey team, I told them. There was no way I woul
interfere in the way he did it. The coaching would be his baby.
would never go in the dressing room between periods or take par
in the coaching at all. If Reay asked me, naturally, I'd say what
thought was wrong. What I'm trying to make clear is that I wa
hired to get players and be responsible for how the hockey clu
made out, not to interfere with Reay as coach in his own dressin
room or behind the bench.

So we talked like this. We were getting close enough that
knew what the decision was going to be. I left the office and calle

my wife and told her what was happening. I said, 'What do you think?'

'What do you want to do?' she asked.

I said, 'I might as well give it a try.'

She said, 'That's all right with me, then. If you want it.'

I went back to Stafford's office and said, 'All right, I'll go to work for you August the first.'

I went back to Springfield then. We had to try to get rid of the house, and naturally we hit a time when nobody wanted it. My wife stayed there trying to sell it. Eventually we had to rent it, and then sell a year or so later.

But the first day I came to work, August 1, I found out pretty well where I stood around Toronto. I went in to the receptionist and said, 'I'd like to speak to Billy Reay.'

'Mr. Reay is not in,' she said. 'Would you care to take a seat?'

There I am, only the assistant general manager – you know? Being treated like a bug-spray salesman. And I realized right then that what went for that receptionist went for everybody else around Toronto, both in and out of the rink. They didn't know me. I was nothing to them, until I made some sort of a reputation with them, some mark.

I said, 'I'll go downstairs and have a cup of tea and come back in a little while.'

When I did come back from the snack bar, he was in. The girl said, 'Oh yes, you wish to see Mr. Reay,' and took me in. He had his little office on the second floor of the Gardens, with a window looking out on Church Street. The whole place has been remodelled since, but then it was just about big enough for two desks, one facing the other. One was his and one was mine.

He and I had known one another in hockey for a long time. We were the same age, born in 1918. We hadn't been friends, but as far as I know we weren't enemies either. He had worked in the shipyards and played for and coached the Quebec City team during the war when I was with the Cornwall Army team. He had won the Allan Cup there. After that our paths hadn't crossed much. He had gone from Quebec to the Montreal Canadiens before I turned up in Quebec as a player. Then he'd been coaching in Seattle and Victoria. He had come back to the American Hockey League at Rochester, but left to take over the Leafs the same year I got into that league at Springfield. Anyway, I didn't really know him. I never had any animosity for him. I've understood since that he had some for me, but that's natural in light of what happened.

At first, though, I had a lot of other things on my mind. I hadn't seen Toronto play at all for seven or eight years at least. When I was in Quebec I'd see other teams in the NHL because often we'd be playing in Montreal or Valleyfield on the Sunday afternoon. We'd go into Montreal on the Saturday afternoon and watch the game at the Forum that night. So I'd see Montreal a lot, and four of the other five teams that were in the league then fairly often. But I'd never see Toronto because in those days they were always in their own rink on a Saturday night. There was only one thing to do – look at the pictures. I used to get out the movies of the previous year's games. Shanty McKenzie at the Gardens would run them for me. 'Who the hell's Number 20?' I'd ask. That was Bob Pulford, of course. Or I'd say, 'That guy there – What's his number? Who is he?' I didn't recognize any of them at first. I did get to the point, by the time we got to training camp, where I at least had an idea of what some of them could do. Of course, one of the good things was that when I walked into training camp at Peterborough I had an open mind. I didn't know who was good or who was bad or what – meaning that so far as I was concerned the team was wide open.

Before that I'd been helping set up the training camp and doing some of the signing of players. The first job I had was to go to Seattle and try to sign Guyle Fielder. Leafs had drafted him in June. He was a good hockey player for a long time after that, but he just didn't want to play in the NHL. Seattle was where he wanted to be and that's where he stayed, always a good scorer and a great playmaker. The year we *didn't* sign him he had ninety-five assists for Seattle and for years he was almost always in the nineties in total points. But he only played nine games in the NHL, three with Boston and six with Detroit, all before I tried to sign him. In the NHL he never got a point of any kind.

So Fielder was my first signing assignment, and I flopped there. But on the way back I stopped on the prairies in Saskatoon, and signed Johnny Bower, whom we'd drafted from Cleveland. That was a good day's work for the Leafs. Also, I had talked my new bosses into having Leafs play exhibition games – including one in Quebec City against Boston. I still owned twenty-five per cent of the Aces and I couldn't see any harm in putting them in the way of making a little extra money. But the big bonus of that exhibition trip to Quebec was the deal for Allan Stanley. I made it right there in Quebec. I went down there with another player in mind, Bob Armstrong. I always liked Bob – and not only because we were both prematurely bald, either. He'd played for me in Springfield the year before. Really played well. Good defensive hockey player. And from watching the movies I knew Leafs were bad on defence. So I tried to get him from Boston.

Well, they weren't going to give up Armstrong. They'd seen how well he played, too, and the fact that I'd coached him, and now wanted him for Toronto, reinforced their idea that they should keep him. So I ended up trading Jim Morrison for Allan Stanley and cash. It's been reported often that Boston got the cash end of the deal, but that's wrong. We got Stanley and $7,500 for Morrison. Stanley went on to play more than six hundred games for Toronto in the next ten years, as honest and dependable a hockey player as a coach could hope for – half of one of the defence pairs in the years when we were going big: Stanley and Horton. Another thing we did in training camp that year was to turn Carl Brewer pro. Eventually he was teamed up with Bob Baun for the other pair in the great Toronto defence of the next few years – so good that later even a first-rate NHL defenceman like Al Arbour couldn't break in and be a regular.

Of course, being still a junior in his first year with us, Brewer had a lot to learn. He developed very quickly. He was a pretty good hockey player by the end of the season. He did a remarkable job for a first-year man.

But as the first weeks of that season wore on, one thing got plainer and plainer. The Leafs just weren't playing for Bill Reay. I'm not going to try to analyse why, or lay blame on anybody, including the players, but they weren't putting out for him and that was that.

Around the middle of November things were getting really bad. Detroit beat us 4–1 in Toronto on Saturday night, November 15, and the crowd booed Leafs a lot. That's a thing you can't ignore, getting booed at home – especially when you deserve it. Something had to be done. Leafs' hockey committee had a meeting right after the game and called me in, before the club took off for a Sunday-night game in Boston. They wanted to fine the Leafs right then and there. I talked them out of it for two reasons. First, Ed Chadwick hadn't played well in goal. If the other players wanted to blame him for bad goals they had some justification. But, more important, I didn't think it made sense to fine a team for a game that was over. If they were going to be fined it would be more useful to base it on a game coming up.

Anyway, I knew what I was going to do. We had two road games in the next few days, the one in Boston Sunday night and one in New York in the middle of the week. We used to travel by train in those days. We got into Boston Sunday morning. At noon Billy Reay and I were up in our suite and I called the players up there. Now, let's see who we had. There was Chadwick and Johnny Bower, the goalkeepers. Stanley, Horton, Baun, Brewer, Marc Reaume, and Noel Price, the defencemen. Then Brian and Barry Cullen, Bob Pulford, George Armstrong, the captain, Dick Duff, Bert Olmstead, Billy Harris, Frank Mahovlich, Ron Stewart, Dave Creighton, and Rudy Migay. They all stood or sat around this room in the Copley. I did most of the talking. I reminded them that the fans were booing them. The moment the fans weren't satisfied, the management wasn't satisfied either. I told them that I'd already saved them some money by talking the Silver Seven out of fines after the Saturday game. But I said, if they lost these next two games, it would cost them two hundred dollars each. You might think that wasn't being very tough with them. All they had to get was a tie in two games to avoid the fine. But don't forget Boston had a good club, Stanley Cup finalist against Montreal the year before. New York was good too. Anyway, that night in Boston we were losing 4–2 in the third when Ron Stewart scored one goal for us and Allan Stanley got another in the last ninety seconds to get a 4–4 tie.

I went to the dressing room after and kidded them over how lucky they were that I wasn't in there collecting their dough.

But nobody was happier than I was when Stanley scored that tying goal. I didn't want their money. I wanted them to play hockey, that's all.

But that was only one night. We lost in New York three nights later, 7–4. Here it was getting on in November and we'd won only five games out of sixteen. When we got back I knew nothing was solved. The hockey committee called another meeting. They were talking over what was wrong with the hockey club. (In another ten years I'd be the guy they were arguing about firing, for the same reasons.) But now some of them wanted to fire Reay and some didn't. It was quite an argument. Finally they asked me.

I said, 'Well, you're paying me, so I'd better tell you what I think.' I told them that the team obviously wasn't playing for Reay. I thought he wasn't tough enough on them; that he was trusting them to do things and they were letting him down. They asked me what I would do about it. I said I wasn't the general manager, I was only the assistant general manager. In a way, I put it up to them. That's when they decided to make me the general manager, to be fully responsible for making the rules for the hockey club and for seeing that coach and players alike stuck to them.

This meeting was in a Toronto hotel. I went back to the Gardens thinking about it. This was the general manager's job that I had wanted, and thought I could handle. Now I had it. I was glad to have it, and glad that it hadn't been somebody else's job – in other words, glad that I got the job without somebody else having to be bounced. I was just wishing that I was more confident we'd get through the whole thing without anybody losing his job. But I wasn't.

This was Friday, November 21, 1958. A big day in my life. I must say that the press and public didn't exactly jump for joy when my appointment as full general manager was announced. Rex MacLeod wrote about it in the *Globe and Mail* the next morning. He put it this way: 'Leafs have won five of their first sixteen games, so in a sweeping move, have promoted George Imlach to be general manager. So meteoric has been the rise of this young hockey executive that it is conceivable he might make it to president if the Leafs lose a few more games.' But he did also quote me as saying that some things were wrong with this hockey club and they were going to be fixed, because 'I'd rather be shot for a lion than a lamb.' No change there from the way I look at things today.

That weekend we tied New York 2–2 and Chicago 3–3. Some sports columnists later accused us of doing what came next while they were away in Vancouver at the Canadian football championship, the Grey Cup, just to get it done without any public uproar. That had nothing to do with it. It was just something that had to be done. The events had been moving for weeks.

That week we had two games with Detroit, Wednesday in Toronto and Thursday in Detroit – the U. S. Thanksgiving. Early that week I went into the office I shared with Billy Reay and I said, 'Look, we're going to have to tell these guys that if something isn't done, if they don't start playing hockey, there's going to have to be a change.' In a way I was trying to warn him. I can't remember what he said. He felt as bad about all this as anybody, maybe worse, but he still thought he could bring them out of it. Maybe he blamed me partly for the trouble we were in. There had been times when we had disagreed on things. I guess the players knew about it. That couldn't help much. But I had my job to do, just as he had his.

We lost 5–2 at home Wednesday night and looked bad. We lost 3–2 in Detroit Thursday night. I came back with the club on Friday. We were going to have a practice at four in the afternoon. I was sitting around with the problems going through my head. We had Chicago coming in here Saturday night. We were going further and further down in the league standings every game we played. Now we'd only won five games out of twenty. We were the league doormat. I can remember sitting around the damned office with these thoughts of what to do going around and around in my mind.

I pretty well knew what I had to do. That Friday afternoon just after lunch I went to see Conn Smythe. I wanted to let him know first, because he was the one who hired Billy Reay. He was sitting there behind that big desk with the pictures behind him of all the Stanley Cup winners he had managed. He knew that tough things had to be done sometimes, in running a hockey club. He'd done tough things himself.

I said, 'I'm going to relieve Billy Reay of his duties as coach.'

He looked at me hard for a few seconds. We talked a little more. Then he said, 'Well, if that's the way it is.'

I went downstairs for a cup of tea. Then I went back upstairs to the little office that Billy and I shared. He was there. It was a hell of a situation, here in one small office with the guy I'd been working with for nearly four months, but I had to do it.

I said, 'Billy, I'm relieving you of your duties as coach.'

He jumped up. He wouldn't believe me. He was mad as hell. It was tough; it's always tough.

'Does Mr. Smythe know?' he asked.

'He knows,' I said.

One of the bad things, for him, was that he could have had the general manager's job. He could have been there in my place, laying the blame on some other coach. He did tell the press that day bitterly that he should have known in training camp that this was going to happen eventually. 'This team will improve,' he said. 'It's much better than its record shows.' He still had a contract, of course, and would get paid, but that never lessens the shock – not much, anyway.

All this had happened between about 1.30 and 3.30 in the afternoon. Now the players were coming in for the four o'clock practice. When they were all in the dressing room and some of them partly undressed I went in and said, 'Never mind practising today. I've got something to tell you.' They listened. 'I've had to relieve Billy Reay as coach,' I said. They all stared at me, saying nothing. 'Now I've got something to talk to you players about,' I said. 'I want you all to stay in this room. I'll call you in one at a time. . . .''

They were in the dressing room. I had each one come alone to the little medical room near by – across the press room corridor. I told each of them to bring all his stuff with him when he came to me, because no one was going to be allowed back in the dressing room once he'd talked to me. I wanted to talk to them that way, without them getting together and one guy telling the rest what I had said. I wanted a response from individuals. They'd talk to me and then go home.

When each guy came in, I would say, 'I want to know one thing from you. If I take this hockey club, *will you play hockey for me?* I think I can help you, and I'm prepared to stick my neck out if you're prepared to give me your promise that you'll play hockey for me. If you won't play for me I'd better know right now.'

I got some pretty classic answers. Bob Pulford's was one.

'Whose side are you on,' he said, 'players or management?' Just like that. That was it. He just let me know. But he said he would play for me. This was a promise. I've never let any of those who promised me that day off the hook. Even ten years later I'd remind some of them of that promise and say, 'You're not living up to it, you know.'

But they all promised they would play for me.

One other I remember was Bert Olmstead. He'd been a pal of Billy Reay's when they were teammates on the Canadiens. But there never was any question about Olmstead. He was a profes-sional. He recognized the way things were and the way they had to be. He realized that something had to happen. He told me he'd do his best. That was a big relief to me. I made him an assistant captain and assistant coach. He was a leader in the dressing room and I wanted him on my side. He publicly quit the assistant coach dodge a few weeks later because he said he wasn't being consulted on team moves. If he was going to be responsible for something he had no part in, he'd rather just be a player, he said. But I respected him for that too. A lot of people tried to create friction between Olmstead and me, then and later. I mean, his character is a lot like mine, or completely opposite, or something. But I never had any real trouble with him. Sometimes he'd start giving me a little argument, or sometimes a big argument, but when I'd crack down — well, he's a hockey man and he knows that the coach can't take any back talk in the dressing room. Many years later, after we left him unprotected in the draft and New York drafted him and he quit hockey, he blasted off at me. But under those circumstances anybody gets mad. I let him do the talking. I'm glad now that when people tried to drag me into it, I kept quiet. No comment. He played well for me. To me, that's the best thing I can say about a player — and I've said it often about Olmstead.

The next day, the Saturday, was the first time I'd ever been in the Leafs' dressing room just before a game, or between periods. As I'd told the Silver Seven when they hired me, I've always believed that the dressing room belongs to the coach. In there he's in sole command, like the captain of a ship or the pilot of an aircraft. And if I was ever working as general manager and someone else was coaching, I wouldn't go into the dressing room, either. It would be his alone. A coach has a tough enough job without anybody interfering in the dressing room.

There we were in the dressing room that night facing each other for the first time in that particular situation: the coach and the team, with a game to be played.

I was forty years old, without much hair left, I swore a lot, and that's about all they knew about me. I was certainly no great leadership figure to them. Some of them had never heard my name, even, until four months before. They knew I'd never been more than a senior hockey player and a coach and manager in the minors. I mean, having Punch Imlach take over as coach right then wasn't exactly one of those big dramatic events in a hockey player's life —

like it would have been if a former great player like Milt Schmidt or Toe Blake had been brought in to coach them.

But we did have something in common. We were both down. If nobody thought much of me in the NHL or among the hockey public right then, nobody thought much of them either. I hadn't even been tried. They had been tried, and had been found wanting. Later a lot of people were going to call us the Cinderella team. Right then the only thing Cinderella about us was that we were down in the ashes, last place, as low as a hockey team can get.

I genuinely don't know what I said to them that night but I tried to get across some of the things I believe in that I thought would help them. And out we went, not knowing or even guessing that ten years from then, some of us would still be together, having hit the heights and then the depths again.

That night we played a good game but Chicago scored in the last few minutes and beat us 2–1. The next night in Boston we won 2–1. I remember Lynn Patrick telling me that night, 'The way your guys came off the bench at the end of the game, anyone would have thought you won the Stanley Cup.'

The Stanley Cup. Right from the cradle, Canadians know what that means. Maybe hockey fans in the United States are getting the idea now too. The Stanley Cup is Canada's World Series, Super-Bowl, Kentucky Derby, world championship fight, all rolled into a set of post-season playoffs that mean money, but much more. The best hockey in the world is played during the Stanley Cup. It's the thing a young kid dreams about, if he dreams about hockey – getting the winning goal in the Stanley Cup; hell, getting any goal in the Stanley Cup. Here we were, in last place. How could we even dream of the Stanley Cup?

All the same, right then I started to say, as often as anybody would listen, that we were going to get off the floor, that we were going to make it into one of the first four places in the league – be one of the teams that would play for the Stanley Cup. I talked loud and long. I did it on purpose. Somebody had to give that team the idea that they could win. Somebody had to stand up for them in public. I tried to do that. The writers scoffed. Some of the other coaches scoffed. I didn't give a damn. I stuck to my guns. It wasn't long before the team began to believe it, too, and show it on the ice.

That win over Boston was the beginning. We went unbeaten in

five more games after that. We were getting pride and spirit. The truth is I could talk to them that year better than I ever have been able to since. Partly this was because neither of us knew much about the other, but we also had this common goal – to start making a respectable showing.

I remember two weeks later, at home in Toronto. We'd been unbeaten in five games then and New York was leading us 4–3. Their fourth goal had been a bad one. Someone had shot it at the backboards and Johnny Bower had come out to try to trap the rebound, and missed. That left him away out of position and Dean Prentice just tapped it in. There wasn't much time left.

I went up and down the bench behind the players. I said, 'Your goalkeeper is a horse's-ass if you don't get that goal back. This is a team, and you don't want anybody on it to be a horse's-ass. So get it back.' With about eighty seconds left in the game Dick Duff scored and got it back, making it six in a row unbeaten. We lost the next night in Boston to end that streak, but in the meantime the team had proved to itself that with extra effort they were as good as anybody.

I still looked on myself as only a fill-in coach for the hockey team then. Certainly if they'd gone out and lost the first six with me behind the bench, that would have been it – I'd have had to hire a coach. But even when I talked to Alf Pike about coaching Leafs, the hockey committee seemed to want me to coach. Especially Harold Ballard, I think. But Pike made it easy for me not to hire him. He looked like the best prospect at that time. He'd been doing well as coach of Winnipeg in the Western League and he had a good NHL background with Rangers, which is more than I had. If he'd been easy to get along with I would have hired him. But he wanted conditions written into his contract that wouldn't be accepted by the Leaf management anyway – certainly conditions that I wasn't asking for myself. Also Jack Perrin, the Winnipeg owner, wanted something back if he was going to give up his coach. He wanted a player, or players. We simply didn't have any to give away. Two or three years before, Toronto's farm club at Pittsburgh had been disbanded and Leafs had lost a lot of those players in the draft in Montreal. That had started a decline in the Toronto club that was still on when I arrived. Apart from the eighteen players on the Leafs, we only had about four at Rochester. In conditions like that you don't give away players to get a coach.

Especially when I knew that what the Leaf management really wanted was for me to keep on as coach right then. Some of them later changed their minds once or twice, of course.

After the Pike deal didn't work, I didn't look any more. I was caught up in trying to get out of last place. Now we were playing better hockey, but we still couldn't gain on anybody. Then I got Larry Regan from Boston. They put him and three others on waivers. I'd had Larry in Quebec. I knew what he could do. He's got a lot of go in him and was a hell of a stick-handler. He also had a pretty good gift for being a positive thinker. Some people have another word for it, something like bullfeathers, but a guy who is thinking positively all the time is going to do any club a lot of good. Regan used to use the line that he'd been bailing me out of trouble all his life, first in Quebec and now in Toronto. That amused the guys. I put him between Dick Duff and George Armstrong and they played the game hard.

The best line was one we put together a little later that season. We badly needed scoring. I got Gerry Ehman from Hershey. Traded Willie Marshall, another minor leaguer and a good one, for him. I knew what Ehman could do. He'd got forty goals for me in Springfield the previous year. I put him on right wing with Billy Harris at centre and Frank Mahovlich on left, and that was one hot scoring line. But the other line, Pulford at centre with Olmstead and Stewart on the wings, was a good line too, both at scoring and checking, especially at checking. But Pulford got 23 goals that season, and Stewart got 21 and Olmstead 15, so they weren't so bad at scoring either.

A funny story about Ehman. When we got him in that trade, nobody was very impressed. Then he went out and got twelve goals in about the last two months of the season. Right near the end of the season, in March, when we were still in last place, Milt Dunnell wrote a column in the *Star* about the deal, telling how it had helped Toronto. It was slanted towards blowing me up as a genius and letting on that in letting Ehman go, Baz Bastien at Hershey had sort of been taken on the deal. Well, Baz wrote a very hot letter to Milt about it. Told him that when Toronto was through for the season, maybe Milt would like to come down to Hershey and watch the other part of the deal, Willie Marshall, in the American Hockey League playoffs. And he was going to reserve tickets for me to come and see Willie Marshall in the playoffs too.

But something told Baz he shouldn't mail the letter until we were out of the playoffs for sure. The way I found out about it is that later that spring I was down in his office, and Baz pulled the unsent letter out of the files, and showed it to me. Ehman was great in the playoffs too; six goals in twelve games. They don't come much better than that.

What a winter and spring that was! On March 4 we were still last, five points out of fourth place – the last playoff spot. Then we had a little slump and by March 9 we were nine points out of fourth. On March 14, a Saturday, we were seven points away from fourth place and had only five games to play – a total of ten possible points if we won them all.

New York Rangers were fourth. They were the team we had to overtake. Then the luck of the schedule intervened. We had two games against the Rangers that second-last weekend of the season. I remember a story by Rex MacLeod in the *Globe and Mail* on the Saturday morning that Rangers came into Toronto. 'A win for Rangers in either game will send Leafs to the embalmers,' he wrote, and he was right. If Rangers won Saturday night we'd be nine points behind them with only four games to play. Even if we won that one and lost Sunday we'd still be seven points behind with only three games to play. We had to win both to stay in contention.

That same morning there was the official announcement from the National Hockey League office on Stanley Cup playoff dates. This is usually full of alternatives, because for television and other reasons the dates have to be set before the final standings have been decided. The system is for the first-place team to meet the third-place team in one semi-final, with second and fourth going in the other. This official announcement from league headquarters gave several different alignments: Montreal against Boston, Montreal against Chicago, Montreal against New York; also, Chicago against New York, or Chicago against Boston. There was no mention of Toronto against anybody.

But that night we beat Rangers 5–0. My guys played an absolutely great game. George Armstrong got one goal and Frank Mahovlich and Dick Duff two each, the shutout going to Bower. In New York the next night it was a fantastic hockey game, ending with the New York goalie out and six forwards swarming around our goal. But we beat them 6–5, with Armstrong getting three of the goals and Bob Pulford scoring the winner on a play with Olmstead and Stanley.

Those two wins put us past Detroit into fifth place, three points behind Rangers, with three games left to play. One trouble was that we'd just won two in a row, and we'd never won *more* than two in a row all season. There was nothing easy about the schedule either. Thursday night we had to go into Montreal. Montreal was in first place with Jean Beliveau having a good year and Dickie Moore shooting for a scoring record, with better than ninety points in goals and assists.

I remember running into a group of Boston players that Thursday at the Montreal Forum when we went for a skate. They'd beaten New York the night before, helping us, and they were in to play the Canadiens on Saturday night. Right then I almost (but not quite) felt sorry for Phil Watson, the coach in New York. We had feuded in the Quebec league, and again in Quebec City when he coached the junior Frontenacs and I had the Aces, and we were fighting for the crowds. He's the kind of coach who suffers even more intensely than the rest of us. I knew all the Boston guys, of course. They were pretty cocky, home and cooled out in second place. I remember saying to Fleming Mackell, 'How did Watson take it last night?'

'He took it as if he was being hit on the head with a mallet,' Mackell said. 'He sank slowly behind the boards, over on their bench. I could see less of him every time I looked.'

I told the Boston guys, then, in public, with some of the Leafs listening and grinning, that we were going to play them in the playoffs, because we were going to finish fourth and they were going to finish second. We would beat them in six games, I said, and would only let them go that far because they had done us a good turn by beating New York the night before. What they said back I couldn't print. But anyway.

That night we beat Montreal. Then we were only one point behind Rangers. But Rangers had one kick left. They went out on Saturday afternoon and beat Detroit. Referee Red Storey gave Detroit a five-minute penalty for some damn thing and New York won it – and if I could have climbed through the TV set to murder Storey, I would have. That put them three points up on us. We had our backs to the wall again. We beat Chicago on the Saturday night (they were in third place) to get back in range. When we got on the train to go to Detroit that Saturday night we were one point down again, and the whole thing depended on the two Sunday night games, Rangers at home to Montreal and us in Detroit. We got off the train in Windsor and went by bus to Detroit, early in the morning. The customs guys kidded that they'd been told to give us a hard time. 'We've got to stop you,' one said. 'It looks like nobody else can.' When we got to the hotel, King Clancy took off for Mass and lit all the candles he could find.

I can always remember that night. Of course, I'd hardly slept at all on the train. I got to the Detroit Olympia early because the New York game started at seven and we didn't start until eight, and Detroit had a sports score ticker in their office. I went into the Detroit office to watch the ticker. Dickie Moore with Canadiens was going for a scoring record that night. I'll tell you I sure was hoping he'd get all the goals he needed. First thing I knew the machine started to rattle away and I read it. *New York had scored the first goal!* Oh, no, no, I said. But two minutes later – bing, bing, two fast goals for Montreal. Beliveau and Moore. So New York was behind. I went into our dressing room just before the game and said, 'Montreal is winning 2–1.' If Montreal beat New York and we beat Detroit, we were in the playoffs.

When we went out on the ice I was still watching the New York score on the scoreboard. But first thing I know we're down 2–0. Norm Ullman got the first and Marcel Pronovost – both of them would wind up playing for me ten years later – got the second. And that's how it was at 16.22 of the first period when the final score was announced from New York – Canadiens had won it 4–2. Now it was really up to us. But we were still down 2–0 when the first period was over.

I've got to give my old buddy Stafford Smythe a little shot here. We're down 2–0 but there's no use me telling Leafs anything. They knew. So I don't go into the dressing room. He comes along the hall.

'Well, at least you had a good try,' he said. 'You have nothing to be ashamed of.'

I exploded, 'What the hell are you talking about? We've come too far to lose now! Don't be stupid!'

When they came out in the second period they were flying. Armstrong told me on the way by, 'We'll get it for you.' I don't know what they'd talked about in there by themselves. Maybe they didn't talk. In the second, Larry Regan, playing the game of his life,

knocked in Armstrong's rebound, and we're only down 2–1. Then
Bob Baun let go a slider off the right point for his first goal of the
season. 2–2. Ullman got them ahead again at 15.16. Carl Brewer
tied it up at 17.08. Regan scored his second goal twenty-one seconds
later to put us ahead 4–3.

I said to myself, 'This is it! We got ahead!'

Then Pronovost highballed down the middle, split between Baun
and Brewer, and let it go – and his angle shot trickled off Bower's
glove into the net and that tied it again, 4–4.

Regan at that point had scored two, got an assist on Brewer's goal,
and wasn't finished yet. Early in the third there was a face-off in our
end. I saw Regan go over to Duff, before the puck was dropped. I
heard later he told Duff, 'You're going to get the winner. I'm going
to give it to you. Just be there!'

Regan got the draw and went down the ice stickhandling like a
wizard. When he hit the defence he beat Warren Godfrey twice
and Red Kelly once and circled around the boards in the corner,
still with the puck. His passout in front of the net got there at
exactly the same time that Dick Duff did. Duff's stick was in the air,
shooting as the puck came out, and wham, it was in, Duff's twenty-
ninth of that season. That was the winner. Later on Billy Harris
made a nice play for our sixth. He passed back to Baun at the point
and when Baun shot it back in, Harris tipped it out of the air into
the goal. I don't remember all the goals I've seen in my life, but I
remember every one from that game in detail. Toronto 6, Detroit 4.
We were in.

We had a chartered plane waiting in Windsor. We got to Toronto
about one in the morning. Some of the wives were out to see us,
along with photographers. We just touched down to pick up some
stuff. Then we flew on to Boston. By four a.m. we were dropping
our gear at the Boston Gardens and then went to the hotel. I never
did get to bed. I put on my pajamas at five in the morning when we
got to the hotel, and I might as well have saved myself the trouble.
King Clancy and I had this suite. The phone never stopped ringing,
from all over Canada. Especially from Quebec. Everybody in Quebec
was my friend. I was still in my pajamas twelve hours later, at five
in the afternoon, and I hadn't been to bed.

That game in Detroit was one of the greatest I was ever in.
Winning the Stanley Cup for the first time three years later certainly
was a thrill but by the time we were winning the Cup we were

expected to win. That spring of 1959, even a week before the season ended, you could have got a hundred to one against us even making the playoffs. I remember hearing later that Conn Smythe had said to somebody on Leafs' hockey committee, 'What did you get, did you get a coach or did you get a madman?' This because I'm saying, 'We're gonna make it, we're gonna make it.' They got a madman, all right, but they didn't know it at the time.

Of course, in the coaching business there is a very thin line between a madman and a genius. Like maybe a couple of goals at the right time. Anyway, for the next day or so in Boston, that March of 1959, life was just one big round of everybody telling me what a great guy I was, and how great the team was, et cetera. Harold Ballard, you know, he's one of the biggest cheerleaders in the whole world – loves hockey, loves the Leafs – Ballard was never happier in his life, because he was one of the people who went to bat for me to take the thing over in November. In the headlines we were being called the Cinderella team. We had captured something in the public imagination that is always rare, but comes when a team gets off the floor and starts winning and refuses to quit. People do like that.

In Boston we lost the first semi-final game 5–1. It was a big letdown, had to be, after what we'd been through.

We lost the second game, too, but I was always sure we were going to win the series. We won the third game in Toronto, with Ehman scoring the tying goal in the third period and the winner in sudden-death overtime, from Harris and Mahovlich. Mahovlich scored the winner in overtime in the fourth game. We won the fifth game back in Boston 4–1, and after that one Ballard pulled a gag on the players. He stomped into the dressing room at the end of the game and said, 'Boys, you played well tonight and I feel this is an appropriate time to introduce your new coach for next season.' When they were all gaping at the door, in I walked – wearing a beatnik-type toupee that one of our fans in Boston had loaned me for the occasion.

We lost the sixth game in Toronto but won the seventh in Boston with Regan playing with a broken wrist, frozen and in a cast. And we gave Canadiens a real run in the Stanley Cup finals. They beat us four games and we beat them one, but every game was close. If we'd had just a little bit of luck here or there we might have made it all the way from last place to the Stanley Cup. In the fourth game

George Armstrong scored a goal that went right through the net. The referee didn't see it. If it had been counted, we might have won the fourth game and gone back to Montreal tied 2–2 in games instead of down 3–1. This goal showed plainly in colour films of the game and later was one highlight of a hockey film put out by one of the game's television sponsors.

But that season was still the greatest thrill of my life. Now people knew that Leafs once again were a team. And a few more knew who Imlach was. One day my wife and I got home to find a letter on royal stationery, several weeks before Queen Elizabeth was to visit Toronto. This letter invited us to lunch with the Queen aboard the royal yacht *Britannia* in Toronto harbour. At first I thought it might have been some of hockey's more imaginative practical jokers pulling a gag on me. But soon the newspapers started phoning – by then they had the invitations list. Naturally it put our household in an uproar. One of the big chuckles I had at that time was this column in the *Globe and Mail* by my co-author* in this book, who was a sports columnist for that newspaper then:

(Punch Imlach is coach and general manager of Toronto Maple Leafs, a hockey team. He is a man of medium height and build, strong views, and a fine head of hair which was given to him as a present last spring by a grateful local chapter of the Mafia in Boston. Besides the colour and virtuosity of his normal speech, he is noted in that it was he, and not Shakespeare, who first said, 'A team that won't be beat, can't be beat.' For these and other proper reasons, he was invited with his wife to lunch yesterday with the Queen.)

TIME TABLE, MONDAY, JUNE 29

12.44 a.m. – Punch Imlach rises from bed in mighty bound. Reads clock. Tears flannelet nightcap from head, flings it into corner, charges into kitchen to get toupee from refrigerator, shouting, meanwhile, 'We're late!'

12.46 a.m. – Mrs. Imlach, already half-dressed, notices that it's dark outside. Draws to her husband's attention possibility that it is middle of night rather than middle of day, when they are expected aboard Royal yacht *Britannia.* He turns on television. Stares moodily into beady eyes of Charlie Chan. Returns toupee to refrigerator. Returns to bed.

*Footnote from S.Y.: I tried to talk Punch out of this, but he roared, 'But it's exactly what happened!'

4.32 a.m. – It is Mrs. Imlach's turn to awake in panic. Still da
outside but she feels this must have been caused by unexpecte
eclipse of sun. Rises to check clock.

4.33 a.m. – Clock shows 4.33 a.m. As double-check, she remov
Mr. Imlach's left hand from a volume in which he has bee
employing hand as a bookmark. Notices that although cover of boo
reads, *Ode on Intimations of Immortality from Recollections*
Early Childhood, Imlach has hidden inside a tome entitled, *Prop*
Forms of Address for Royalty. Slumber disturbed, Imlach mumbl
politely, 'So I said to these censored deleted sportswriters, You
Majesty, I said, you guys just stay against me and I'm really in
you . . .' His wristwatch confirms time.

7.10 a.m. – Alarm sounds. Imlach swings feet over side of be
and sits rubbing face for first five minutes before he realizes wh
day it is. Roars briefly, arousing wife and children. While breakfa
is being prepared he practises shaking hands with air in corner o
bedroom, each time bowing low and murmuring, 'How do you do

7.16 a.m. – Has sensation of being spied upon. Turns. Is bein
watched from doorway by goggle-eyed son and daughter. Out-stare
them. When they leave, he curtsies thoughtfully. Not that he *he*
to, of course; but any man is better if he can play more than on
position.

7.18 a.m. – Recalls that in addition to being day when he an
his wife lunch with Queen, it is day when Conn Smythe's filly
Wonder Where, goes in Woodbine Oaks. Considers prayer on he
behalf. Decides it would be sacrilegious to pray for any filly that ca
run that fast anyway. Prays for Major Flight in Queen's Plat
instead.

7.22 a.m. – Roars, 'When do we eat?'

7.24 a.m. – Sits down to orange juice, ham, sausages, pancake
eggs, sweet rolls, honey, four cups of coffee.

7.45 a.m. – Wife asks if he wishes more. Says no, hasn't muc
appetite, must be the excitement.

8.00 a.m. – Being calm, sensible woman, wife completes house
work before she showers, dresses, and sits quietly awaiting time t
leave. Imlach shaves, showers, dons lounge suit and is pacing floo
by 8.58 a.m.

9.02 a.m. – States to wife that his lounge suit is rumpled. Sh
presses lounge suit five times in next one hour and 58 minutes.

11.00 a.m. – Leave for Royal yacht. Route is west along Kingston Rd. (55 mph).

11.04 a.m. – Makes unscheduled stop to inspect detachment of Metropolitan Police and receive memento of occasion, which will cost him two deleted points.

11.30 a.m. – Arrival at Orchard Park Tavern.

11.32 a.m. – Departure from Orchard Park Tavern. Proceeds west on Fleet (22 mph), south on Jarvis (47 mph; no cops in sight); west on Queen's Quay.

11.50 a.m. – Imlachs are piped aboard Royal yacht. While crossing gangway, he doffs hat at white ensign. Toupee drops in water. 'Good deleted gracious!' Imlach comments, peering over the side. But it is gone.

12.32 p.m. – Meets Queen. Tells her of early days in hockey with Ed Wildey's Young Rangers.

12.45 p.m. – Local offices of Audubon Society flooded with calls from citizens claiming to have sighted a mallard drake wearing a toupee.

2.00 p.m. – Imlachs debark from Royal yacht and proceed home quietly, agreeing that it has been a long way indeed, from last place.

Me and Clancy . . . and Kelly

One thing for damn sure, at the end of my first season with the Leafs I felt we had the impetus to be the next club to rule the roost in the National Hockey League. If you look back you can see how it goes in cycles. In the late forties Leafs were the ones to beat for the Stanley Cup, and they weren't beaten often. Then Detroit took over for a few years, with Montreal the main challenger. Then Jean Beliveau arrived with the Canadiens, along with Boom-Boom Geoffrion, Jacques Plante, Tom Johnson, Dickie Moore, the Pocket Rocket. All these guys joined Doug Harvey and Rocket Richard, who were getting on but were still great hockey players. For a while Montreal had it all its own way. Now Leafs were challenging. But I knew as well as anyone that we had holes in the team. They all played like hell for me that first year, but I knew I would still have to make moves if I thought I could better the team. Canadiens were the powerhouse; to win a Stanley Cup we had to beat them; to beat them we had to make changes.

The biggest and best change that we made in the second season I had the Leafs was to get Red Kelly from Detroit. I guess this is the obvious time to say something about King Clancy, because I don't know if we ever could have got Kelly right then without Clancy's particular combination of persuasiveness, fun, trustworthiness, and just general likeableness.

Over the years reporters used to ask me to give them a rundown
on how King Clancy and I split our duties, how we got along when
we were together so much. Well, I don't know how he got along
with me – it must have been tough sometimes. But who the hell
couldn't get along with him? It would have been an impossibility
not to. As to who did what, well, if there was something to be done,
t was done. If I didn't do it, he did. That's it in a nutshell. If I
didn't make the practice he took over. If I wanted him to go somewhere, maybe to talk to a player or another club about a deal, or
almost anything, he'd do it. As I saw it, we weren't manager-coach
and assistant manager-coach; we were partners. I needed his help.
I was getting so I knew a little about the league – but who knew as
much about it as Clancy? Thirty years earlier he'd been a great
player for the Leafs. He'd played for Conn Smythe and worked for
him, was loyal to him, and knew how to advise another guy like me
in dealing with him. He'd known Stafford since Stafford was a kid.
He had refereed in the league for years, so he knew the personalities.
Then he had coached the Leafs. He had friends everywhere, and
the kind of big-league background that helped me an awful lot all
the time we were together, especially in that first few years. We had
our battles. Sometimes anybody else listening to us arguing might
have thought we were mortal enemies. But in that kind of a job,
facing problems that sometimes couldn't be talked over with many
people, we tended to brace each other. When he was down, I seemed
to be up and could get him up. Same the other way – when I was
down, he was the guy who could get me moving. The Kelly deal was
typical of the way we worked.

Kelly was one of the great hockey players of his day. In all the
modern acclaim for Bobby Orr – and I'm not trying to take anything
away from Orr – it's interesting to look at Kelly's record. Back in
the 1950-51 season, when it was a lot tougher to score goals in the
NHL than it is now, Kelly had 17 goals playing defence for Detroit.
A couple of years later he scored 19. A year after he scored 16. For
seven years in there he always had 15 goals or better. There was
one eight-year stretch in the 1950s when he was a first all-star six
times and second all-star twice. He won the Lady Byng Memorial
Trophy three times, won the James Norris Memorial (for the
league's best defenceman), and several times was in the league's top
ten scorers, rare for a defenceman.

He was also everybody's idea of a gentleman and still is. He didn't smoke or swear, and he had about one drink a year – something mild after the last game of the season.

But around the time I got to the Leafs, Detroit was sagging. They were tied for first place on the weekend I took over coaching the Leafs, but from then on they went steadily down. They finished last that year. The next season, 1959-60, they were fighting us for second place for the first few months of the season. But they didn't look as if they could hang on. Jack Adams, general manager at Detroit, could see that and he wasn't one to stand on sentiment. He knew he had to shake up his club, and in early February of 1960 he made a deal he figured would do it – he traded Kelly and Billy McNeill to New York for Bill Gadsby and Eddie Shack.

But Kelly, who hadn't played for any team but Detroit as a pro, took it hard. There was more to it, as we'll see, but not many knew that. Anyway, Kelly announced he wouldn't report to New York. Billy McNeill decided he'd refuse too. That killed the deal. But Adams wouldn't back up, either, and take them back. Instead he suspended them both.

Well, I knew Kelly could help us. As I said before, my big aim at that time was to build a team for one function: to beat Canadiens. To do that we had to be more powerful at centre. Red had played a little left wing for Detroit from time to time. I knew how well he skated, checked, made plays, and so on. I figured he could play centre and that he was one guy I could put out against Jean Beliveau and make the big guy fight for any goals he got.

But, as I hinted a minute ago, there was a background to this situation. This was February. Seven months before, in the previous summer, Jack Adams had called me. He was a guy who'd been in hockey as a player, coach, and manager for forty years – Jolly Jack, they called him. But he wasn't laughing much those days. He'd had a last place team the previous spring and was looking around for ways to make sure it didn't happen again.

'How'd you like to make a deal for Kelly?' he asked me.

'Sure, I'd like to make a deal for Kelly,' I said.

It turned out he was having trouble signing him. When a general manager is signing players after they'd finished last the year before he doesn't figure he should get too many arguments. He was getting arguments from Kelly.

So Jack and I started coming up with names, for a deal. I mentioned Marc Reaume. He'd been our fifth defenceman the

revious season, once we'd got straightened away with the Horton-
tanley, Brewer-Baun combinations. I also mentioned another
oung hockey player; I can't even remember now who it was. But I
aid I'd give him Reaume and this other young hockey player for
Kelly. Jack said he was interested. He'd think it over.

Well, deals don't often happen all at once. You talk and think,
alk and think. I thought about it for a long while. The more I
hought, the more I thought maybe I had offered too much. If
Adams couldn't sign Kelly anyway, maybe I could get him for less.

A month later I called Jack.

'Lookit, Jack,' I said, 'I don't think I'm so interested in Kelly. I'm
rying to build a hockey club and I just figure I can't give two young
layers for an old player, at this time. Maybe one, but not two.' I
vas thinking maybe I could get Kelly for just Reaume.

But Jack said, 'Well, it's just as well. Kelly has agreed to the
ontract and everything is all right.'

But that was a tip-off about the way that Jack was thinking of
Kelly. I mean, I figured he'd offered a contract that Kelly didn't
vant, but Kelly had signed it. That usually doesn't mean you've got
happy hockey player. So when he did try to deal Kelly to New
York five months later, everybody else was surprised – but not us,
ecause we'd known all along that Jack was ready to trade Kelly if
e could make the right deal.

Anyway, now Kelly was refusing to go to New York. He wouldn't
ven talk about it. And Adams had suspended him.

I remember that Saturday night King and I were sitting together
n the plane on the way down to Boston. We talked about our own
ame for a while. Then I said to King, 'What about Kelly? Do you
hink maybe we should try to make a deal for him?'

'That's what I think,' King said in that gravelly voice he's got –
vhat you'd call a whisky voice, except that King never drinks.

We agreed to talk about it later when we were alone. No use
omebody happening to pick up a word or two about a deal like that
rom a conversation on an airplane, where the acoustics are some-
imes pretty strange.

The next morning in Boston King went to church as usual.
When he came back to our suite we talked about Kelly again. We
vanted him. The way I recall it, I said, 'Look, you're a Catholic
nd Red's a Catholic – why don't you call Jack, isn't he a Catholic
oo, and ask him for permission to talk to Red?' I mean, this was a

Sunday, and religion was on everybody's mind, eh? Nothing personal.

King remembers it a little differently. He said that when he got in from church, I was up. Usually when he got back from church on a Sunday morning – we were almost always on the road on a Sunday – I'd still be asleep and he'd eat breakfast and then crawl back into bed for a few more hours too. But this morning I was up. King says I didn't say anything about religion, but just said, 'Remember last night we were talking about Kelly?'

'Yeah,' King said, 'would you like Kelly?'

'Yes, I would,' I said. I thought about it a little more and then said, 'Call Adams and see if you can get permission to talk to him.'

Well, he picked up the phone. We had Jack's number somewhere. King called him and I could tell from the way King was talking that Adams wasn't being very polite. King told me later how it went.

King said to him, 'Punch made you an offer some time ago for Kelly.'

Adams: 'Yeah, the son-of-a-bitch.' (I'm not sure whether he meant me or Kelly.)

King: 'Well, Punch would like to get him. If he'll play for us, Punch'll give you Reaume. Will you let us talk to Kelly?'

Adams: 'Yeah, you can talk to the (censored). You can do anything you like with the (censored).'

King: 'What's his telephone number?'

Adams: 'I don't have his (censored) number. You'll have to get it someplace else.' He had the number of course, but he was just feeling miserable enough about the whole situation to make us sweat for it. 'You've got permission to talk to him. If you can make a deal we'll take Reaume.'

King and I talked some more about how we should go about this. We decided we'd try to arrange a meeting with Red in Toronto.

King called another former Leaf player and coach in Toronto, Joe Primeau. From Joe he got the number of a priest at St. Michael's College where Kelly had played as a junior and Joe had coached. This priest was a good friend of Red's. This is the way we got Red's number, which was unlisted and unobtainable through normal channels.

So King called Red and got him on the phone. Again, I could hear part of it and King told me the rest. King asked Red what his plans were and Red said he was going to quit the game. You could tell he was feeling low.

King: 'Hey, wait a minute. Punch wants you on his hockey club.'

Red (after a pause): 'Well, I don't know.'

King: 'It's hard to talk over a thing like this on the telephone, but would you come up to Toronto for a day? We'll pay your transportation and expenses and I'll meet you at the airport and then we can pick up Punch and we'll go and have dinner and talk the thing over.'

But Red still gave us the ho-hum treatment. He said to phone him again when we got back from Boston. So Monday we did that. I don't know how many times we talked to him on the Monday, but finally he said he'd come over on Tuesday night. We had a game with the Canadiens on for the Wednesday. King went out to the airport. It was the old Toronto airport, where you could look out of the waiting room window and see people getting off. It was late afternoon and pretty dark. At first King thought Red hadn't come. He was looking for a guy with red hair and no hat, because Red never wore a hat in those days.

Then suddenly King saw Red walk in wearing a fedora. It was so different it was like a complete disguise. We'd also arranged a reservation for him at the Westbury under some other name. We'd done it that way because we didn't want a lot of stuff in the papers and on the radio and television at this stage. As long as Red was suspended nobody could make a deal for him. And if it got out that we were in the midst of making a deal, there might have been action from some other clubs. I mean, somebody else might have wanted to give Detroit more.

Anyway, King and this guy in the fedora drove downtown. On the Church Street side of Maple Leaf Gardens there is a door set into the wall, near the corner of Carlton. This leads to the executive offices so you don't have to pass a lot of guys lined up at the ticket wickets to get there. King brought Red up and we sat down and talked. He agreed to play for us. We settled the money side of it. Then we phoned Jack Adams and said, 'The deal is made.'

'That's fine,' Adams said. 'Send Reaume.'

Then he hung up the phone.

No good luck to Red, good luck to you, or anything.

It was around seven o'clock at night, I think, by then. A lousy night, blowing and slushy. We wired the league's central registry, the place where all deals have to be recorded. Also I guess we must have let Stafford Smythe know down in Florida. There was a governors' meeting on there at the time.

Then the three of us went downtown to eat. We still wanted to keep this quiet until it was officially cleared with the league. We went to a restaurant called the Embers in the Prince George Hotel. Trying to keep it quiet, I'm damned if I know why we picked that one – it was right across the street from the *Globe and Mail,* down the street from the *Star,* and next door to the Toronto Men's Press Club. Reporters were swarming around there like bees. Maybe it was our version of the old story – if you want to hide, be where they least expect you. As we were parking the car who do we see coming but Al Nickleson, one of the guys on the hockey beat for the *Globe and Mail.* He was just leaving the press club. But he had his head tucked in against the weather and he didn't see us. I know he kicked himself later – he had the story right there in his lap, if he'd happened to look up.

Then we went into the Embers and who were sitting around the place eating but a lot of the Canadiens! They'd come in early for our game the next night. Rocket Richard looked up at Kelly and said, 'Hi, Red,' and then looked at King and me, a little surprised. He knew what was up right away. But he wasn't the kind of guy who ran to tell a newspaperman.

Anyway, we ate and Red went to his hotel. Then all hell broke loose. The next morning the papers had stories from Miami quoting Clarence Campbell, the league president, as saying we couldn't make a deal for Red or any other player who was under suspension. I said to hell with that, we've already *made* the deal. Adams had agreed to it, Red had signed, and that was that. Which it was.

In the middle of all this, Red came around to the team meeting that morning. He said a few words to each player who came in, shook hands with some, and put on a Leaf sweater for pictures. Tommy Nayler, the equipment man, had been around the Leafs a long time. Away back when Red was a young kid playing for St. Michael's College, he used to come in and say, 'Can I get my skates sharpened, please, Mr. Nayler?' That was long before. Now Tommy asked me, 'What number you gonna give him?' He looked at his list. 'Nobody's got Number 4.'

When Red skated out as Number 4 of the Maple Leafs that

night, he got a tremendous ovation. He'd always been a favourite in Toronto. That's the number he wore playing great hockey for us, for seven full seasons after that – including four Stanley Cups. He did handle Beliveau. Yet when Red joined us, and even before, some people said he was through.

I liked one remark Red made after that first game. He was going to fly right back to Detroit and get more clothes and so on. One of the writers asked him if he had meant to stay when he had come up the night before; if he'd had his mind made up all along.

'I only brought a small bag with me, so it wouldn't look as if I'd made up my mind,' Red said, with a grin. 'But I had it packed real tight, with everything I'd need to stay.'

When I look back on it, we tried a lot of things that winter to improve the team. The core from the year before was still there. We'd sent Barry Cullen to Detroit and Brian Cullen to New York before the season started. Among the transients, who played a few or a lot of games for us from time to time as we experimented to get a lineup that could stop Canadiens, were Ted Hampson, Gary Collins, Dave Creighton, my old pal from Quebec Joe Crozier, Ken Girard, Pat Hannigan, Al MacNeil, Rudy Migay. We also had a very popular line that everybody called 'the Rocks' – Gerry James, Duke Edmundson, and Johnny Wilson. When things needed shaking up I'd send out the Rocks. The hum that would go through the rink was the same as we'd get later when Eddie Shack joined us. Everybody kept his head up when the Rocks were out there.

We had a tough, aggressive team that year. Bob Pulford led the team in scoring, with 24 goals, and he also had 81 minutes in penalties. Carl Brewer led the league in penalties, with 150 minutes, and tied for the league lead in misconducts with 5. We also led the league in major penalties, with 19. Allan Stanley got 10 goals for us. And certain other patterns were beginning to show. The previous year Johnny Bower had split the goal tending with Ed Chadwick, until I went with Bower exclusively at the end. He never let me down. So this year he played 66 games, and Chadwick, except for 4 games, was in Rochester.

But the big change was the Kelly deal. Until he came, we'd been life and death with Detroit for second; but right away we started to pull away from them. We finished second and they were fourth, twelve points behind us. Adams got razzed a lot by fans in Detroit when we went on to eliminate them in the first round of the Stanley

Cup. In the last game (of six) the crowd was yelling to Gordie Howe that he was going to be traded to Toronto next year too. But we still weren't strong enough to handle the Canadiens in the final. They took us in four straight. We were still a year or two away.

7

The First Stanley Cup

When I think about the team that did win the first of my four Stanley Cups, I really think about two whole seasons: 1960-61 and 1961-62. We didn't make many player changes in those two years and we should have won it both times, instead of missing in 1961. I've read a hundred articles by so-called experts saying that we got so tired out in 1961 battling Montreal for first place that we had nothing left for the playoffs. I've got my own idea about that. If it hadn't been for something that happened in Detroit on the Sunday night of February 12, 1961, I think we would have been home and cooled out in first place long before the end of the season. With that kind of a breather before the playoffs, nobody could have stopped us from winning the Stanley Cup.

The game in Detroit that I'm talking about was our fifty-sixth of the season. We were in first place. We won it 4–2, putting us six points ahead of Canadiens. At 7.17 of the third period we were leading 3–2 when a puck came down into our end, and Howie Young was trying to get to it for a shot on goal. Johnny Bower skated twenty feet out of his net to beat Young to the puck and clear it. But Howie was a different player in those days than he was a few years later. He had all kinds of personal problems that everybody knows about now – he was drinking hard and some nights he was just about the roughest and most reckless player in the game. This

83

time when Johnny got to the puck first, Young just kept right on coming. Johnny was too busy clearing it to brace himself. Young leaped into the air as he hit Johnny and just plain steam-rollered right over him. Johnny was crashed over backwards to the ice, with one leg back under, injuring his left leg high up in the thigh or hamstring muscle. When he was trying to get to his feet I could see he was hurt. I yelled at him and waved him over to the bench. He could hardly stand on that left leg. He lost a tooth, too, because Young's stick had hit him in the mouth. And he didn't have too many teeth left to lose. Anyway, we managed to get him into the dressing room to be patched. There wasn't much we could do about the leg. I asked him if he wanted to sit out the rest of the game. He refused, and insisted on going back out. He was leading for the Vezina Trophy, the goalie award based on least goals against, and had been almost unanimous choice for all-star goalie in the first half of the season. So he had a lot of his own to protect, but mainly he was thinking of the team and first place. That's the kind of man he is. But it was pitiful to watch him. Every time he had to go flat on the ice, he could hardly get up.

When the play resumed we had a power play going. Young had been given a five-minute charging penalty. Alex Delvecchio broke away and seemed to have John at his mercy when at the last second John flopped to the ice and stretched out with his stick and blocked the shot. A minute or two later he made another great save on Vic Stasiuk. I'll never forget the sight of him out there playing the last twelve minutes of that game. When he was standing in the goal he had to hold on to the crossbar with his left hand to take the weight off his leg. But he kept them out. Talk about guts. Nobody ever, anywhere in sport, had more than Bower. He was out for five weeks after that, but that night he wouldn't quit. Wings knew he was hurt and they really put on the pressure for the rest of the game, but he stopped them every time.

Dr. Jim Murray couldn't even examine his injury properly for a few days because there had been hemorrhaging. Meanwhile, he kept Johnny in hospital. When we played Montreal at the Garden on Wednesday night of that week, Johnny was watching it on TV in the hospital while Gerry McNamara played goal. We'd had to call him in from Sudbury, in the Eastern Pro League. He played well, too, and I'm not taking anything away from Gerry or from Cesare Maniago who played later in the season while Johnny was still out – and played well enough that he still won the Vezina. But the night that Bower missed his first game because of that Howie Young charge, Montreal beat us 3–1, and from then on we sort of levelled out as a team. In a week we were back in second place.

We got back to first and actually had a six-point lead again early in March. But we just couldn't keep ahead of the Canadiens in their closing drive, with Boom-Boom Geoffrion suddenly spurting towards 50 goals. He got his fiftieth against Maniago in the last week of the season, and in the end we finished second, with 90 points to Montreal's 92. I've always thought that if Bower hadn't been hurt in that senseless way back on February 12, we would have been so far ahead by the last week of the season that nobody could have caught us, and nobody could have stopped us in the playoffs. As it was, even when Johnny came back he wasn't in top form – he couldn't be, after that layoff. Also, Shack was hurt, Olmstead was hurt. Detroit put us out in five games in the Stanley Cup semi-final, while Chicago was disposing of Montreal in six. Then Chicago beat Detroit in the final while the Leafs, to my mind the best team in hockey that year and the next three years as well, missed the finals for the first time since I'd taken over as coach.

I have to say more about that team, though, to explain why I thought Leafs were the best team in hockey right then.

That was the year that Frank Mahovlich came into his own as one of hockey's superstars, scoring 48 goals. That was the year Dave Keon came to the Leafs. We weren't counting on him at all. He'd been a good junior, but in a pro tryout at Sudbury hadn't been impressive. But from the way he played in training camp there was no way he could be kept off the team, proving that training camp is of some use after all. That was also the year Bob Nevin came to the Leafs. We *were* counting on him. He'd scored 32 goals in Rochester the previous season and we knew he was good.

Early in that year, too, New York finally got fed up with Eddie Shack and let us have him for Johnny Wilson and Pat Hannigan. I'll never claim that my old pal Eddie is the world's greatest hockey player, but on the nights that he was going his best he helped us plenty.

And, finally, that was the year I made a deal that I think would have given us first place and the Stanley Cup even with Bower hurt – except that I couldn't convince Don Simmons in time that this was what I had in mind.

In January of 1961 I had a chance to get Simmons from Boston. I don't think anything could have helped Boston much that year, but early in the season Simmons had played eighteen games for them and then they decided to go the rest of the way with Bruce Gamble. They sent Simmons to Providence. In ten games there he had a goal-average of about five a game, I think reflecting his discouragement with being sent down. I knew Simmons from when I was in the Boston organization and I had a lot of faith in him. I thought he would be the ideal backup goalkeeper for Bower. In those days the two-goalie system was being used only by a few teams – and even then usually by a team trying to decide which of two men deserved to be Number 1. Johnny was my Number 1 all the way, so when I traded Ed Chadwick from our farm club at Rochester for Simmons, I intended to have Simmons play at Rochester and be available for immediate call-up to the Leafs in an emergency. But he was so disgusted with himself and the game right then, he wouldn't even report. He said he was tired of being shunted around. I tried to convince him that the way back to the NHL was for him to play for me in Rochester, draw his NHL salary, and bide his time. The trade stood, but, because Simmons wouldn't report, Chadwick stayed in Rochester for the rest of that season. When Johnny was hurt a few weeks after I'd made the deal, Simmons would have been the guy called up, if he'd been playing. But by then he hadn't even been playing for weeks and that was that. In the following summer, Simmons and I did get together. He agreed to go to Rochester. I felt a lot better with him there, and as events happened it paid off both for him and for us in the spring of 1962.

All through the 1960-61 season, of course, there were the usual controversies and arguments and battles and so on that come along in one form or another every hockey season. But nothing got more space in the newspapers than the big run Frank Mahovlich made to become the second hockey player in history to score 50 goals in one season. There were times when I, along with everybody else, thought that he couldn't miss.

People have often asked me what Frank did that season that he didn't do later for Leafs.

Well, I'll tell you one thing – he was aggressive. Take a look a his penalties. He had 131 minutes, about one-third more than an average year for him. And the number of goals he got was a lo higher than his lifetime average too. Of course there were a lot o other factors. It wasn't only that Frank had a big strong centre, Red Kelly, feeding him passes, or that Kelly was made to look good by the way Frank was going. It was a little bit of both. Add to that the fact that Bob Nevin on right wing was a good playmaker himself, an excellent checker, and could score goals, and you had quite a line. But I'd like to get back to the aggressive part. Frank has always been one of the most naturally talented and skilful players in the game, ever since he entered the NHL and won the rookie award in 1957-58. One other contender that year was Bobby Hull. But the 1960-61 season was the only one he spent with the Leafs when he really played up to his potential. That year if he couldn't go around a guy he'd go over him. That's the only year he spent with the Leafs that he played aggressively all season long. That year he was as good a left winger as ever played the game. And his aggressive play set the tone for the whole team.

I remember one night in New York early in the season. He scored two goals, both unassisted. On the first one, Dave Balon was trying to carry the puck out of the New York zone and Frank went in, knocked the puck off his stick, and zigzagged back through the defence to beat Gump Worsley from about fifteen feet out. For his second goal he checked Harry Howell right in front of Worsley, got the puck, and scored again. Both goals came from one kind of aggressive play – forechecking, hitting the other guy before he hit you. That was just one game. That's the way he played nearly every game that season.

He was aggressive that year in other ways. Like, one night in a game against New York, Big M was breaking down his wrong wing with the puck. Bill Gadsby was the only guy back for New York and there was no way he could stop Frank legally, so he high sticked him to slow him down and sort of hooked him at the same time. Down Gadsby went and pulled Mahovlich down with him. Now, Gads was one of the oldest and toughest guys in the league then, and Frank was just a kid, but they no sooner hit the ice than Mahovlich was swinging at him. That kind of attitude – quick retaliation, letting the other guy know that he can't play games with you and get away with it – doesn't score goals by itself. But the attitude that goes with it, always being aggressive, scores goals.

I remember another night early that season. We were beating Canadiens, and in the third period Mahovlich was wheeling out of our end with the puck. Pocket Richard was coming in after him.

Frank shot the puck. I don't know to this day what he had in mind when he shot the puck. It doesn't matter much now. He says he was just clearing the puck and I believe him. But it hit the Pocket on the face and knocked him down and out. Canadiens were burning! They were mainly burning because they were being beaten, but this happening near the end of the game gave them a chance to let off all their frustrations on Frank. They called him a lot of names from their bench, claiming that he'd shot the puck at the Pocket on purpose. Boom-Boom Geoffrion was yelling to Marcel Bonin to spear Mahovlich, and Dickie Moore was trying to get at him, and suddenly Mahovlich just threw down everything and was ready to take on the whole Montreal bench. The way he was that year it would have taken a lot of them to handle him too. It got straightened around, but that was typical of the kind of year he had. Canadiens tried to get him the next time we were in Montreal and he took on anybody who came along that time too. Wherever the action was, he was right in the middle of it. He was only twenty-two that year, you know. He was still living in the house he'd helped get for his parents and his brother Pete, over in Leaside, because I remember that on his birthday his mother made him a big birthday cake. Off the ice he was the same as ever – always a gentleman, a very high-class guy. But on the ice he was mean when he had to be. Every place he went he was the centre of attention. Jack Adams said, explaining our success in one of the game's really classic remarks, 'The big guy puts 'em in and the old guy [Bower] kicks 'em out.' The headlines were full of Big M. He scored three against Chicago, two against Boston, four against New York a few days later. He got another four in Chicago. He was our home-run hitter. He was leading in league scoring by February, with 43 goals and 26 assists for 69 points at the time Bower was hurt.

Then, I guess it was inevitable, he got tired. With Rocket's record in sight and needing less than a goal a game to break it, he was carrying two guys on his back every time he got the puck, instead of just one. And when a game was over, there was no relaxing for him. Every magazine in the country, it seemed, was doing a story on him. The interviews were at all hours. And all the time he was working harder. I know on the night he got his forty-eighth goal that season I had him on the ice more than 24 minutes, because I was giving him every chance to break Rocket Richard's record of

50 for one season. Later in the season Boom-Boom Geoffrion, who'd only had 32 when Frank had 43, caught fire and did get to 50.

So that was Frank's best season (until years later, when I'd traded him to Detroit). And I say it was his best year because of the extremely aggressive way he played. This is part of my philosophy of hockey, that it is basically an aggressive game and that if a team hasn't got a large dose of aggression it hasn't got a chance.

Aggression, to me, doesn't mean that you have to be fighting all the time, or taking stupid penalties. The year that Mahovlich had his aggressive year was Dave Keon's first with the Leafs. It was Red Kelly's first full year. Same with Bob Nevin. Now, those three players never got many penalties. That year Keon got three two-minute minor penalties and scored 20 goals; Kelly got six two-minute minors and scored 20 goals; and Nevin got four minors and one major penalty, and scored 21 goals. But those players never backed away from a challenge either. So they never weakened the general aggressiveness of the team.

That team and every other good one I ever had used to show its toughness of spirit where it counted most – on the road. It's easy enough to be aggressive at home. You've got the crowd with you. Any bunny rabbit can look like a tiger at home, especially if his home rink is Boston or Chicago. In there every time a home-team player looks hard at his check a cheer goes up as if he'd just won the world heavyweight championship. But you take a team from another city into one of those rinks and it is something else again. When every guy in the place is howling for the home team to clobber you, that's when toughness of spirit counts. You skate out knowing that everybody in the rink is hostile to you, that even the referees sometimes react to the emotion of the home crowd. Then you've only got two choices. You take the hostility and ram it back down their throats, or you let them intimidate you. The Leafs in those early years in the 1960s never let anybody intimidate them. The big tough clubs would come out running at us and we'd come out running right back at them.

Once a team is playing that way, oddly enough, even the injuries don't seem to knock it down. The next season, 1961-62, we had a lot of injuries, but finally we had reached the kind of solidity that we needed. We had Johnny Bower in goal, with Don Simmons down in Rochester ready to come up when needed. He played nine games during the season for us to spell off Bower, and got two shut-outs, playing as well as I always knew he could. We had Bob Baun and Carl Brewer on one defence, and Tim Horton and Allan Stanley on another. As fifth defenceman we used Larry Hillman some, but eventually wound up with Al Arbour, the only player in the league who wears glasses during a game. Al was good enough to be a starter on most NHL defences. So when there was an injury on defence we were still okay.

On the forward lines, when everybody was healthy, we had Kelly centring Mahovlich and Nevin; Keon between Dick Duff and George Armstrong; and Bob Pulford between Olmstead and Shack.

In that full-strength situation we still had a few good ones in reserve – Billy Harris, who wasn't a powerful checking centre but could handle a puck and make plays beautifully; Ed Litzenberger, who I'd picked up on waivers for $20,000 from Detroit, and who could play any forward position, even though his skating, never the greatest, was beginning to slow down; Ron Stewart, one of the smoothest and most competent right wings around; and John MacMillan, a very fast kid who never quite made it in the NHL, but never hurt us when he was out there. Once, when Keon was hurt, Harris took his place and scored seven goals in five games. Another time, Shack was hurt and Stewart filled in and made us better, if anything. Litzenberger filled in very strongly at centre for Kelly in one stretch. There was one time when we had Litzenberger playing for Kelly, Harris for Pulford, and didn't have a centre left when Keon got hurt – so I sent out Al Arbour and told him to play centre. All he said was, 'Give me my stick-handling stick!' and over the boards he went to play centre for the last few shifts of a game. He didn't hurt us at all.

With all those injuries (and more that I haven't mentioned, to key players like Armstrong and Duff) we weren't really in contention for first place for the last two months of the season. We finished thirteen points behind Canadiens. But that year we *were* ready for the playoffs. Simmons had broken a cheekbone playing, but was still working out with the Leafs, using a mask. That way he got used to our club and our players. He was with us all through the semi-final series with New York. That was the year Doug Harvey was playing coach for Rangers. Gump Worsley played very well in goal, and Andy Bathgate was still the big player that he'd been for years. We needed six games to put them away. Meanwhile, Chicago had knocked off first-place Montreal, and so that left us and Chicago in the final.

Chicago had a tough, hard team that year. We beat them in the first two games in Toronto, but when we got back to Chicago it was a different story. I don't say the Leafs were intimidated by running into the Black Hawks in their home rink, because they'd been there often before and never backed up. But this time, as it happened, Chicago decided to try to run us out of the rink in the first few minutes of the third game. They didn't run us out of the rink, but they did knock us off balance. Two of their biggest checks in the first minute or so of the game – one by Pierre Pilote and one by Dollard St. Laurent – nailed Dave Keon. The Hawks went on from there to out-bump us and outscore us 3–0. In the fourth game we played better, but something else happened. Before the halfway mark in the first period Bobby Hull let a hard shot go from just inside the Toronto blueline, and headed straight for the corner at Bower's left. Bower did the splits to get to it – nailing the shot with his glove hand, and getting his left foot over in time to give his hand some backing. Some of Hull's shots travel a hundred miles an hour or better, so a shot taken just with the hand might still drive the hand right back into the goal.

But as Johnny stretched, he felt something snap. I could see that he got up very slowly. He played for another six or seven minutes. They got one goal. It was a deflection by Bobby Hull and came in on Johnny's left, the side that he was hurt on. A few minutes after that Johnny came to the bench. In those days there wasn't the rule that a team had to dress two goalies. Don Simmons was up in the crowd. The game had to be held up while he changed. He had to go right in there cold and he played well enough, but Chicago got three more goals and beat us 4–1 to tie up the series.

I think our pride was stung by some of the things people started to say then. Chicago had this reputation as a bruising team. They had slowed Montreal to a walk with heavy checking a couple of times in the semi-finals, and everyone was saying that now they were doing the same thing to the Leafs in the final. In fact, one guy I know figured we were through, that we wouldn't win another game against them. But we had something left – including a whole team of players who didn't scare.

Simmons had needed that part game in Chicago, and probably more, to get his playing edge back. After all, he'd gone two months at the end of the season and then another nine games in the play-offs without having a puck shot at him in anger. I was confident he would come through for us. This was the exact situation that I'd had in mind when I'd made that trade for him more than a year before.

Also, Bert Olmstead had been out with a broken shoulder for six weeks. He was a player whose spirit and professionalism had meant a tremendous amount to us ever since he joined the club. He was especially good – the best in the league – at working in the corners. You have to have courage as well as skill to work the corners well, with defencemen trying to cream you into the boards. Bert was so tricky in corners that defencemen were almost afraid to commit themselves against Olmstead for fear they'd find them-selves in there with him, but with the puck out in front and into the net. Olmstead was deadly on his passes, and at figuring who was in the best position to take one. Anyway, without him, we just weren't at full strength. He still wasn't quite ready, but I decided to put him back in. And the first time he was on the ice he did what we hadn't been doing for a couple of games. From the open-ing face-off Pulford got the puck and carried it into the Chicago end. Bert got in front of that Chicago goal and created so much havoc in around there, refusing to be pushed out, that when Pul-ford got away a high backhand it hit Glenn Hall on the chest and the puck dropped in around his feet. Bert was keeping the defence so occupied that there was nobody free to clear it. Hall couldn't get to it. It rolled in for a goal, seventeen seconds from the start of the game. It wasn't a stylish hockey game, but we went on from there to win it 8–4.

However, the doubters still weren't fully convinced. They said, 'Okay, the Leafs won it – but it was at home. Wait until they go back to Chicago for the sixth game.'

Well, those doubters are still waiting. Normally, you like to win the last game of a series at home. For one thing, the home fans enjoy being in at the kill. But this was one time when I had a hankering to wind it up on the road, just to make a point.

That was one of the toughest hockey games I ever paced through, behind the bench. The Chicago crowd is something that you just have to see, and hear, before you can believe it. There are trumpets, noisemakers of all kinds, and everybody there seems to have brought something special to throw. Not just beer cartons and programs and hats and eggs, but about everything a man might carry into a rink sometimes gets thrown onto the ice at Chicago. And the noise the crowd makes at a body check or a goal is deafening, and lasts sometimes for a minute or two. That was the atmosphere, as I paced and watched the line changes Rudy Pilous, the Chicago coach, was making, and made my own, trying to bottle up their big guys like Hull and Mikita. In a way, what I was doing that night led all the way back to Ed Wildey, to the days in Cornwall, and to the early days in Quebec – but I can't say I gave any of those matters much thought right then. I was living minute to minute. In a game like that there is no other way.

It was a tough, even game. Both teams played it hard and without backing up, neither giving a thing away to the other. Simmons and Hall were playing such great goal that halfway through the third period neither team had scored. The tension of many near misses had built up in the crowd to the point that, when Bobby Hull did score, the place went mad. The crowd threw so much stuff on the ice that it took about ten minutes to clean things up. That ten minutes didn't hurt us. Chicago, instead of being able to go right back at it all buoyed up by the go-ahead goal, had ten minutes to cool out. When the puck was dropped again Bob Nevin scored and tied it up almost immediately. And then a few minutes later Tim Horton started out from our end with the puck, the way only Timmy can burst out when he's going his best. On the way up the ice he handled the puck three different times, passing and getting it back, before he made his final pass to Duff, who put it in. That was the goal that won Toronto its first Stanley Cup since 1951.

It was only after the game that the public found out a couple of things we'd been keeping very quiet. Bob Pulford had torn the ligaments in his shoulder in the first game of the series. We had his shoulder frozen every night before a game. His shoulder was all colours of the rainbow. He'd scored three goals in the fifth game, but still hadn't been able to shoot as well as usual, and without the freezing could hardly lift his arm. Also, Ron Stewart had some cracked ribs that were so painful he couldn't play without them being frozen. All through the series the press had been sore at us for keeping the dressing room door locked for fifteen minutes or more after every game. We'd had to do it so that Bobby Haggert could help Pulford out of his gear and he and the other injured players could get enough clothes on to hide the injuries.

I can't speak for some of the others about the way they felt, winning the Stanley Cup. But when the game was over Simmons ran out of goal and sprang off the ice right into the arms of the nearest player to him. They were all yelling. The guys I hadn't been able to dress – Bower, Litzenberger, and Johnny MacMillan – were jumping around and hollering and slapping the players when they came down. I remember going around and shaking hands with all the players, as I always do at the end of the season, thanking them. It was Easter Sunday, April 22, 1962 – late at night. When I got to Bert Olmstead he was sitting on the bench where he'd gone right when he came down. He hadn't moved. Most of the younger guys were still yelling their heads off and the place was bedlam. But when I shook hands with Olmstead I had to lean close to him to hear what he said. He didn't bother getting up. I didn't blame him.

'It's been a long haul, Punch,' he said.

When we flew into Toronto a few hours later there were a lot of people to meet us at the airport. Then someone at City Hall called to say that the city would like to give us a parade, if we wanted one. Ballard took the call and came to me about it. But after I've won something like that, after being 'up' for so long, I sometimes feel depressed. I said, 'Hell, we won it – anything more would be an anti-climax.' But they kept pressing and finally I said, okay. A few days later we rode up Bay Street in open convertibles to the old City Hall. There was such a big crowd, packed from the buildings right out into the street, that the cars could hardly move. Police Chief Jim Mackey told me later it was one of the biggest crowds ever to watch a parade in Toronto. The square around City Hall was just a sea of faces. It hit me, as well as the team, very hard. I was glad we'd done it, when it seemed to mean so much to the people.

In the next few weeks, I often thought of that handshake with Olmstead. One of the most trying times of any year for me comes in June, when the annual hockey meetings are held – always, so far, in Montreal although probably one of these days they'll be moved to a United States city. That year I had a Stanley Cup champion and naturally wanted to protect all the guys who won it for me. But the league rules then were that, for purposes of the major league draft, a club could put eighteen players and two goalies on its protected list. All others were available to be drafted by other clubs, so that the strong clubs couldn't just bury good players in the minors who could help other major league teams. Deciding on who is going to be left unprotected is where the strain on a coach's loyalties starts.

Of course, when I go to the meetings I go pretty well prepared. As soon as the season is over I start a series of meetings and discussions with scouts, coaches, and managers in the farm system checking over how all our promising young players are doing. Also, I'm looking at my own roster and making lists of guys who absolutely have to be protected. Then there might be a few left over who might be used in trades or deals where it is possible to get a little more than the straight draft price.

All the other general managers are around at the meetings. Sometimes they come to you trying to make deals, and sometimes you just meet and start chewing things over in a corridor or in a hotel room, coming up with names: this guy I have available if I can get the right deal for him, that guy or guys he has available. You have to look not too eager for the ones you really want. Most deals take a long time and a lot of talking. Some of them hang fire for years, waiting for the right combination of names to come up.

In the spring of 1962 I only made one deal. I had the best defence in hockey already, but there was a player with Eddie Shore at Springfield that I thought was the best young defenceman in the minors – Kent Douglas. He'd been in the Toronto farm system at one time, but had a lot of trouble with his temper, and was inclined to do some teams more harm than good, so he'd been allowed to get away. But in four years under Eddie Shore he had developed very well and seemed to have himself under better control. Shore wanted my right arm for him, but finally we made a deal; we got Douglas, and Shore got five young minor leaguers. My reasoning was that, if Douglas worked out for us (and he did, especially for that first season), he'd be our fifth defenceman, and would give us extra power in the good shot he had from the point in power plays. And that would leave Al Arbour and Larry Hillman expendable one way or another.

But all that was pretty straightforward. When I went to Montreal for the meetings in June of 1962, I had some much more special problems. One in particular. It was one that was always with me, I think, more than with other clubs. Many of the key guys on my team were getting on in years. When the years catch up on an athlete it is usually a very sudden thing. One season a man is okay, slowing down a little maybe, but with his know-how better than ever. The next year suddenly the know-how is still there, but the legs won't do what the mind says has to be done. For that reason, a coach has to protect the veterans he is sure are going to help him, but he also has to protect some of the young players coming up in the farm system. Otherwise they are gone, drafted, when he needs them to fill in for an older player who suddenly is over the hill.

One of the toughest things I had to do at the 1962 meetings was leave Bert Olmstead unprotected. We had at least three young players in Rochester and other parts of the farm system who would be snapped up by other clubs if we didn't protect them — Bruce Draper, Larry Keenan, and Jim Pappin. The fact that Draper and Keenan never did make it in the NHL, and Pappin didn't work out as well as I thought he might, didn't alter the situation at the time. Olmstead had been able to play only about forty games the previous season. The way he played the game was all out, all the way. He played the danger spot, the corner, as if there was no tomorrow. In close quarters or at passing or taking a pass he was as good as he ever had been, if not better. But when end to end skating was needed he had trouble.

I hoped to keep him around, but I had to leave him unprotected for at least a round or two of the draft. I'd told him the previous autumn when I signed him that probably I would have to leave him unprotected in the draft the following year. I thought I owed it to him to let him know. And I know that he went out that season and in the 1962 playoffs to show me that he still deserved to be protected. Some people thought he was a dominant figure in our last two games against Chicago, when we won the Stanley Cup, and I wouldn't argue with that. But I had to take the chance — and I lost. New York picked him up for the $20,000 draft price, and after a certain amount of agonizing about it, Bert quit the game.

I know he felt he could still help the Leafs, because we were deep enough in talent that he could be played sparingly some times to save his strength for other times. New York had finished fourth in 1962, but basically that had been a triumph for Doug Harvey as playing coach more than anything else. Olmstead felt that New York would be depending on him to play almost every game, and even though his old buddy from Canadiens, Doug Harvey, was running things, he didn't feel up to the demands that would be made on him.

He said some bitter things about the Leafs, and about me, when he was left unprotected. The press tried to get me to reply to Olmstead at the time, when he shot off, but I wouldn't. I remember one thing he said about me that sums it all up. 'I've done a lot for that s.o.b.,' he said. 'A heck of a lot. And I'd do it again.'

Another thing that happened that spring bothered me a little, but not so seriously. The federal government, John Diefenbaker's Progressive Conservatives, had called an election. The Liberals, trying to pick up seats wherever they could, got Red Kelly to run for Parliament in the York West constituency of Toronto. Red certainly wasn't any silver-tongued orator in those days − he's become pretty good since at public appearances and television − but he won in a breeze.

We talked about it and he said he thought he could handle both jobs: working in Ottawa as a member of Parliament and still play-ing hockey. It was a killing pace he set himself; sometimes flying to Toronto for a practice and then back to Ottawa to sit in the House of Commons. It was made tougher because the Liberals had picked up a lot of seats, and left the Conservatives with a minority government that could be toppled at any time, so absenteeism in all the parties was very much frowned upon. The closest parallel I can think of in another sport would be if, say, somebody like Mickey Mantle had become a Senator and had to go straight to Washington from Yankee Stadium after every game. But Red made it work. They used to call him the Member for Centre Ice. He never missed a game for us, but I can't say that I liked the idea of sharing him with anybody − even Liberal leader Lester Pearson, who the next year, 1963, won enough seats to be prime minister, but then had a minority government himself and needed Red more than ever.

I also figured that, as those years went on, Red got more and more tired and it showed on the ice. But he could come up with the big game when it counted. When he did decide not to run again, in the fall election of 1965, for a while there he played like a kid again, great player that he was.

But the next big rhubarb of my life didn't involve either Kelly or Olmstead, but centred around the guy who played left wing for the Member for Centre Ice – Frank Mahovlich.

The First Mahovlich Deal

On the night of October 4, 1962, a Friday, Clancy and I were in the lobby of the Royal York Hotel in Toronto. The place was full of hockey people because that was the night of the NHL all-star dinner. I hadn't had a drink, either at the reception or the dinner, and I was about ready to go home to bed. But Clancy and I had been invited to a party that the league governors were having in one of the suites. Or maybe it wasn't exactly a party – more like an extension of the other festivities. They'd had a drink or two before the dinner, I guess, and now it was over and nobody was quite ready to go home. Anyway, we're standing there discussing whether to go home or to show at this party. Finally we decided to go up.

'Just a few minutes,' I said to King. 'And I'm not drinking.' Which made two of us, because he never does. It *was* just for a few minutes – but pretty hectic ones.

We no sooner got in the door than Harold Ballard grabbed me and said, 'Come here.' He took us into the next room. Jack Amell, an athletic-looking, prematurely grey member of the hockey committee, was there. Ballard looked at me with a real glint in his eyes. He's hard and strong, built like a tank. He said, 'Norris has offered me a million dollars for Mahovlich. What do you say?'

Jim Norris owned the Chicago Black Hawks in those days, a

multi-millionaire better known in the United States as a fight-game boss, or a race-horse owner. But Jim always said he liked hockey best. His father had helped make the NHL solid in the early days. Of course, Chicago's top left wing was Bobby Hull. He'd scored 50 goals in 1961-62. But in 1960-61 Frank Mahovlich, with 48 goals to Hull's 31, had been the league's all-star left wing. They seesawed, year by year, and in those years there were plenty of arguments about who was the top player of the two. Anyway, nobody would mind having both of them.

There are two other things to remember about that night: first, Norris had the money to pay a million for a player if he felt like it; second, everybody in the suite had been drinking and I hadn't.

I heard later through Tommy Ivan, the Chicago general manager, how the deal had got that far.

Ballard and Norris had been talking. Ballard mentioned the troubles we were having signing Mahovlich that year.

Of course, Frank — or The Big M as everybody was calling him by then — had plenty of reason to be holding out. He'd scored those 48 goals in 1960-61, teamed up with Red Kelly and Bob Nevin for the first time in one of the best forward lines in the league. He'd dropped to 33 goals and second all-star left wing (behind Hull) in 1961-62, but in the spring of 1962 we'd beaten Chicago for the Stanley Cup and Frank had played well.

Anyway, when Ballard complained about the trouble in signing Frank, Norris immediately said, 'I'll take him off your hands any time. I wouldn't worry about signing him — we'd sign him.'

Ballard apparently was in that kind of a mood that he started saying, 'Make me an offer.'

Norris said, 'Ah, you wouldn't sell him.'

Ballard said, 'Everybody has his price.'

This was all before King and I arrived. Norris stepped out of the room and called Ivan over from where he'd been talking to another group. There were three rooms in the suite and a lot of governors and executives around. Stafford Smythe wasn't there at the time, but most of the others were. And there were a few newspapermen — one anyway, Gordie Campbell, from the Toronto *Star*.

Norris said to Ivan quietly, 'How good a hockey player is Mahovlich?'

Ivan said, 'Pretty good.'

'Worth five hundred thousand dollars?'

'Yes.'

'How about seven-fifty?' Norris asked.

'That may be a little high.'

'I think I can get him,' Jim said. 'I think Ballard would sell.'

So Norris went back into the other room and brought up the subject of Mahovlich again. He said to Ballard, 'Would you take two hundred and fifty thousand for him?'

Ballard said no.

'How about five hundred?'

'No dice.'

Over the course of the next few minutes Jim worked the price up to a million dollars. That was where I came in.

Now, when Ballard told me about it, he and I and King and Amell were alone in this one room. I didn't think it over as long as it has taken me to tell it, but I did think it over for a minute or two. Then I said, 'As general manager, I'd make that deal. But as coach I couldn't because the million dollars can't play left wing for me.'

Tommy Ivan and Jim Norris were waiting in the next room while we talked. Tommy says that while they were sitting there with us not around, Jim took a piece of notepaper and wrote on it, 'I promise to pay one million dollars for Frank Mahovlich. Signed, Jim Norris.'

Tommy also says that the later reports that the partying had affected Jim's judgment were entirely off base, and that Jim always knew exactly what he was doing.

Then the four of us came in from the next room: Ballard, Amell, King, and I. Jim shoved the piece of paper at Ballard and said, 'Sign this.' Ballard and Amell didn't have the power to make the deal. Nobody did without clearing it with me, unless I was fired first. But they wrote the word 'accepted' on the paper and signed it for Leafs' hockey committee. Then Norris took out his roll and said, 'How much earnest money do you need?'

Ballard said, 'You're good with us, you don't have to pay anything down.'

But Jim insisted on peeling off a thousand dollars in U.S. bank-notes and giving them to Ballard.

It was around that point that Ballard tried to get me to shake hands with Jim Norris, to seal the deal.

'No,' I said. 'I won't shake hands. There is no way I'm going to shake hands on this deal or any deal tonight.'

Remember I hadn't had a drink. Maybe if I'd had a few drinks,

I might have shaken hands, but I doubt it. I talk deals sometimes over a drink, but I wait until the next morning before I do anything that can't be taken back.

But Ballard hadn't yet taken no for an answer. He wouldn't accept my no. There was a certain amount of loud discussion and argument, but Jim Norris didn't get sore at me for holding things up. He knew it was my job.

In the meantime, word had got out through the other rooms that the deal was made. After all, Ballard and Amell had signed the paper. Pretty soon everybody in the place knew about it and was arguing and laughing.

I said to myself, I'm going to get the hell out of here. And I did. Clancy and I left. I don't think anybody missed us.

What happened after we left (I went home and Clancy went down to the lobby) was that about 12.30 Jim – who had this signed piece of paper, remember – asked Ballard, 'How do you want to handle the release?' Meaning the press release. There was a discussion with Tommy Ivan and a few others about what should be on it, and then Jim said, 'All I want is to be able to say right now, "The Chicago hockey club has purchased Frank Mahovlich for one million dollars." When can we break it?'

Ballard said, 'Right now, if you want.'

So Tommy Ivan phoned Johnny Gottselig, the Chicago publicity man, to spread the word. Now this was definitely one of the biggest sports deals of all time, up until then. It got out about the same time in Toronto. I heard it on the car radio on the way home. They broke into a program to say that Mahovlich had been sold for a million dollars to Chicago.

In the meantime, Clancy hadn't left the hotel. And I guess about the same time that Tommy Ivan was phoning Chicago, Stafford Smythe was walking into the hotel, heading for the governors' suite. He didn't know a thing about what had happened. But Clancy grabbed him and told him what was going on.

'Where's Punch?' Stafford said.

'Gone home. I'm just on my way home myself.'

'You'd better come back up with me.'

So King went back up to the suite. He told me later he never heard such an uproar in his life as there was over this deal. Phones ringing, people talking long-distance, being interviewed, everything else. Stafford tried to cool the thing off a little by saying that any deal first had to be approved by me. But then he laughed, strutting around in that way he has, and said, 'Well, I guess we knock the World Series off the front page today.'

Which they did. The World Series was on right then, between San Francisco and the New York Yankees, but the top front-page line in Chicago, Toronto, and a lot of other places later that day was about this deal.

I also think that Stafford could see even then that this had got a little out of hand. He kept saying that I'd gone home and nothing more could be done that night. I think finally he got Bruce Norris, Jim's brother who owned Detroit Red Wings, to tell Jim to hold everything until the morning.

That's the way it ended, for that night anyway. Except that by the time I got home, after hearing about the deal on the radio, my phone was ringing. People wanted me to comment on it. I just told them, 'Don't bother me about that,' and then left the phone off the hook.

The next morning I went in to our regular Saturday team meeting at the Gardens. When I got there the place was full of reporters and cameras and radio people. Also, down at the hotel there were TV cameras set up outside Jim's door. The first thing Jim had thought of in the morning was finishing off the deal, according to Tommy Ivan. They had an early breakfast together and during it Jim said to Tommy, 'I'll write out this cheque and you take it up to the Gardens and complete the deal.'

He was going to write it out in longhand, a personal cheque for a million dollars. Tommy told him, 'Give me a blank. I'll go down and get it typed out.'

Jim gave him a blank. Tommy went to the public stenographer in the hotel and had it typed out. Then he took the cheque back, Jim signed it, and Tommy took a taxi up to the Gardens.

I'd talked to Stafford, and I had told him flatly, no deal. Of course, they could have fired me and made it themselves. But I think Conn Smythe had got to Stafford by then and told him to go easy, too.

When Tommy got there he walked in and handed over this cheque for one million dollars. 'My boss made a deal with your club last night for Frank Mahovlich,' he said to Stafford. 'Here's the cheque.'

Stafford said, 'We're not accepting the deal. We need a directors' meeting before we can decide on it.'

Tommy argued with him. Stafford wouldn't budge.

Then Tommy had to phone back to Jim and report, 'They won't accept.'

I'm told you could have heard Jim's reply all the way from the Royal York, without using a telephone at all. *'What do you mean they won't accept – I made a deal!'*

It was another week before the thing was killed. Some of Leafs' directors were for it as a real cash windfall. Some were against it. But it was the following Thursday before Stafford announced definitely that the offer would not be accepted and that Frank Mahovlich would continue to play for Toronto Maple Leafs.

So you can see it wasn't really a phony publicity stunt, as some people said. It was real enough in all particulars but one – the guy who was authorized to make deals was me, and I never agreed to it. On the other hand, hockey always likes to have something special going in the way of publicity in the World Series time. That's the time our season is starting and it's hard to get much space in many of the U.S. papers, with them full of the Series. This was one year we scored. And though it didn't start as a publicity stunt, it certainly wasn't ended prematurely to cut off the publicity that flowed from it.

Looking back on it, nobody could blame Jim Norris for wanting to make the deal. He was a promoter and he knew what sold best – quality. Chicago already had won one Stanley Cup for him, in 1961. Who could have taken the Stanley Cup away from Chicago in the next few years if they'd had Mahovlich added to all the big shooters they had? This was a matter I often thought about later in that season of 1962-63 – where we would have ended up that season, and where Chicago would have finished, if they'd had Mahovlich.

As it turned out, with only four weeks of the season left, Chicago was in first place with an eight-point edge on Montreal and nine ahead of us. Late in February the Hawks came to Toronto for a Wednesday night game, swaggering more than a little. Rudy Pilous was still coaching them then. He could just about smell that first-place finish. We hadn't been able to beat Chicago in our previous four games and Lord knows where we would have been in the standings if it hadn't been that right up there among the league's leading goal-scorers was Frank Mahovlich. He and Bobby Hull each had 30, one behind Gordie Howe of Detroit.

Anyway, in any season where a team is going to make it big,

there is usually one game that you can pinpoint as a turning point. This was it for us. Frank had missed one game because of a charley horse, and it didn't figure that he was going to be at top form for this one. Instead, he turned in one of his better and more aggressive games. Both teams came out trying to out-bump the other, a sort of matching of muscles that was natural between the two most muscular teams in the league. We got a little the better of it, especially with the referee, because Chicago had two players in the penalty box in the first period when Mahovlich scored our first goal.

From then on he was harder than ever to stop. In the second period, Kent Douglas and Reg Fleming, who used to be called Mr. Kleen in Chicago because of his powerful, almost barrel-like neck, had one fight that resulted in major penalties. A little later, back on the ice again, they swung their sticks at one another, got slashing penalties, and started to fight again in the penalty box and on the floor of the aisle behind the box. Jack Evans, another tough Chicago defenceman, had been in the penalty box when they arrived. Mahovlich, skating by, thought Evans was going to interfere in the Fleming-Douglas battle. He grabbed the top of the six-foot safety glass barrier and vaulted over it to make sure that the sides were even. Some recovery from a charley horse.

As I've said before, any time Frank was showing that much interest in a game, the whole team was lifted. In the third we still had only a 3–2 lead when he really took charge of the game. His long, perfect pass sent Ron Stewart in for our fourth goal, and two big plays he made later in the period resulted in rebounds that Bob Pulford cashed for one goal and Stewart for another. We beat Chicago 6–3 to move past Canadiens into second place. A few nights later, against New York, Frank scored with 62 seconds of play left, to win another game for us. In that streak we eventually went ten games unbeaten. Within two weeks we went into Chicago tied with them for first place; we outshot them 40–19 that night, showing superiority even though we could only break even in goals, 1–1.

We had a tie against Montreal later that week, while Chicago won. That put us one point back again and set up a Saturday night game against Chicago at the Gardens as the real test for both teams. Scalpers got $25 a ticket for that game. If Chicago could beat us they'd be three points up and we'd be in trouble. But we never gave them a chance. They didn't have a shot at Simmons in our goal until halfway through the first period. Over the game they only had 15 shots to our 36. We won it 3–0 on two goals by Stewart and one by Pulford. That put us alone in first place, with only four games left to play. We went into New York the next night and won, to go three points up. In the eight games since the night we'd beaten Chicago 6–3, we'd won six and tied two. Not many teams can stand up against that kind of pressure. Now Chicago was behind us, and faltering. When Hawks were beaten by Detroit two nights later, all we needed against Montreal in a home game Wednesday was a tie to cinch first place for us.

In the last minute of that game Montreal was leading us 3–2. I pulled Don Simmons out of goal to put on an extra attacker. Montreal had one shot on the empty net and missed. With only twelve seconds left, Bob Nevin shot the puck into the corner at the left side of the Montreal goal. Dick Duff got in there, a pretty good homer-hitter in his own right. Terry Harper, about twice his size, was in the corner too, battling Duff for the puck. But Duff got the puck out to Dave Keon at the edge of the crease. Keon tapped it in. There were eight seconds to go in the game.

We had needed the tie to cinch first place. We got it.

The only thing that didn't work out right for us that season was that I would have liked to finish first, and then beat Montreal in the Stanley Cup final. But they had finished third, so we had to play them in the semi-final. We won the first three games, they took the fourth, and then we beat them 5–0 in the fifth game. That seemed to be decisive enough to make up for the times they'd beaten us in earlier years.

Meanwhile, Detroit knocked Chicago out in the other semi-final. But I never had much doubt about our ability to beat Detroit, especially after Dick Duff scored twice in the first sixty-eight seconds of the first game for the Stanley Cup. They won one game, the third, but we wrapped it up in the fifth 3–1. We were tied late in the third, 1–1, when Bob Pulford won a face-off in the Detroit end and got it back to Kent Douglas at the point. Douglas shot it. Eddie Shack was cruising in front of the net. The puck hit Detroit defenceman Doug Barkley and headed for Shack. 'I was trying to get the hell out of the way,' Shack said later. 'It hit my stick and went in.' Dave Keon had got our first goal in the first period. Alex Delvecchio got theirs in the second. But it was a wild finish. After Shack's goal Keon scored into an empty net – with

Pulford in the penalty box and Detroit playing six attackers against our four and Bower.

One of my souvenirs from that year is a headline from the Toronto *Star*: 'City Salutes The Conquering Leafs,' said big red letters on the front page. '40,000 jam Bay Street eight deep.' This was for another open-convertible, ticker-tape parade to City Hall. 40,000 people – but it still wasn't as big as the one the year before. I guess they were getting used to it.

The funniest remark of all that spring was made by Ed Litzenberger. He'd been with Chicago in 1961 when they won the Cup. Then he'd been shuffled off to Detroit, hadn't made the grade there, and I had picked him up on waivers in time to help us win the 1962 cup. And now this one.

'This is my third Stanley Cup in a row,' he told a reporter, while sipping champagne. 'You can say I'm getting tired of meeting all these mayors.'

Static from All Over

I can't say that I had much trouble with Stafford Smythe or anybody else in management back in the years when every springtime – well, all right, three springtimes in a row – brought a Stanley Cup. But he'd second-guess me from time to time in public. For instance, we went one stretch where Montreal didn't beat us in a league game for more than a year. Then in November of 1963 they came in and did beat us 3–1, and Staff was right in there to let the public know whose fault it was – good old Imlach's.

'Blake used every man on the Canadien bench,' Staff grumbled after the game, as Red Burnett quoted him in the *Star* the next day. 'We had three fellows – Al Arbour, Ed Litzenberger, and Johnny MacMillan – who didn't hit the ice. And Billy Harris made only three token appearances. That's like paying $40,000 a season for window dressing. Our regulars looked jaded, ran out of steam. That's when the reserves should have been moved in.'

His $40,000 figure was low. We certainly paid those players a total of more than that. But what the hell, he was one of the owners; I guess he felt he had to say something once in a while. But second-guessing is second-guessing. My idea always has been, you play the best players you have as much as you can. And playing that way, my win-loss record wasn't all that bad. Also, sometimes you get criticized both ways. I remember Dick Duff later that year saying that his scoring decline had set in back in the 1959-60 season when I'd started using four lines once in a while, meaning the regulars weren't getting quite as much work. And he had figures to back him up, not just an offhand opinion like Stafford's. Duff had scored twenty-six goals two seasons in a row, and then twenty-nine, and then for four in a row hadn't been able to do better than nineteen.

But people change. I've always had a long memory about criticism of my way of running a hockey team. One thing I know for damn sure is that if I changed my way of coaching and managing every time some sportswriter or owner or player said I was doing something wrong, I'd never know what I was doing, and neither would anybody else. That night when the Canadiens beat us in a league game for the first time in a year, their coach, Toe Blake, made a comment that was a hell of a lot more to the point than Stafford's or anybody else's. Blake mentioned one time when Claude Larose had about six swipes at a puck and missed before he finally put it in.

'Last year Leafs would have put him on the seat of his pants after the first miss,' he said.

Now that was an expert opinion and one I agreed with.

An excellent example of how little use some sideline opinions are, whether they're for you or against you, came out of what happened to our club that year. Blake put his finger right on it. We had the same team that had finished first the previous spring and had manhandled Montreal and Detroit in the playoffs. But by midseason I knew that we were in trouble. There were a lot of things you could point to. Red Kelly was having his worst scoring year in a long time, maybe because mixing Parliament and hockey was too much. Frank Mahovlich was dropping off into being just an average player, except on rare nights. But two of the most serious declines involved two of our best young players. Dick Duff didn't score a goal at all until November, and by January he only had six. Bob Nevin was the same. I became more and more convinced that we weren't going to win a Stanley Cup that year, or even come close, unless I shook up the hockey club. I tried some minor moves, like sending Litzenberger down to Rochester and later sending Douglas down there too. We tried Bronco Horvath for a few games – enough to find that he couldn't help us. But this was tinkering around the fringes. I felt that I had to do something right at the core of the team to get these guys going again. And that's when I started thinking seriously again about a trade that I'd been trying to make off and on for years – to get Andy Bathgate from New York.

One thing that helped was that New York wasn't going anywhere. I think they finally realized that they were going to have to sacrifice their one genuine superstar, Bathgate, to get some good young players. They were helped toward this decision by the fact that Bathgate was having a bad year. The season before, he'd scored 35 goals. Now with the season about two-thirds over it looked as if he'd be lucky to get 20. They began to realize that if they put off trading him too much longer, they wouldn't have anything left to trade.

Around New Year's they mentioned to me that they might be interested in trading Bathgate. But they were going to drive a hard bargain. Quite a few names were mentioned, including Nevin and Duff and Ron Stewart from our club, and Vic Hadfield – a player I'd always wanted – from theirs. I'm not sure exactly what happened then. I've heard that in mid-January of 1964 the New York owners suddenly realized that the trade-Bathgate talk in the papers wasn't just the publicity gag that it had been other years, and really had some substance behind it.

At that point, anyway, negotiations were broken off. In fact, the statements made by both clubs didn't leave much chance for a deal at all.

One night after Boston bombed us 11–0, Stafford got into the act. 'There'll be no trades this season,' he said. 'All these rumours do nothing but hurt a team. Maybe if the Leafs know this, they'll settle down.'

Also, Red Sullivan, the New York coach, said flatly after the January negotiations broke down: 'Andy won't be traded this season.'

In New York, about the middle of February, we had a meeting with Muzz Patrick, the big former player who managed the Rangers. At that one, a Bathgate deal was discussed again and also a straight swap of Don McKenney for Dick Duff, which we wouldn't go for. Muzz told reporters after that meeting, 'Gentlemen, I've been wrong before, but I have to say we're dead on this thing now. I can't see us getting together.'

And on Friday afternoon, February 21, when Rangers came in from Chicago to wait over for a game with us the next night, somebody called me at the Gardens for a quote and I said, and believed it: 'Sure, we may talk to them. But I'd say it's a thousand to one against a deal.'

Well, that very night Clancy and I went down to the hotel and had a few drinks with Patrick and Red Sullivan. I think Emile Francis was around, too. Rangers had been swamped 7–2 in Chicago in the middle of the week. Bathgate had played 56 games by then and only had 16 goals, less than half what he'd got in the full season the year before. He was getting to the stage where he couldn't skate. He never was the big strong hockey player. He was slight, the perfectionist, you know, with all the tricks. Of course, if a player like that is skating well enough things are okay but when he can't skate he can't do the other things either. And of course, they could see that he was going down and they had to make a move if they were going to get anything for him. So they decided to do it, which was smart on their part. I mean, what the hell, they got a pretty good hockey team out of it.

Actually, we agreed on the deal that night. But I'd had a couple of drinks and so had the guys from New York. We had two separate meetings. Suddenly they said okay. They wanted to seal it right there. I backed off. After all when you're moving human beings around a lot is at stake. I figured that when we'd waited this long, there was nothing that could be hurt by letting it go until morning and seeing how we all felt then.

The next day we met, and because of one thing and another we didn't make the final decision until mid-afternoon. That meant Duff and Nevin attended our usual Saturday team meeting. And Bathgate and McKenney ate their game steaks with the Rangers before they were told. The deal was basically two deals – Duff for McKenney in one, and Bathgate for four players in the other. The big man they wanted was Nevin, of course. He was only twenty-six and they could see him as a future captain, which he became (Bathgate was their captain at the time). But also they got Arnie Brown, a first-rate young defence prospect who was at Rochester; Bill Collins, a pretty fair minor-league forward; and Rod Seiling, a fine young defenceman who was still a junior then, but had been one of the most sought-after prospects of his time.

There has been a lot of controversy and some criticism of me over that deal since. It was pretty plain that we were going to get the short-term advantage but Rangers would get the long-term advantage. That was okay with me. I thought the addition of Bathgate and McKenney, plus the mental shaking-up the trade would give the rest of the Leafs, would win the Stanley Cup – and it did. The Rangers got good young players who would help them a lot in the future, and have. Instead of having one superstar they got several hockey players who balanced their team up over a period of time. Also, I had the players, and how the hell were Arnie Brown or Rod Seiling, both defencemen, going to play for me when I was winning three Stanley Cups in a row and had Stanley and Horton, Brewer and Baun, on defence at the time.

And for us, Duff had 7 goals in 52 games and Nevin had 7 in 49. McKenney had 9 goals for them in 55 games.

You might think to look at those figures that, what the hell, we weren't dealing for a bunch of star hockey players but more for some who, for one reason or another, weren't playing well where they were. That's always the ideal situation in which to make a trade – sometimes the change gives all the players concerned a new lease on life.

The deal was effective immediately. Bathgate and McKenney played for us that night – and we beat New York then and the next night in New York, too, with Duff and Nevin playing for Rangers. Arnie Brown reported to New York right away from Rochester. Collins wound up at the Ranger farm team in Baltimore. And Rod Seiling was due to become Ranger property at the end of the season. Right then he was with Marlboro juniors, and would play for the Canadian national team in the Olympics in a few weeks.

From our standpoint, I didn't like giving up Duff and Nevin of course. They had come up through our system and both were very high-class players and men. I particularly liked one comment Dick Duff made after the first shock of the deal had worn off. He told an interviewer that his time in Toronto had all been fun but he had slipped. He didn't know why. Now he had to re-establish himself as one of the good players in the National Hockey League, he said. Well, he didn't do that in New York. He never did seem to cotton to their system, the city, or anything else. But before the next season was half over, New York traded him to Montreal for Bill Hicke – and in Montreal Duff blossomed again as one of the best money players in the game, the most dangerous man on the ice when there was a big game to be won, especially in the playoffs. He still is, for my money. One other point: Duff was my daughter

Marlene's favourite player. She cried when she heard that I had traded him. It sure left me in the doghouse.

In light of what happened later, it's worth reminding a few people of how enthusiastic Andy Bathgate was to join the Leafs – which meant, also, joining me. 'You dream of something like this but it just doesn't happen,' he said. 'This is the biggest break of my life.'

I'll hand it to both Bathgate and McKenney: in the next two months they did exactly what I'd had in mind when I made the deal. McKenney fitted in with Keon and Armstrong and was a particularly pleasant surprise. He'd scored 9 goals for New York in 55 games and now he got 9 for us in the last 15 of the season, and 4 in the playoffs before he got hurt. Bathgate, Kelly, and Mahovlich made quite a line. Bathgate picked up only 3 goals but had 15 assists for 18 points in 15 games, finishing out the season with us. But he was deadly in the playoffs with 5 important goals in 14 games. He didn't have much left in his legs, but in that seventh and deciding game against Detroit in the Stanley Cup he proved he could turn it on one last time as he streaked in from the centre zone and beat Terry Sawchuk for the only goal we needed – although another 3 later took the heat off Bower's 4–0 shutout.

That was one Stanley Cup we won the hard way. We finished third in the league, and then went 7 games against Montreal, never ahead until the last game when Dave Keon scored all 3 goals as we won it 3–1. And even in that one, we went into the third period only leading 2–1 and could have lost it a dozen times in the next 20 minutes. I wanted the Leafs to play it cosy, but first thing I knew both teams were racing up and down and I had no control. Canadiens would break on our net and all pile in there desperately. Then they'd lose the puck and, of course, with them trapped our guys would break for the other end – all 5 of them. They'd nearly score, but when they lost the puck then they'd be trapped and Canadiens would be racing in on us again. I almost died right there behind the bench: the Stanley Cup on the line and we should have been playing it carefully, and they just never stopped.

In the final against Detroit we were behind again. In the sixth game Baun broke a bone in his leg, and in the third period Detroit should have won it. I can say now, they should have won it a dozen times – and if they had, they'd have had the Stanley Cup because they were ahead then 3 games to 2. But Bower was absolutely great. He robbed them time and again. And in the sudden-death overtime Baun came out with his broken leg frozen and scored the winning goal. That kept us alive for the seventh game and even in that one we were only ahead 1–0 on Bathgate's goal until midway in the third when we pulled away.

One picture that got a lot of play at the end of that season was Bathgate holding the Stanley Cup triumphantly above his head. Now get this. He'd been a professional since 1952. He'd won the Hart Trophy as the league's most valuable player in 1959. He'd been a first team all-star twice and a second team all-star twice. He'd tied Bobby Hull for the league's point-scoring championship once, although Hull had more goals. But never before he joined the Toronto Maple Leafs had he been even close to winning the Stanley Cup, which is the goal of every pro hockey player who ever pulls on a pair of skates.

You would think that would have indicated to him that, whatever else he might think about me, I at least had some kind of an idea of how to coach hockey teams to win. But no. A year later, in the spring of 1965, after we finished fourth and got knocked out in six games by Montreal in the Stanley Cup semi-final, he was a different Bathgate from the guy who had said being traded to Toronto was the biggest break of his life – the guy who had hoisted that Stanley Cup the year before as the climax of a great hockey career. I don't know the circumstances and I don't care much. But he told a reporter that I was doing things all wrong.

'There's a limit to an athlete's endurance,' he said. 'Imlach pushed a few of the players past that limit physically and mentally.'

He talked about how I had tired out Ron Ellis and Pete Stemkowski, that they'd complained of overwork and I'd paid no attention. The older guys like Kelly, Stanley, and Bower could stand the pace at one time, he said, but not any more. We had played some of our best games in practice. Stuff like that. Horsefeathers.

I didn't say much about it at the time. I don't mind getting in controversies over some things but I don't like the idea of getting in controversies with a player. But he talked about limits – pushing players beyond their limits of endurance.

There is no limit to what you can do. Who says there is a limit? Only you! *I live by the creed that you can always be better than you are.* I don't care what it is that you do, you can always do it better. I don't think anything is ever perfect. It can always be made a little perfecter – more perfect. That's the way I feel about it. And the same thing with endurance. Nobody would have run a mile in under four minutes if they'd said, well, four minutes to run a mile is as fast as anybody's endurance will stand.

Every standard like that is made to be broken.

Bathgate talked about Kelly, Stanley, and Bower. The same three guys won us four Stanley Cups eventually. Two years after Bathgate said I was pushing them too hard they helped us win the 1967 one. That refuted anything he had to say. I'd talked like this to the older guys for years, and they'd believed me. 'The older you get the harder you have to work,' I'd tell them. 'That's all there is to it. The day that you quit is the day you are gonna go downhill.' I'd tell that to Bower. He believed me and he went on just about forever.

Actually, if I have done anything for hockey at all, one good thing is to get older players playing hockey longer. At one time, at thirty years of age they were finished. I wouldn't even get some of them until they were thirty or older. That's the way I feel about age. If I worried about a guy's age, and thought I'd have to baby him along at his own pace, I never would have got Bathgate or a lot of other guys to start with.

I'll admit, right off, that a lot of people feel the way Bathgate does. For instance, Clancy, my best friend, doesn't subscribe to some of my theories about long practices. He feels that if you get 45 minutes of good practice out of them – 'real whoop-de-do practice', he calls it – you're better than if you go an hour and a half and have them die on you out there. When he'd run the club, as he often did when I was sick or away, he did it his way. I didn't interfere. But my way was different. I figure the same way as those track coaches who say that if you're going to run a mile, you practise for it not by running one mile, but by running ten miles. If you're going to play a hockey game in an hour, you should be able to practise two hours. That's the way you build endurance. You can't build it in a half-hour practice, because then they're not used to going the distance.

King's theory is that when a player gets uninterested, it is time to call it off. He feels that stamina comes from going out and powdering the other team for the first two periods, and that that gives a team the stamina it needs to hold on and powder them again in the third – while they're still down from being powdered early. But I feel that anything that builds the body stronger fits a player to meet any situation he finds himself in. No matter how tough the game, if he's in good enough shape, from long hard practices, he's always ready to make a comeback, and his body is ready.

I try to push a guy along, that's all. This is for his own good. Bert Olmstead certainly didn't like our long practices. But years later when he was coaching in Oakland, he told me one time, he finally realized what I'd been trying to do with long practices, and he started using them himself. The players will rebel, of course. Like Bathgate did. You can expect that. But you run double practices two or three days in a row, and then have a game, and whatever happens in the game, it isn't because the guys have run out of stamina.

The thing is, you also have to convince the players that this is the best thing for them. What you are doing is selling. You're selling them in practice on the idea that the stamina they're building up is everything. From behind the bench you're selling them the idea that they can win if they put their minds to it. You sell them on the idea that if they want to give the effort, they'll win. You've got to be a super-salesman. Starting right from 1959 they all believed in what we were doing: long practices, double practices, and all.

Now, just to finish off this line of talk about something I believe a lot – and won't change no matter how many players claim they're being overworked – I should say that when Bathgate did sound off that way, I knew he wasn't going to play for me again. It seemed pretty clear he didn't want to play for me, anyway, so what was the use? Detroit knew that I wasn't going to keep him so they wanted to make a deal for him. So Bathgate went to Detroit with Billy Harris and Gary Jarrett for Marcel Pronovost, Ed Joyal, Larry Jeffrey, Lowell MacDonald, and Autry Erickson. Pronovost was the key man for us in that trade, but some of the others also helped us win the Stanley Cup in 1967.

And when we lost three of those guys in the expansion draft in 1967, this brought in hundreds of thousands of dollars. Two Stanley Cups and a lot of money in the till – much as I hated to see those young players go in 1964, it wasn't a bad deal for us at all.

And even if New York goes out one of these days and wins two Stanley Cups with the players they got from us, they'll still just be breaking even with what we did because of that deal.

10

The Dressing Room and the Rink

One other thing that Bathgate said about the way I run a hockey club was, 'Imlach never spoke to Frank Mahovlich or myself for most of the season and when he did it was to criticize. Frank usually got the worst. We are athletes, not machines, and Frank is the type that needs some encouragement, a pat on the shoulder every so often . . .'

Although that second and final season Bathgate spent with Leafs was also the one in which Frank missed some weeks because of a severe depression, rather than answer the criticism directly, I'll give you an idea of the way I operate in a dressing room – not just with Bathgate or Mahovlich, but with everyone. For both praise and criticism, I always tried to deal with the team as a team, rather than as a group of individuals. I think that's the only fair way. There are exceptions, but they have to be big ones to cut any ice with me.

Very seldom would I go into a dressing room and tell off one player, once or twice a year at the most. Only twice can I remember really blasting Mahovlich in front of everybody. Once was later, in the spring of 1967, and another time was in Detroit in the play-offs in 1964, when he'd given away the puck for Detroit's winning goal. I used to talk team effort. Maybe I'd swear like hell at all of them, but there wasn't one who hadn't been told at one time or another that swearing was just my way of saying what I had to say. I told them: 'If I swear at you, if I call you a stupid son-of-a-bitch some time, take it as a term of endearment. That's the way it's meant to be taken.'

Whatever I said in criticism usually was said to the team as a whole. I'd tell them what was wrong but not specifically who did it. What the hell. They knew. Each guy knew what he was doing and what he wasn't doing. He could take out what was meant for him. If he was playing perfect hockey, of course, none of it applied to him.

That isn't to say that I didn't ever consider deeply the other way of doing things: talking to individuals. I was aware that some individuals could do with extra praise, that they really needed it. But would that be fair to the others? For instance, suppose the crowd boos one particular guy. Usually – not always, but usually – if the crowd booed a guy, he was doing something wrong. So because he's a sensitive guy should I go in and tell him a bloody lie, that the crowd didn't know what it was all about, that the booing had been wrong? That he's really the greatest player on skates, and stuff like that? Suppose I'm going in night after night to this dressing room, and three-quarters of the guys are playing their hearts out and making very few mistakes and not needing anybody to hold their hand, but this one guy is making mistakes and I'm giving him all the attention. I don't think that would be fair and in the long run I think it would hurt the team. Those guys who were doing their jobs eventually would start thinking, how come that guy gets all the attention all the time? So if I was going to give praise I would do it on the plane or bus or in a hotel room when we were on the road.

Anyway, individual treatment isn't the way to promote my main idea – that this is a team, everybody has to work as a team, be part of the team. One of the greatest football teams in the world was the Green Bay Packers. There was no nonsense about them. It was strictly team. If a guy didn't like it, they got rid of him. This is the way any team effort is. It's *not* individual. It's individuals that make up the team but the team is the whole. The team is everything.

You get this crap that some people feed young players now – 'You're being used, exploited. You're just a puppet.' Some believe it. They get a little backing on it, and they rebel against it. But in the long run sticking to the team idea is the only way you ever win.

I've even said to some of the guys when they're talking about individuality, okay, you're so individual, you go take the puck, go on in, and score the bloody goal. You're so good, go and get me a goal, I need it. They can't do it. Even Hull can't do it. He can do it more than anybody else, but he can't do it all the time. If he could do it, Chicago would win the Stanley Cup every year. So you've got to have a team effort. Somebody else has got to be doing some of the work that you're not doing. And this is the way I try to operate as a team.

When they complain, of course, I don't get it directly. They don't come up and say to me, lookit, you're lousing up my individuality, I'm different than everybody else. They'll give it to the newspaper guy on the beat, or give it to a radio guy, or their friends. Their friends will tell somebody else. And that's when you get it back. But no matter how many times I get the feedback that this guy or that is unhappy with me, I still say you don't try to weld a team to the individual. You've got to weld that individual to the team. And this is where the difference is in their thinking and my thinking.

Now, for a lot of the time I was with the Leafs, most players accepted that team idea. I felt, and still feel, that they were the important guys on the team. Even Carl Brewer, who was a really great defenceman, didn't give me any trouble until we'd been around together for quite a while. He was an emotional, high-strung kind of a guy and sometimes he'd blow off quite a bit of steam. But he was a team guy. He and Bobby Baun stuck pretty close together, with a lot of loyalty between them, and then the two of them had a lot of loyalty to the team.

All the same, I was told one time by a doctor on our hockey club, 'Someday he's going to quit on you. Mark my words. He's just going to walk out.' Well, he had Brewer pegged. But to my mind Brewer would still be with the Leafs today if some of his influences outside of the club had been different. I'm talking now about Alan Eagleson, the lawyer for the Players' Association. Eagleson is a rebel himself. He got into hockey as the players' lawyer and he started trying to work a revolution. Now maybe some of the things he was working for needed to be done – I'm not going to argue down the line, right or wrong, on every item. But one thing I do know is that he was very chummy with Brewer, who was a bit of a rebel himself. So you have two rebels talking together, bracing each other up, telling each other that they're great guys and Imlach is the bloody villain, and pretty soon something is going to happen.

Hell, as I say, when he first started I had no problems with Brewer. I gave him the best of it every time. But he just got in with this guy and he got filled in that I was always trying to screw him. The words he used to me were to the effect that I was taking advantage of him, exploiting him. 'We're just puppets,' he told me once. 'You want us to dance when you holler.' This conversation took place in a plane. We were talking about contracts, or something.

I don't blame Brewer in a lot of respects. I realize his problem. He's very nervous and tension gets to him easily. And he's a guy who could be told that I'm taking advantage of him and he isn't getting enough money and he shouldn't have to do this, and he shouldn't have to do that. He can be led, and I think he just got the wrong guy for him. He needed somebody who, instead of aggravating his problem, would cool his problems down. But this guy Eagleson aggravated the problems all the time, made them bigger. I mean the game itself aggravated Brewer enough without having somebody standing behind him always giving him the rebel treatment.

And yet he played his best damned hockey when he was going sky-high emotionally. And he had a terrific amount of ability. He could skate like hell. He couldn't finish, couldn't get it through his head how to finish, this was one of his problems. But try to tell him. It was a total block. You were telling him to do something that he didn't want to do and that was the end of it. He got to the stage, before he walked out on us in 1965, that everything I said created more disturbance, more trouble, so I was better to leave him alone. This is what it got to at the end. I never talked to him.

This all had to have some effect on other players on the team. But the point I want to make is that not everybody on the team, by a damn sight, was offended by the way we did things. For years there I'd walk into that dressing room and look around and some of the faces I saw were with me all the time I was with the Leafs, and never gave me any serious trouble. We had our fights. You show me a bunch of guys thrown together for ten or eleven years in a really tension-filled occupation who don't fight – they'd be (censored) saints. But most of them, as far as I knew, never disagreed seriously with the way I did things. In that category you might put my captain George Armstrong, Red Kelly, Dave Keon, Tim Horton, Allan Stanley, Johnny Bower. And then there were some guys who may have disagreed with things I did, but didn't disagree enough to start a rebellion, right? Frank Mahovlich was the greatest hockey player I had some years, and things did prey on him quite a bit, but I never heard Mahovlich tell me, or heard that he told anybody else, that his main trouble was me. Bob Pulford and Bob Baun and I had our scraps and disagreements, but if either of them thought it was *all* my fault he never told me that. Later there were guys who came along like Marcel Pronovost, Terry Sawchuk, Ron Ellis, and some of the others who never gave me less than a hundred per cent of what was in them. To my mind, the people who were mature in their minds accepted that playing on a National Hockey League team was bound to bring about tensions in personal relationships that didn't exist, say, in the banking business. But like me they tried to roll with the bad times and enjoyed the good.

A dressing room is a remarkable place. When you walk in there, close the door, and look around at eighteen or twenty guys who are in the game with you, it is something like a family. One, the coach, is the boss. No player with any sense will disagree with that. But you are all dependent on one another. Some guys might be more energetic than others, some more talented than others, but all are pretty damn close to the top of their profession or they wouldn't be there, and they have that bond between them even if on some teams the bond sometimes gets pretty thin.

People sometimes ask me who was the most interesting guy I ever had in a dressing room. Eddie Shack. You never knew what was going to happen with him in a dressing room. I was always mad at him or laughing at him or giving him hell about something, either for something he'd done out on the ice or for something he was doing right then.

Mahovlich never opened his mouth, a quiet, deep person. Keon never said much either. Sometimes I wished that either of those guys, who were natural leaders on the ice, would do the same thing in the dressing room – but that wasn't their personality. Keon is a really amazing athlete, of course, when you see the size of him out there and then see what he can do against men much bigger. Of course, sometimes a man who is thin and sinewy can stand more than one who is big and muscular – more in the way of skating and keeping going, I mean. Naturally he can't take the bumps; he has to be able to get out of the way.

Then there was Tim Horton. He never said much either. Or listened much, for that matter. He's a stubborn so-and-so. The story with him is that he just keeps on getting better all the time, so naturally he has faith in the way he does things. But this can be aggravating for a coach sometimes. He's going to play it the way he wants to play it. Period. There is not much you can do about it. I've seen me say to him, lookit, you did this or that wrong. And he'd say, what the hell, I've been playing this way for fifteen years, what's the sense of changing? That would get me mad. Sometimes I'd say to him, 'I don't care the way you played fifteen years ago, this is the way I want you to play now. After all,' I'd say, 'if everybody else played it his own individual way, we're gonna lose.' But with Tim sometimes I'd just save my breath. I'd just look at him and walk away. But in his own way sometimes he'd listen to what I said and if *he* decided it made sense – if *he* decided – then maybe he'd do it my way.

Then there'd be guys like Armstrong and Stanley. They had it all in their heads. On the ice they knew where to go and where not to go. In all the time they'd spent playing pro hockey, you know, they knew – but in later years, of course, they weren't staying as strong physically as Horton was, I mean in skating and everything else. It was a case with them that they always knew where to go, but maybe in the last couple of years they were having trouble getting there.

But, all the same, a lot of times it's better to have a guy who knows what to do than a guy who has been in the game five or six years and still hasn't learned to get there – won't go into the openings, won't give up the puck and try to get it back again. They only give it up and then watch the play. Some people never learn, but the good ones do.

Watch Armstrong working his way in on the net from the boards; in places like that he didn't need the speed, because in close quarters it's know-how that counts, not speed.

And Stanley got a lot of goals for us because he could see two or three plays ahead just what was going to happen to the puck. He could read the play and he'd be moving into where he knew the puck was going to be two or three plays from then. Lots of times he'd come off the point and land in front of the net just when the puck got there, and he knew what to do with the puck in that position too. Not many defencemen got more goals. And he could check too. One of the last of the big body-checkers. When he was at his best over on that left side of the defence he'd play forwards coming in on him as if he had them on strings.

Of course, all these guys were remarkable in their own ways. But Johnny Bower! Now we'll start out by saying he was, in his time, the world's greatest athlete. I'll defend that against anybody.

Bower is simply not a normal sort of guy. He had so much desire that he was able to continue to develop all the time. I say to any kid, 'You can be the best junior in the world, but when you step into pro you've got to learn some more. You can keep on learning and learning and learning. How much you learn dictates how great you're going to be. If you can continue to learn to play we'll say for ten years after you get out of junior you're going to be the greatest hockey player in the National Hockey League.'

But somewhere down the line they stop being able to get better. Bower never did stop. He came in, well, we'll say he came into the NHL at forty years of age, damn near, and he was able to keep on getting better. On top of it all, he had the heart, the will. By wanting to be the best so badly, he overrode the aging process. Let's face it, he would go out and practise at things that would kill most people at fifty years of age. He's got to be damn close to fifty now, you know. Now how many people on the street could go out and skate around that rink? Or go back and forth across the rink the many times I'd make him go? They'd all die, every one of them. They'd all die. It's easy to go trot around the park with running shoes on. There's no weight to them at all. But Bower would do all I asked and carry a lot of weight at the same time. It's fantastic what that man could do. Absolutely fantastic. That's why I say he was the greatest athlete in the world. I don't give a damn if anybody wants to argue it. Just bring the guy along and we'll put him in the same position as Bower, even right now, and we'll see who finishes. There is nobody who'll finish. I couldn't do what he does.

You know what he did to me once in training camp? This is quite a few years ago. I heard from the grapevine that he had a birth certificate.

They'd say, 'Has he showed you the birth certificate yet?'

And I'd say, 'No, he hasn't showed it to me yet but he will.'

About a week after he's in camp, everybody else has seen it except me.

Finally he said, 'I want to show you something.'

I said, 'Sure, let's have a look at it.'

'Take a look at this,' he said, and brought out the birth certificate.

I read the thing and I said, 'That's pretty good, Johnny. I didn't think you were that young. But I'd like to ask you a question.'

He said, 'What is it?'

'If you were born on this day here that you're telling me, you had to be overseas with the First Division, in 1939, when you were thirteen,' I said. 'And in the Canadian Army I know they were stupid but they were not that stupid.'

He turned around and took the thing and put it in his pocket and I never saw it again or heard of it.

I don't care about his age anyway; in his prime he was the world's greatest athlete, and whether he was 30 or 50 didn't alter that.

As far as playing goes, the only trouble I ever had with him was convincing him that he was the best ever, and that he should play the same way all the time. If they started to beat him he'd start to wonder why and then he'd try new tricks. He'd try to change and I'd tell him not to change, just to stand up and cut the angles like he always did. I kept telling him, 'You're the best in the game. Make them beat you – that's all there is to it.' He was going to get beaten once in a while, what the hell, who isn't?

In the dressing room, Bower was a very sensitive sort of person. We had a few run-ins. I mean, hell, if he did something wrong, I'd have to tell him because I got other people in the room, and it's a team, everybody treated the same. Sometimes he'd get a little hepped up and sore at me.

One of the worst times I remember concerned Shack. Oh, there were two or three things involved. Like right at that time John had a very sore hand. He'd been playing with it for about three weeks and it was bothering him a lot. Then, in a game against Canadiens, John Ferguson got upset going across the goal-mouth and he wound up in the corner banging his head against the boards or something. When the play stopped, Bower skated right out of his net and went over and inquired if Ferguson was okay. I didn't like that. I told him and he got sore. Then a day or so later, maybe even the next day, I come out on the ice and he's sitting there on the bench. And Shack, kibitzing out on the ice, yells to me, 'Hey, Bower wants to see you.'

Well, what happened was that Bower was having a smoke on the bench. Shack knew that, and was playing his kind of joke by sending me over. Johnny had this cigarette hidden in his hand, but I didn't know that. I went over and talked to him. I just couldn't figure it out. I was telling him to get out on the ice or something and he wasn't moving, and I guess the cigarette was burning his hand. So he got sore at me, and when he didn't move I told him to get off the ice. Then we went into the dressing room together and had a bust-up. He was just tied too tight. He said something about the hand and I told him to get out of there and have a doctor look at it. He was overwrought, and he did go out of there and there were stories in the papers that he was going to quit. But what the heck, we both cooled down and he came back and we got it straightened out.

The thing is, there was a real bond between us. He knew how much I admired him, no matter what little incident might come up that made him sore at me. I know he once said that when he was through, when his reflexes had gone, I would be the guy who would tell him. But we never talked about things like that much, except maybe when he was signing a contract.

He was never hard to get to sign. That's one thing that bothered me a little, because if he'd been like some of the other guys he might have been demanding more money and getting it. That's why his contract was torn up one time in mid-season and he was given a new one. Every fall he'd say he didn't know how much longer he could play, and I'd tell him, 'Just come to training camp and if you're good enough, you're good, and if you're not good enough, hell, there's nothing you can do about it. You've been around a lot longer than anybody expected.'

I remember signing him once back about 1964. I wanted to give him a three-year contract. He said he didn't know if he could last another three years. But he signed it, and he fooled himself and was still playing long after that contract was up. If every hockey player in the world had the same attitude towards himself and the game that Johnny Bower had, coaches and general managers would live forever and never have ulcers.

I think everybody will realize that a lot goes on inside a dressing room that has a fair amount to do with the well-being of a team, without really having any direct connection with hockey. For instance, there are the stars and there are the other guys who might be the backbone of the team, but who aren't stars. They know there is a difference in what they get paid, but I don't think that bothers them if every guy can be made to feel that in his way he is just as important to the team as the stars – each guy doing his bit. There are various ways you can do this, one being to treat everybody alike. One principle that I have in this line goes right back to Quebec, when Jean Beliveau was playing for me. In those days when we sold the program a lot of the advertisers used to like to put up some kind of a gift for any player who got, for instance, a 'hat trick' – three goals in one game. One place would give away a suit of clothes, another a hat, another a pair of shoes, shirts, ties, and so on. The advertisers would use it for publicity, of course – like get Beliveau or Gaye Stewart or one of the other big wheels picking up his free suit, have a picture taken, and put it in the window.

Some guys get a lot of hat tricks and some don't. On the team idea, I always figured that the guy getting the hat trick couldn't really get it by himself, so the loot should be shared around. So I had a deal. The players all went along. The first time a guy got a hat trick, he got the works, all the prizes. But the second hat trick he got, he would pick one thing, and all the rest went to other players who'd draw for the stuff, out of a hat. That way everything got spread around the hockey club and it wasn't a case of Beliveau or another star getting everything and the other guys getting nothing.

With the Leafs we had a modified form of the share-the-wealth idea for a while. Any time there was a deal made for promotion or publicity that involved the club as a whole, or individual players, everybody shared to some degree. If it was an individual player who was going to do a commercial, for instance, the player would get a third of the fee, the club would get a third, and the rest of the players would split the other third. If it was a team deal, the club would take a third and the players would split two-thirds equally. But that way there were still conflicts; some guys always got more than others, naturally. And sometimes there were arguments on individual contracts, about endorsements and so on.

Well, then Maple Leaf Gardens sold program rights and all commercial rights to the use of the team or individual players. It was a package deal. The people buying these rights were MacLaren Advertising and the club had a right to do it, under our contracts.

But when this deal was being made I saw a chance to do something that I thought would be good. A separate company was set up by MacLaren's to handle all these extra rights. It was called Maple Leaf Sports Productions. My idea was that, instead of this outfit dealing separately with each player, meaning that some of them would still get a lot more than others, we should sell the whole lot as a package. I got Maple Leaf Sports Productions to agree to pay the players a lump $27,000 a year. This would be split on a daily basis so that players who maybe were with the club only part of a season would share it too. But everybody would share equally for each day he was with the club. It came to $1,500 a year for a guy who was with us all year long. This was a tough arrangement to get from the Maple Leaf Sports Productions people. They didn't think it was worth the money and in strict terms they were right. But from our standpoint there were other considerations. It was a tidy arrangement that left no room for bickering or animosity among the players and that was what counted with me.

However, after selling the idea to the company, I then had to sell it to the players. At a team meeting, I put it to them as a team effort. 'After all,' I said, 'when some of you came in here first you weren't worth a nickel to anybody in this endorsement line. Some of you still aren't. But some day you might be the guy who'll get a $10,000 endorsement and then this company will get their money back on you.'

Two or three of the players were against; some of the guns on the team, you know. But Frank Mahovlich went for it right away. He was always a great team guy, and he could see the sense in it. Well, when he went for it everybody else naturally came in – because if Frank would go for it, who else could complain? And I told them, this is the one thing you get whether you're playing well or not. I made the deal for five years, with an option to renew for another five. This was tied to the TV contract. Not a bad deal, I thought. Every player who gets the full $1,500 share was getting exactly the annual amount that he puts into the NHL pension fund. He puts in $1,500 and the club puts in $1,500. So in effect he's getting his pension for nothing.

Of course, there were still exceptions. We didn't stop an individual player from making a deal of his own to get a free car to drive, or something like that. Or maybe they go into a hockey school with a deal where they're going to get paid after they quit hockey, or when they leave the Leafs. No deal is perfect. But this one is just about as good a one as can be made, in my opinion.

One bit of trouble we had with Eddie Shack a few years ago was over this particular deal. He was supposed to show up to do a commercial, and the way I heard it he checked with Eagleson or somebody and was advised not to. I had set up the appointment and everybody was sitting there in the studio waiting for him and he never showed up. Then he phoned the office and said he hadn't appeared because he wasn't getting enough money out of it. That's when I had the papers made out transferring him to Victoria, which caused a bit of a stir. Of course, Shack went up to the studio a day or so later and did the thing, and later on we just let the Victoria thing die. But we didn't let it die so soon that he didn't know we meant business. Eagleson and some of those other guys talk about me moving people around like puppets, and all that horsefeathers. To my mind when a guy agrees to something, and it's in his con-tract, and he's taking the money for it, he's got a responsibility too. It's bigger than just one player. And this deal was just the basic one, the minimum. It was also arranged that any time a player went on television or radio, he'd get a hundred dollars. Or if he went out for a sponsor like Esso for a personal appearance somewhere, he'd get expenses and a hundred dollars a day. I think it is the best over-all club deal in the league, and the best part of it is that it treats all the players alike.

Of course, there are some money things that go on in the dressing room that aren't entirely to their benefit – they figure, anyway. One with Leafs was that I was allowed to fine them up to $500 for things they did wrong. This rule might get changed some day, because some people do abuse it. I didn't fine people often except in serious matters of discipline. But there was one regular fine we had – $5 for give-aways. You give away the puck to the opposition, and it cost you five. The money went into a pool for the players to have a party at the end of the year. It made a pretty good party at the best place in town. You might think that $5 isn't much for a bad play made by a guy who is making maybe $20,000 or $25,000 a year – and you're right. But it was a penalty for a poor play and I think it helped them look twice before they got rid of a puck.

For a lot of these reasons, plus others that have more to do with the actual hockey playing itself, I think I probably did more talking in the dressing room, at team meetings, or before or after practices, than I did at other times. I didn't spend much time in there during a game. For instance, I'd never go in right after a period. Didn't matter where we were, in the Gardens or some rink on the road, I'd stay outside in the hallway not far away. The reason for not going in is this: almost certainly in the period just over somebody did something wrong. Maybe three or four guys. So if I spent too much time in there I'd be bound to raise a few points and before I was finished someone might say something back. Then maybe there'd be an argument going and the team wouldn't get a chance to rest and relax.

Also, if you talk to them too long and try to cover too much, probably you're going to wind up knocking down this guy or that – in criticism, I mean – and maybe you'll forget to get them all back up again before the game starts.

So I'd go in about two minutes before the game was due to get going again – and all I'd do, usually, was to pick on one thing they were doing wrong, maybe raise a little hell, and then tell them they could do better than that. A lot better. Then I'd try to bring them back up again. Maybe I didn't always succeed but that was the theory.

When they'd go out for the game I had a lot of little things I used to do in the dressing room. Just to get some tension out of my system before I went out there. Supposed to be for luck. Anyway, I didn't feel right if I didn't do them. Knock the sticks and put an arrow on the blackboard and kick the pails and things like that. Tommy Nayler, the assistant trainer, would wait around until I finished that nonsense. Then he'd hand me some gum to chew and follow me out and close the door.

At the end of a game there was a routine too. For instance, we never let much get into the press about injuries but we sure as hell wanted to know all about them ourselves. So at the end of the game the doctor would go around to every player and check to see if there were any injuries picked up during the game.

You want everything reported so that you can get it treated. A player gets hurt tonight and he hides it and plays tomorrow night and by Wednesday the team's playing again and a small injury may have become a big one and maybe you're going to lose the guy for two weeks now. But if he had told you Saturday night you might not have played him Sunday night, or you might have treated him and had him fit for Wednesday. These are the things that happen.

We had trouble with players hiding injuries one year, 1967-68, a lousy year anyway but we played with three broken wrists to boot. Duanne Rupp, Wayne Carlton, and Ron Ellis. Rupp played with his and we knew but nobody else did. But this is the thing that tends to happen: Carlton didn't let us know that his wrist was that bad and we went along with it until finally, maybe three weeks later, we had it X-rayed and had to put him in a cast. Same thing with Ellis. Finally we get it X-rayed. Well, he'd played with it for two or three weeks before this happened, and he played another month before anybody on another team knew about it. In the long run this certainly didn't hurt Ronnie Ellis because he was the best hockey player I had that year, by far the best. But he had to have an operation after the year was over and have it put in a cast.

Here's the thing about injuries – I want to hear from the players but I don't want to let anybody in the press know. So if a guy is playing with an injury it's a good reason to keep the dressing room door locked a while at the end of a game. The reason I don't want the press to know about it is that if an injured player can possibly play I don't want other teams knowing he's hurt. I only go on what I would do myself. If I knew a guy playing against me had a bad leg, well, everything is fair in love and war. If he's got it, what the hell, exploit it. It's just like on the battlefield. There is a hole in the line. You know it's weak there. What are you going to do, go and attack some place else? You try right where the weakness is. So I don't want to let another team know I have any weakness. I let the guy play. If the other team doesn't know he's hurt, he may get through the game without any trouble. If they know he's hurt, he's going to take more abuse because they've been tipped off that he's been hurt, and exactly where.

Another reason for keeping a dressing room door closed after a game is that everybody gets a chance to settle down a little bit. It just saves trouble. I remember when Howie Young hit Johnny Bower that time in Detroit, Fred Cederberg from the *Telegram* came to me and said, 'Would you say that was a deliberate attempt to injure?' I was mad, but if I'd said, 'You're god-damned right!' it would have come out that I said it was a deliberate attempt to injure and maybe a lot of other things I'd wish I hadn't said. When you're hot, there's lots of times some serious accusations can slip out. If you've got a chance to cool down you're not apt to make those mistakes. Taking it over the years, it's usually better to say nothing in public about things like that.

Another thing, a lot of times we're leaving right after the game. So we have to pack all that stuff. If there's been a big schmozzle in the game and the room is full of reporters and we're trying to catch a plane, or a train, we're in trouble. So I would keep the dressing room closed until everybody was undressed and getting into the shower. Then the three trainers would get a chance to pack the bags and get them to hell out of the road. Then we're in not bad shape.

The pants and gloves and the pads are all put into the bags as they are taken off. The clean underwear is already in the bag before the guys come in — clean jock and clean socks and clean sweater. So then they get their skates checked and put them in the bag and they throw the bags over and the trainers put them on the truck and take them out.

So those are the three reasons I kept the dressing room closed a while — injuries, letting myself and the others cool off, and getting packed for the road. Of course, I know the press has a job to do and we try to make the job as easy as we can. But I couldn't make the press job easier at the expense of making my job harder. Anyway, this sort of thing works both ways. One time in the spring of 1960 I closed the dressing room to the press entirely after one game. This made Milt Dunnell, sports editor of the Toronto *Star*, sore enough that (I was told later) he instructed his staff not to use my name in any of their stories. I didn't ask him if this report was true. But if my name did appear on his sports pages for the rest of that season I must have missed it.

The Most Satisfying Stanley Cup — Centennial Year

In the fall of 1965, we had a very eventful training camp. Bob Baun was a holdout and this had made Carl Brewer extremely unhappy. I think this fact had something to do with Brewer leaving the team and retiring from hockey, although like most things that have been building up for a while the final blowup seemed to be related to a single incident.

We were playing an exhibition game in Peterborough this particular night when the puck went into the corner and Johnny Bower yelled at Brewer to get in there and get it. All I could see from behind the bench was that Brewer went into the corner, got the puck, and then shot it right out in front. Somebody on the opposition team took a swipe at it and it almost hit Bower in the face. Then the puck went back into the corner and damned if Brewer didn't go in for it and shoot it out in front again, and once more Bower almost got creamed. I took Brewer right off the ice that time, but I didn't really know what was going on – all I could see was that Brewer was giving the puck away in our own end.

Then when we were coming off the ice at the end of that period (I heard this later from some of the players) Brewer was behind Bower and shoving him, maybe accidentally for all I know, but Bower turned on him and told him to quit. Then they went into the dressing room (I stayed outside) and Bower told Brewer that there were three goalies in the camp trying for the big job. 'I need all the help I can get,' he said. 'And I don't need you throwing the puck out in front on me.'

Brewer said, 'Don't take your old-man frustrations out on me.'

Now, they often kidded Bower about his age, everybody does, but this time Bower wasn't taking it. 'I may be old,' he said, jumping up, 'but I'll be around this league longer than you will.'

They kept on jawing at each other and then Brewer threw an orange. Nobody knows whether he tried to hit Bower with it, or what, but it wasn't far off the mark.

Now you can imagine my situation; I didn't know anything about this at the time. But just before the intermission was over I went in. What I did know was that Brewer had made two bad plays out there and there'd been others not playing well either. So I go in and I'm giving them hell and one thing I say is, 'If any of you don't want to play, stay in the room. Otherwise somebody might get killed.' I said more, but that was the gist of it. And then when the team got up to go to the ice, Brewer didn't get up.

The rest of the players went out. I stayed in there a couple of minutes or less. Brewer was badly upset by this time. I said something to him and he told me a lot of stuff and finally I said, 'If you feel that way, take your uniform off.' He started to do that and he was obviously in such an unsettled condition that I was worried. When I went out to the bench I got someone to find Clancy and I told him what had happened, and asked him if he'd go into the dressing room and stay with Brewer – make sure that, in this frame of mind, he at least had some company when he walked back to the hotel. King did that. And it was the last walk Carl ever took out of a Leaf dressing room. The next day the papers were full of it: Brewer had quit.

Well, just to mention one side of it, he left us in a hell of a hole. Earlier that year I had traded Ron Stewart to Boston for Orland Kurtenbach, Andy Hebenton, and Pat Stapleton. That was June 8, just before the annual draft. But I figured one thing I didn't really need was a defenceman. We had Horton and Stanley, Brewer and Baun, and I didn't see how Stapleton could crack that lineup at all. So I left him unprotected in the draft and Chicago got him. He played good defence for them, as I knew he would. But if I'd known then that Brewer was going to walk out on the club, I certainly would have protected Stapleton. A lot of people tend to take the part of a player in any dispute, arguing that it's unfair for him to be tied to one team the way he is. But here was a case where a player could walk away, apparently feeling no responsibility for leaving his team and his teammates in a difficult position.

However, a lot of people blamed me for what had happened with Brewer and I never told anyone about the Bower incident. And this gave Stafford a little ammunition.

All the time I had anything to do with Stafford he wanted to have more say in running the hockey club — more say, actually, than the deal that I had with the Leafs allowed him. Stafford, John Bassett, and Harold Ballard became the principal owners of the Gardens and the Leafs in November of 1961, buying out Conn Smythe. In the next three years we won three Stanley Cups in a row besides finishing first once, so Stafford didn't really have much chance to tell the world how much he could improve on what I was doing. In June of 1964 I signed another three-year contract as manager and coach, so legally, at least, I was fairly safe. But as soon as there was this opportunity to start cutting me up, Stafford grabbed it — the Brewer incident, along with some moves I'd made, like sending Eddie Shack and Pete Stemkowski temporarily to Rochester.

This came to a head in November of 1965. We were making some changes in the team, rebuilding here and there and testing once again what we already had. Orland Kurtenbach was new with us, giving us some muscle we needed. Brit Selby was starting off well towards winning the rookie award, which he did. Mike Walton played a few games with us but needed more seasoning. Pete Stemkowski seemed on the verge of making it. Ron Ellis had arrived in a big way the previous season, only nineteen but playing with poise and never quitting. With Brewer gone, our defence wasn't as good — after all, he'd been an all-star. Johnny Bower and Terry Sawchuk were splitting the goalkeeping, and there was nothing wrong with them. They were playing as they had in the spring of 1965, when they won the Vezina Trophy between them; Sawchuk had played 36 games of the 1964-65 season and Bower 34.

But there in the fall of 1965 we weren't getting goals. We had nineteen in our first eleven games, and five of them were in one game against New York. Stafford took that opportunity to give the same old interview that had been hanging around my neck for nearly twenty years by then: I was doing too much, trying to be both coach and general manager. I'd have to be relieved of some of the load.

Stafford did say, rather generously I thought, that he wasn't planning to fire me. 'I've given him too much work to do,' he said. 'Next year he'll only have to worry about the Leafs at training camp.' He claimed that by handling all of our teams at training camp in Peterborough, I'd got so tired out that I couldn't think straight.

'You can't expect Punch to spend from seven or eight in the morning until midnight on the ice for four weeks of training camp and then be sharp enough to make decisions,' he said. He also said he and the other members of the hockey committee intended to help by travelling with us on the road. I was never quite sure how that was intended to help us win hockey games.

One of his offhand opinions was that we weren't playing well enough on the road because we didn't have enough of what he called National Leaguers on the Leafs, despite the fact that some of them had helped us win three Stanley Cups before we'd lost out in the playoffs in the spring of 1965.

Anyway, at a hockey luncheon in New York a few days later I was asked about all this. All I said was what I've always said: 'I run the club as I see fit. If anyone wants to disagree with me, he can – I'm not right all the time. But as long as I'm general manager, my decisions will have to stand. If the decisions are not good enough, they'll just have to fire me.'

Just to show how much importance there really is in an exchange like that, right after Stafford sounded off about our performance on the road we went into Montreal (a road game, of course) and beat the Canadiens 3–1. They were in first place and we were fourth or fifth at the time. But even more satisfying to me was that our three goals all came from one new line – Larry Jeffrey, who had come to us in the Detroit trade for Bathgate, Eddie Shack, who I'd earlier sent to Rochester hoping it would shake him up into playing the kind of hockey he could play, which it had, and Bob Pulford. Right after that Montreal game we had two with Chicago Black Hawks, who were in second place. We beat them 3–1 in Toronto and then went into Chicago (another road game, where Stafford said we were lacking in spirit) and slathered them 7–3.

I knew that, even with that kind of a record over the short haul, we were rebuilding. I'd like to point out that Shack never had as good a season in his life as he did after I'd sent him to Rochester to straighten out a little. But the main thing is that if you're going to blame me for being overtired when the team isn't scoring, who are you going to give the credit to when the same team, under the same 'tired' coach, knocks over the best teams in the league? We went on at that time to go ten games unbeaten.

There were some decisions I'd had to make in the previous few months that were a hell of a lot more important than arguments with Stafford on details. At the annual meetings in June of 1965 I'd tried every trick in the book to hang on to Gerry Cheevers. Actually, I tried to keep him as an ordinary player, listing him with the forwards and defencemen. But the league ruled against that. I'd always thought he'd be the next goalie for the Leafs after Bower was finished. But at the same time how could I leave Bower or Sawchuk unprotected after they'd won the Vezina Trophy between them that very spring? No matter what I thought of Cheevers, the two old guys were the proved goalkeepers. I had to keep them. So Boston picked up Cheevers in the draft and he has been a great one for them since. I also lost Don Simmons at the same draft, to New York.

It's interesting to look back over those years from winning the Cup in 1964 to getting knocked out of the semi-finals by Montreal in four straight in 1966. That way you get an idea of the ebb and flow of a club, even of individual hockey players, in a way that you don't see it when it's all day-by-day, life and death to get ready for the next game. Imagine us getting Sawchuk for $20,000 in the draft in 1964. He and Bower went right out and won the Vezina. Dickie Moore played thirty-eight games for us in 1964-65. I tried him for the same reason I give any older guy a chance: he'd been a great one and he still had some of it left. Jim Pappin came up to the club first in 1964. He was an ornery guy in some ways, but when he was at his best he helped us plenty. Litzenberger and Harris and Ehman and McKenney were all gone from the club, one way or another. In 1964-65 I used Horton at right wing quite a bit and he did all right, although it might have cost him the place on the all-star defence that year. I played my son Brent a few times, including once at centre against his old idol, Beliveau. He was in London going to the University of Western Ontario and playing junior for London Nationals. Bruce Gamble played his first few games for us, and we knew we had another goalie who could play in the NHL. We had our moments here and there, but nobody knew better than I did that we were labouring, that we didn't have the gas any more. Guys were getting older, that was all. And the replacements we tried – Ed Joyal, Larry Jeffrey, Pete Stemkowski, Wally Boyer, Mike Walton, Jim Pappin, Brit Selby and some others – weren't quite enough to arrest the process.

It might be indicative of what was going on that I had more run-ins than usual with referees in those years from 1964 to 1967. I know one time I said, and it got in the paper, that the league could have saved a lot of money one night just by taking somebody out of the crowd and giving him a whistle – he couldn't have done worse than the referee we had. Another night I teed off on another referee who loused up a Montreal game something awful – gave Kent Douglas a match penalty for swinging his stick at Dave Balon, but didn't give Balon anything for swinging his stick at Douglas first. That was the night Rocket Richard reached over and punched Douglas when he was going off the ice. You can imagine what the league would have done to some other club executive – Rocket was a vice-president of Canadiens at the time – for doing that sort of thing. Even the league president, Clarence Campbell, got into the act one night, sounding just like a Montreal fan, by saying that we had tried to intimidate the Canadiens with rough play, notwithstanding the fact that they weren't so intimidated that they didn't beat us.

I appreciate the jobs referees try to do. I believe they are all honest. I believe that they do what they can. If they rob me, okay, they rob me. The only thing, at the time I'm not going to let them get away with it. There are always going to be games when you're going to be hosed by the referees. Let's face it, that's part of the damn game. Well, at those times I'm going to say what I think. But it's like I tell my hockey players, no matter what I say to you you're my friend at the start of the season. And when the season is over, I hope you're still going to be my friend. But with referees, I suppose it's a little tougher because I'm going to call some of them everything in the world and it's going to appear in print. They can't say anything about me, sure. But they can give me a screwing that could cost me a game or maybe my job or maybe an awful lot of money. That is a hell of a lot more than their reading five or six lines where

I call them names in the paper. That's the way I look at it. But when it's all over, it's all over. I don't hold any grudges against any of the referees.

Thinking back to the remarks by Stafford Smythe quoted earlier in this chapter, they must have seemed a little ironical if he thought of them at all six months later. We finished third in the 1965-66 season but, as I said, Canadiens knocked us out in four straight in the Stanley Cup semi-final. I had the flu and so did some of the players. A lot of people thought that would probably be it for me, even though I still had one year to go on the three-year contract I'd signed after winning the Stanley Cup in 1964.

But on April 20, 1966, just before I took off to watch our farm club at Tulsa in their playoffs, the Gardens signed me for an additional three years as *general manager and coach.* Isn't that just a little ironical, after Stafford saying I'd been working too hard?

'This action was taken to forestall any further speculation that Imlach was leaving the organization at the end of the 1966-67 season,' the statement said.

I didn't ask my old buddy, Stafford, for this contract, incidentally. Even apart from the fact that it put an end, for the moment, to the rumours that Stafford wanted to take over the managing himself, with Kelly or Stanley or Armstrong as coach, two matters about the contract are worth noting.

First, it eliminated any possibility that I would leave Leafs to join one of the expansion teams when they started to organize in the spring of 1967. I'd had two or three offers.

Second, it also gave me a big raise. But one funny thing, to me anyway, was that the raise did not start for another year. In other words, they were giving me a raise of close to $10,000 a year – but right then, with only six teams in the league, I would still get paid at the old rate. It was only the following year, when the league would be raised to twelve teams, that I was worth the extra. In a day when raises are often retroactive one way or another, this was the first one I ever heard of that was postdated for an entire year.

It isn't hard for me to work up a gnawing pain in the stomach when I think about that season that followed, the one of 1966-67. In that one I was in the depths and I was on the heights. We'll start with the depths. In a ten-game stretch leading from mid-January to mid-February, we never won a hockey game. What can you do in a situation like that? Well, there's no magic way to get out of a slump. Here I had these players who'd done pretty well for me, some for years and some for less time than that, and suddenly nothing would go right for them.

The only answer I had was to make them work harder. That's all. Work, and something's got to give. If you sit back and say what the hell, so we're having a bad time, and don't do anything about it, well nothing ever happens. So you try to do something, and my way was extra work. The players got to feeling they'd never get out of it. They were so worried that they made it worse. We were scoring so little that they all got extra sensitive about not letting the other team score. This made them extra scared of making mistakes. That in turn made them play more conservatively – meaning less goals. It was a vicious little circle. As the pressure mounted, I just kept on getting after them, just kept on trying to get them going, that's all.

As the losses mounted and we slid down to fifth place, I got so I couldn't sleep at all. I would show up for practices as tired as if I'd already been out there practising myself for ten hours. I'd doze off at night and then snap awake with things going through my head that I might do. I remember one of the last things I did after we'd gone ten in a row without a win was to invite them all up to my office to sign contracts for the next season. But even that was sort of a half-hearted rib. I didn't have any takers.

On Saturday, February 18, we had a team meeting. Boston was in for a game that night and things were a little better. We'd had three ties in a row, which was practically a winning streak. This was the usual eleven a.m. meeting. After I'd spoken to them briefly, they were straggling out or doing little things around the dressing room. I sat down on a bench beside Clancy. I had a bad pain in my left side, and sort of congestion there. I told him I felt lousy. He said I should see the doctor. I said to hell with that, we had a game that night. A little later we were having a pot of tea in the Gardens lounge and Dr. Tate McPhedran came in. He was one of the club doctors, Dr. Hugh Smythe being the other at that time. I was feeling worse. I told the doctor about it. He told me I should have an examination and I agreed. Clancy dropped me at the Toronto General Hospital at 2.30. I told him I'd see him later for the game.

Well, I didn't. Dr. McPhedran examined me. He said I should be admitted to hospital right away.

I told him, dammit, that I had the game that night.

'Now,' he said.

They put me in a private room. About five o'clock I phoned Clancy and asked him if he'd run the club for me that night, because they had me locked up. I know there were a lot of rumours then and later about how sick I was, but this is exactly what happened. All the doctors said was that I was completely exhausted. I think maybe if I'd let it go on further, I would have been really sick. But as it was, it was bad enough. I had a lot of time to think in the hospital.

Clancy didn't tell the Leafs much before that game. He just said I wouldn't be there and asked them to give a hundred per cent. They did, and won the game 5–3. They wouldn't even let me watch the game in the hospital, but I knew who had won. My wife came in and told me. Maybe she wouldn't have if we'd lost.

Leafs started to win after I'd wound up in the hospital and it gave some guys in Toronto a lot of ammunition to start repeating the lines, fire Imlach, retire him, do anything, but don't let him coach again. I can't say that it did much for my peace of mind when Stafford came right out in the Monday paper with a quote that Leafs weren't going to be run from a hospital bed. The body was still warm, you know. Also, I think something not many people know is that he phoned Joe Crozier in Rochester and asked him to come up and handle the Leafs. Right away quick.

Joe said, 'Why doesn't Mr. Imlach call me and ask me to come? When Punch asks me to come up, I'll come up.'

It must have been aggravating, to have me flat on my back and not be able to persuade somebody to come up and start taking over before I could get back. All this before there'd been any kind of a final diagnosis at all. I mean, Ontario Premier John Robarts had to go to hospital about the same time. I didn't notice anybody rushing to grab his job while he was still on his back not able to defend himself. Anyway, Leafs went on from there to break out of their slump the way I knew they could. Right away, Clancy was hailed as the wonder coach, the inference being that if I had killed them, Clancy was curing them. By winning, Clancy was also curing me. I always knew Clancy would do a good job of anything that was asked of him.

Maybe it's not very becoming of me, but with all the other stuff flying around I was happy to read what a couple of the players said in interviews with Red Burnett of the *Star* about then.

One was Tim Horton. 'King's been doing a great job – don't get me wrong,' said Tim. 'But Punch had us straightened out before his health gave out. He proved he was a real man during that ten-game losing streak. He could have blasted us in the news media, made a lot of lineup changes, and taken us apart verbally behind closed doors. He did none of those things. Instead of criticizing he went out of his way to try to build up our confidence and kept impressing us with the fact that we had too much ability to keep skidding.

'It took patience and courage on his part to wait out the slump. The only corrective measures he used were to work on basic funda-mentals during practice. I'd just like to make it clear that I'd be giving just as much if Punch were here, instead of King.'

Larry Jeffrey talked to Red, too. 'After we lost five in a row I expected two moves,' he said. 'The first was a spot on the bench and the second a ticket to Rochester. It would have been an easy way out for Imlach – blame it on the younger players.

'Instead of abuse and threats of demotion, I got sound advice and encouragement. I finally was forced out of the lineup through injuries, not because I was part of a slumping team. It gives you a good feeling when you realize you're not going to be used as a whipping boy.'

I was in the hospital two weeks. When I got out it was a Saturday afternoon. I went to the Gardens thinking I might even stick around for the game. But I found I was very tired. I'd been in bed too long. I went home and watched it on television. That was good therapy. The visiting team was Chicago. They were in first place, a mile in front of everybody. We beat them 3–0. I also didn't mind it the following Saturday night when I came back to coach my first game since getting sick, and again Chicago was in there. Bobby Hull got his fiftieth goal of the season that night but we beat them 9–3. So we weren't exactly patsies any more. A couple of weeks later Chicago finished the season in first place, a full seventeen points ahead of Montreal.

I talked about this season being one where I experienced both the depths and the heights. The depths were behind me. Even when we lost 5–2 in Chicago in the first game of the Stanley Cup semi-final, I had a feeling that we were going to get to them. Every-thing worked. George Armstrong got hurt and I put Brian Conacher into his right-wing spot, and Conacher never played better hockey in his life than he did from then on, all through the playoffs. Same with Larry Hillman, on defence. Same with a lot of others. We won the second and third games, dropped the fourth. In Chicago for a Saturday afternoon game, the fifth of the series, I had a tough decision that was typical of most of the ones I was making that spring. That is, it worked.

At the end of the first period we were tied 2–2, but Johnny Bower – who hadn't been playing much – really was juggling the puck. I called him over to the bench during the first period. He admitted he was shaky, but said he wanted to finish the period anyway. I let him. We talked again in the dressing room after the period. I could see he wasn't himself and he knew it too. He agreed with me that he should come out and we'd put Terry Sawchuk in.

Terry had played the first four games of the series and was so battered and bruised that he had asked to be allowed to sit that one out. He was on the bench, of course. I'd asked him in the first, when Bower looked shaky, if he felt well enough to go in. But Terry said he'd rather wait until the start of the second if he had to go in at all, so that made it unanimous.

He hadn't been in the game in the second period for more than a few minutes when Hull let go one of his bombs. It hit Sawchuk on the shoulder and glanced up and hit his mask. Down Terry went as if he'd been axed. Bobby Haggert went running out and kneeled over him and asked him if he was okay. Terry looked up at him and said, 'I stopped it, didn't I?' And he got up and shut the door on them for the rest of the game while Pete Stemkowski scored the winning goal and Jim Pappin got the clincher. That put us up 3–2 in games, and we won the sixth one back in Toronto 3–1 to move into the final against Montreal. The winning goal was scored by Brian Conacher. He knocked down Ed Van Impe, retrieved the puck, and went right in and scored the winner. Brian and I had our troubles the following year, but in that 1967 Stanley Cup he did everything a coach could ask.

I guess nobody who saw that final series against Montreal will ever forget it. I know I won't. We started out the same way as we had against Chicago – we got slaughtered, 6–2. We were through, finished, done with. Everybody said so, right away. I phoned home that night after the game and my wife was so mad about the television coverage she just about came straight over the telephone at me. Apparently TV had written us off entirely. Even the guys from Toronto television, who might just have held back a little for a game or two to see how the wind blew, talked as if the body was ready for burial. The next day one of the Toronto writers called it humiliating. Another said it was like jet fighters (the Canadiens) against Sopwith Camels (us).

I don't know what got into me the day after that game, except that I had too much faith in our team to think that one game made a series. I got Clancy out of bed and told him, 'You come with me. We're going down to the press room and show the flag.' The press room is a sort of league hospitality suite where the writers go to exchange wisdom with one another, I guess. And drink. Anyway, coaches just don't go in there. Especially coaches who have just lost 6–2 and have been given up for dead by every hockey writer in the land. But I went in. I told these guys that we were going to beat Canadiens. I was really jacked up, the way I hadn't been, I guess, since back in the spring of 1959 when we'd surprised a few people too. Of course, they argued with me. Before long I was making speeches in one part of the room and Clancy was making speeches in another part and we were both telling them that we were going to jam it down the throat of every one of them before this series was over.

It must have been great. I remember a sportswriter from Los Angeles coming up to me. They had been admitted to the league, and would start playing that fall, but this was his first Stanley Cup. All he did was peer at me for a long time and then say slowly, 'Are you for real?'

Then I asked George Gross of the *Telegram* if he wanted to come for a walk with me. He came along. We went down the street. A lot of people recognized me, and gave me the business about the game the night before, just one long razz-berry all the way along St. Catherine Street. I kept telling them not to bet their whole wad on Canadiens. Finally I wound up at the place that had been my destination all along, a tailor shop. I told the guy, Tony, to make me a suit. 'It has to be something special, because I want to wear it on the night we win the Stanley Cup,' I said.

Tony just looked at me and said, 'If you want to wear the suit when you win the Stanley Cup, I think you're going to wait a while to wear it.' He meant years.

'Look,' I said, 'just get the suit ready.'

I picked out a green check that I figured would look good on colour television. Then I picked out the accessories, including an

Oleg Cassini tie. And on the way back I straightened out a taxi driver and a bellhop about who was going to win the Stanley Cup that year too.

Well, I had started Sawchuk in the first game. He hadn't looked so hot and had got two more injuries – a bashed ankle and a bashed nose – in the first two periods. I'd put Bower in for the third period and he had looked pretty sharp, although the game was gone before he arrived. I started him in the second game. He shut them out 3–0. It was the first time Canadiens had been beaten in something like seventeen games. We forechecked them crazy, bumped them around. Bower locked the goal entirely – even though in the course of the game he got hit on the head three times by John Ferguson's stick, including a whack across the bridge of the nose, which was swollen and bleeding at the end of the game.

Just to give you an idea of what Canadiens were up against that spring, back in Toronto for the third game Bower kicked out 60 shots. That game went 28 minutes and 26 seconds of sudden death overtime before Bob Pulford beat Rogatien Vachon to win it for us. And then in the fourth Bower pulled a muscle in his leg during the warm-up. Sawchuk had to be sent in without preparation and Montreal again dumped us 6–2. Bower still wasn't back in shape in time for the fifth game. In fact, he was through for the season although we didn't say so. He didn't even come to Montreal for the fifth game. And the way Montreal started that game against Sawchuk, it looked as if they were happy he was around, figuring the two easy games they'd had against him gave them an automatic win. But they should have known Sawchuk by then. We hardly touched the puck for the first few minutes. But after robbing Ralph Backstrom point-blank on the first rush of the game, Sawchuk showed them that the two six-goal games they'd had against him earlier in the series didn't mean any more now than any other thing that is in the past, gone forever. The only goal they got on him deflected off Tim Horton past Sawchuk and he didn't have a chance. Pappin got our first goal, to tie it. Brian Conacher scored the winner, with Marcel Pronovost and Dave Keon getting the others.

Bower still couldn't walk without limping for the sixth game back in Toronto. I dressed him anyway. To hell with it. He couldn't have played if Terry Sawchuk had been hurt. But if we won that one we would have the Stanley Cup. I figured we were going to win it. I was wearing my new green-checked suit, just like I'd said I would. And I wanted all my veterans in uniform for what I figured was going to be the last game some of them would play for the Leafs. We were sure to lose some of them in the expansion draft. Anyway, I wasn't taking all that many chances, dressing Bower. If Sawchuk had got hurt, Bower would have conveniently reinjured his leg when he skated out to warm up. Then I would have hauled in Al Smith. He was fully dressed in his goal stuff, watching the game on television under the stands.

But, as it turned out, Sawchuk didn't need any help. Ellis and Pappin had scored for us, and Dick Duff for the Canadiens, by the time we got to the last minute of play and Canadiens forced a face-off in our end and took Gump Worsley out for six attackers.

Then I did what some people later called a sentimental thing. I won't argue. We needed to keep those guys from scoring in the last minute. Where better to turn than to my old guard?

I sent out Allan Stanley, Tim Horton, Red Kelly, George Armstrong, and Bob Pulford, in front of Sawchuk. They did the job. Six Canadiens crowded in behind our blueline. Stanley faced off against Beliveau at the left of our goal, shoved him off the puck, and hung on to his stick while Kelly picked up the puck. He got it up to Pulford near the boards inside the blueline on left wing. Pulford saw Armstrong moving up on right wing. He got the pass over perfectly, all calm, the way old pros are. George took the few strides that would get him across the centre red line so that if he missed the open goal there wouldn't be an icing call to take it back to our end. Then, nice and easy, he shot the puck into the empty Montreal net. That capped the most satisfying Stanley Cup I ever won.

The only sour note that season was that when we showed up at City Hall for the usual parade and speeches and so on, Bob Baun missed it. I know his pride was hurt because he'd spent most of the playoffs on the bench. But I just didn't feel he was playing as well as the guys I was playing. He'd been with me long enough to know there was nothing personal in that. He said he didn't show up because he hadn't done much towards winning the Cup. But he showed up to collect his playoff money, all right. I thought him staying away took a little of the lustre away from the guys who did win it. It's a team, you know. Baun had won other Stanley Cups with some other pretty good hockey players sitting on the bench. In sport it is always somebody's turn for the limelight, and somebody else's turn for the shadows.

It was like Dave Keon said when he was accepting the Conn Smythe Trophy after being voted by the league governors as the most outstanding player in the 1967 playoffs. He'd only got three goals, but in two series where we took two of the most powerful teams in hockey and stifled them, his forechecking and penalty-killing had been absolutely magnificent. He said he thought there were other guys who might have won the Smythe Trophy instead of him. But the big thing was winning the Stanley Cup, he said. There are eighteen players on the hockey team, he said. My sentiments exactly.

The other main candidate for the Smythe Trophy that year was Terry Sawchuk – and that was another satisfying thing for me. No more than three or four people knew that the previous September, in training camp, he had come to my hotel room and said he was through, he was quitting the game. 'Why quit?' I asked him. 'Nobody's asking you to.' This was at contract-signing time, but he wasn't trying to do me for some more money. He was just the way players sometimes get; he figured he was through and should retire. We talked off and on for a couple of days before I got him to agree to stay and give it one more shot. And then he played such great goal for us. I'd have hated to have had to try to win that Stanley Cup without him.

The Very Expensive Mr. Shack

Baun probably doesn't know it, and won't until the day he hears about it from this book, but I wanted to protect him in the expansion draft in June of 1967. That didn't mean I felt I should have played him in the Stanley Cup the previous spring. The way Larry Hillman was playing, the greatest hockey of his life, there was no way I could have benched him and put in Baun. But all the same, I wanted to protect Baun. I thought he'd lost some of his effectiveness but maybe it was only temporary; he had played some great hockey for me. I don't forget a guy who plays for me on a broken leg. In fact, I wanted to protect all the big defencemen. I knew that with the number of players we were going to lose in the special draft to stock the new expansion teams in Los Angeles, Oakland, St. Louis, Pittsburgh, Philadelphia, and Minnesota, we were going to need as strong and tough a defence as we could keep.

I've talked about the annual meetings before. They have an atmosphere all their own. Everybody in hockey is always there. Toronto always had its headquarters at the Mount Royal Hotel. The various leagues have their officials and owners and managers and coaches there for meetings – Central Pro League, Western League, American League. If any club is looking for people to hire, they often hire them there. Now, there were certain things about the 1967 meeting that were strictly as usual. The group that I had

147

helping me was the same. Bob Davidson, the head scout, always looks after the amateur draft. He knows that field inside out, as well as having some pretty good ideas in all the other fields too. Then there was Buck Houle, general manager of our Western Hockey League team, to advise us in that league. Joe Crozier was around, as usual, as the expert on the American Hockey League. And Ray Miron, the general manager of our team at Tulsa, along with Johnny McLellan, the coach. Then there would be Stafford and Harold Ballard and usually a few other members of the hockey committee.

The meetings have been held in the Queen Elizabeth Hotel in Montreal for quite a few years. And with that hotel swarming with hockey people, an important deal might be made as the result of a chance meeting in a corridor. That is, we all have our lists of who we're going to protect. We also have our lists of who we wouldn't mind dealing. Every club usually has two or three players that they'd like to get rid of for one reason or another – usually reasons that they are going to keep to themselves. Like maybe, for instance, I'm going to protect Bob Pulford and Mike Walton but I wouldn't mind making a deal for either or both of them, if I could improve the team. The trouble is, of course, everybody wants a battleship for a rowboat. Maybe I'll run into Tommy Ivan from Chicago and we get talking and I say, 'By the way, are you interested in Pulford or Walton?'

And he'll say, 'I'm interested in Pulford.'

'What will you give for him?'

And then we start bandying around names. Maybe he mentions Chico Maki. Well, I just don't think that's a good deal. Maybe he mentions Doug Mohns, but wants Pulford and somebody else for Mohns – which I don't think is a good deal either. Maybe Mohns for Pulford, even up, I might think about seriously. We talk for five or ten minutes and we find out, both of us, that there are no bargains going in that direction.

Then maybe I run into Emile Francis from New York and I mention a couple of names and he comes back with Reg Fleming. Well, I don't like that either. I got my own idea, you see, of who I should get if I trade Pulford or Walton. Like, I'd take Jacques Lemaire from Montreal for Walton. But Montreal wouldn't give him up. Maybe I've got too high an idea of who I should get because nobody ever offers me what I think they should. But that's the way it goes. If a deal gets past the casual stage, maybe you'll go to a room and thresh it out more. Some of them jell and some don't. All the time the draft is getting closer, with the trading deadline even before that. Something is done, or nothing is done, but each conversation adds a little grist for some later mill.

The expansion draft of 1967 presented problems to all the old teams, of course. Maybe especially ours, because we had the Stanley Cup and I would like to have protected every man who helped win it. But 1967 was a special year because, instead of being able to protect eighteen players and two goalkeepers as we usually could, that year we were committed to stock the six expansion division teams with twenty players each. The arrangement was that we could protect one goalie and eleven other players. Just for openers, that meant I could only protect one out of my three goalkeepers – John Bower, Terry Sawchuk, and Bruce Gamble. The system was that, if a player was taken, you could fill with another player. So in the end I could only lose one of these three. But of course I didn't want to lose any of them.

Weeks earlier I had started the necessary figuring. Among the eleven I could protect besides one goalkeeper, I felt I had to protect Tim Horton, Marcel Pronovost, and Larry Hillman from the defence, as well as forwards Dave Keon, Frank Mahovlich, Ron Ellis, Bob Pulford, Pete Stemkowski, and Jim Pappin for sure. That left only two places open for Mike Walton, Bob Baun, Brian Conacher, and Larry Jeffrey. The way Conacher had played in the playoffs gave him a big edge. And I also wanted to keep Baun. But whoever I protected among these twelve, it would mean I had to leave open George Armstrong, Red Kelly, Allan Stanley, Eddie Shack, and Kent Douglas among guys who had played fairly regularly, and also Milan Marcetta and Aut Erickson, who had been on that team although they hadn't played much. Well, it was a wrench, but all sentiment aside I had to do what I thought was best for the team in the long run.

One decision I had had to make weeks before was to leave Armstrong unprotected. Well, heck, you know he was nearly thirty-seven and all the forwards I was going to protect were a lot younger. I called him into the office and told him. He got upset. He said he was going to retire, and that he'd call a press conference and announce it, to spare both himself and us the idea that the club he'd played with all his life, much of the time as captain, didn't want him.

'Look,' I said, 'sure as hell if you just announce that you're going to retire, everybody will think it is a dodge designed to beat the expansion draft. They won't believe it, and somebody might draft you anyway. But if you retire and I get mad at you for retiring, that might make them believe it. . . .' If he was going to retire anyway rather than leave Toronto — well, I had an idea in the back of my mind. It wasn't a deal between us at all that he would retire and then come back in the fall. It was just an idea I had that that might happen.

So we did it that way. He announced he was going to retire and publicly I blew up. I said that I thought he owed it to the club not to retire. We were going to lose twenty players anyway, I said. But if he retired, I'd still lose some other player, meaning in his case I'd lose two instead of one.

This worked pretty well as I had figured. When I teed off on Armstrong about retiring, everybody got on my back — 'A fine way to treat your team captain!' they were writing and saying. 'First you don't protect him and then you get sore at him for exercising his right to retire!'

Oh, I got hell all right. But I figured it was worth it if by all that I still had Armstrong around and maybe could get him to reconsider in the fall and play for me again. Which is what happened.

I also was going to be in the same box with Red Kelly; well, not the same in all details, but the same in that I was going to lose him as well as the twenty that were going to be drafted from me.

After we'd won the Stanley Cup, Red came in to see me and talk about going to Los Angeles to coach. He asked my advice on some things and I told him what I could. The thing is, I couldn't stand in his way but I sure didn't want to lose him. He was one of our big players. I knew he could play for years more if he wanted to. A guy like Red is just about impossible to replace. We never would have finished out of the playoffs in 1967-68 if we'd had him, and we would have done a lot better in the playoffs in 1969 if we'd had him. In 1969 we just didn't have a player who could contain Phil Esposito, the Boston gun. But Red could have done it.

My hating to lose Red back in 1967 was why I did some things I did in the draft meeting that made Red and his owner, Jack

Cooke, sore at me. But I'll come to that. The time we're dealing with is the few weeks between winning the Stanley Cup and going in to face that expansion draft.

Instead of just losing guys in the draft, which I was going to do anyway, obviously it would be better to make the best deals I could for guys I couldn't protect and therefore was going to lose. If I know I'm going to lose a player, I might as well try to trade him for two or three before the draft.

I knew that I wasn't going to protect Shack or Kent Douglas, for two. So any deals we could make for them in advance would leave us that much better off. I'll put it another way. Each of the new clubs was paying $2,000,000 to get in. This gave them the right to draft twenty players each. Therefore, as a matter of straight arithmetic, you might say they were paying $100,000 a player. But if I took somebody I wasn't going to protect, who was sure to be drafted, and traded him for three or four players, and those three or four were drafted, I'd really only be down the one player I'd used in the trade. So I'd be better off in players and money when it was all over.

I also could have figured on making a deal for Baun on the same basis, because I knew he'd go on the first round if he was unprotected. But because I hoped to be able to protect him somehow I didn't go out and deal for him. Maybe his name came up a couple of times in talking deals with other clubs. But my thinking was, I wanted to keep him around.

Detroit was interested in Douglas. I still don't understand exactly what their thought processes were when I was talking to them. I told them I'd take Bob Wall and Real Lemieux for Douglas. They weren't going to protect either of those guys. But they said that price was too high. So what happened – both Wall and Lemieux were drafted from Detroit, and Douglas was drafted from us by Oakland. Then several months later Detroit traded Bert Marshall and Ted Hampson, both guys they had protected, to Oakland to get Douglas. Seems to me they would have been better off to take my deal. Like about a hundred times better off.

Anyway, about the same time I was trying to make the Douglas deal I was in Portland at a Western Hockey League meeting when I got a call from Milt Schmidt of Boston. They had wanted Shack the year before. They'd offered me $50,000 cash for him. Now Milt figured that Shack wasn't going to be protected in the expansion draft. He wanted to get him before one of the expansion teams did.

I said okay, what would he give for Shack? After we argued up and down, bandying names around, I said, 'All right, I'll tell you what I want. I'll take Oliver and Don Awrey and . . .' I think I named a couple of other guys.

'I'll call you back,' Milt said. He did. He wouldn't go for that deal. Some time passed, maybe a few days, and then he called me back again.

'I'll give you cash for Shack,' he said.

'All right,' I said. 'I want a hundred thousand dollars and Oliver for Shack.'

'You're kidding!' he said. He couldn't believe it. But I convinced him I was serious and finally he said he'd call me back. He had higher-ups in the club that he had to consult.

He called me back a little later. 'It's a deal,' he said.

'Right,' I said. 'I give you Shack and you give me Oliver and a hundred thousand in U.S. money.'

'Oh, no!' he said. 'Not U.S.!'

'Look,' I said, 'you're in the States, you pay me in U.S. funds.'

'Gotta call you back,' he said.

So he called me back and gave me an argument. But I knew he was pretty eager, and didn't think I had to give anything away. I said, 'I don't care if you take it or not. That's what I want.'

'You got a deal,' he said.

A guy can go to the bank with a gun and walk out with three or four hundred dollars, get picked up, and get ten years in jail for armed robbery. But as you can see, there are legal ways to do it better. Of course, there couldn't be anything said about the amount of money involved at the time. People knew we'd got Oliver and cash, but nobody knew how much. When we got in touch with Shack to let him know he'd been traded, he was playing golf at Oshawa. He got the message on the second tee but he said he knew what it meant, a trade. He was interested in knowing what I got for him, but not interested enough to interrupt his golf game to find out. But he did come down later and ask. John Andersen, my assistant, told him it was in the vicinity of the draft price ($30,000). What the hell, I had to go along with Milt Schmidt on that. If Shack had known he'd been sold for $100,000 in U.S. funds, plus Murray Oliver, he would have been down to see

Schmidt with a lawyer, demanding $50,000 a year. I couldn't do that to old Miltie after what I'd already done.

This looks like a deal slanted very much in favour of Toronto, but just remember Boston knew at the time they were going to receive $2,000,000 in the expansion draft for the loss of twenty players to the new clubs. They'd get as much for the eighteenth man they lost as they had paid for Shack. As good a deal as it was for us, it was a good one for Boston too.

I remember just after I made that deal. I was still in Portland where I'd been during those telephone conversations with Milt. Nobody on our club knew about it, of course, because I didn't have to check with anybody. But Stafford was also in Portland at that time, busy making what I thought was a lousy deal – selling the Victoria Hockey Club. The reason I didn't like the deal is that we'd sold the Rochester club too, and we were going to lose another twenty players out of our system in the expansion draft, meaning we were getting stripped down pretty badly for players. It was okay for Stafford; he and the other owners got the money. But I'd built up that farm system and I didn't like to see it cut seventy-five per cent that way. I was the guy who had to find players to win hockey games.

Anyway, Stafford said, 'I've been looking for you to tell you about selling Victoria to Phoenix. What a hell of a deal we made.'

'Yeah?' I said. 'What'd you get?'

'Five hundred thousand dollars. A hundred thousand the first year and then, starting four years from now, a hundred thousand a year for four more years.'

'That's a hell of a deal, Stafford,' I said. 'Now I'd like to tell you about the one I made.' I told him: Oliver and $100,000 to us for Shack. He just sat there staring at me. He was so flabbergasted he didn't say a thing.

I think the deal he made, selling Victoria to Phoenix, was the worst deal Toronto made in the eleven years I was with the club. The conditions were so vague that arguments will continue until the end of the contract. A suit was later filed by the Phoenix Hockey Club against Maple Leaf Gardens and at this writing is still unsettled. One of my last recommendations to Maple Leaf Gardens was to let Phoenix have the club outright and forget it. It has been said that when I was fired in the spring of 1969 I left the club in bad shape for players. This forgets that the decision to sell hockey clubs and all the players on them was not mine. I was left with the mechanics but the decisions were Stafford's. He sold Rochester to Vancouver for $400,000 cash and then Phoenix for whatever they eventually will get out of it. If Leafs still owned those teams they would be in a position to trade fringe players to expansion clubs for future amateur draft choices, the way Montreal and Boston have done – ensuring that for years they'd always have a corner on the good young ones coming up, and would have been able to trade even more older players for future draft choices. In 1969 three players were drafted for $30,000 each from Vancouver, showing the calibre of players that Stafford had sold off. They could have been exchanged for draft choices instead. And then he was quoted as saying he should get the $90,000. He had sold the teams and still thought he should be able to sell them over again.

Anyway, to return to 1967, we get to the draft meeting. Stafford and most of the hockey committee were there. While I had a pretty good idea of who I wanted to protect, it was agreed that, as was usual before all drafts, we'd have a meeting on the subject before we turned in the final protected list. I had my list made out – the guys I mentioned before, plus Baun and Conacher. Not Walton. He'd got seven goals for us in thirty-one games in the 1966-67 season, and he'd got four more in the playoffs. That was good but wasn't overpowering by any means.

So I go up to Stafford's room. The members of his hockey committee are around. I laid down this list and said, 'This is who I recommend protecting.'

Now, I should make some things clear. There never was anything sacred about a protected list. Sometimes when I made up a list of guys in my own system, like Clancy or Crozier, would put up a hell of an argument for one guy or against another. Usually it was over one of the last guys I'd put on anyway, so sometimes I'd change just to keep peace in the family and because it didn't matter all that much anyway.

This time was a little different because of the different size of the list, of course.

But right away I began to sense something: that as far as Stafford was concerned, Mike Walton was the Number One guy to be protected, the untouchable. He certainly didn't rate that kind of treatment. I nearly forced the issue right there but I didn't. At first I couldn't figure out why Stafford was so adamant about

Walton. But later when I came to think about it – of course, Walton had married Stafford's niece that spring. That made him part of the Smythe family. The only thing I can assume, and it is pure assumption, is that Stafford had made some kind of a family commitment, or had decided himself, for family reasons, to have Walton protected so that he could play in Toronto. Anyway, I can't think of any other good reason why Walton had to be rated absolutely untouchable.

I told Stafford and the others that if we left Baun off, he would go first crack out of the box. This turned out to be pretty close to the truth, as soon as Clarence Campbell started calling the roll for draft choices. I had decided we would protect Bower as our first goalkeeper. That meant Sawchuk and Gamble were open. All the clubs are sitting at tables in a big semicircle around Campbell. Los Angeles had first pick and they took Sawchuk. That allowed me to fill with Gamble and give us our two goalkeepers, which I did. But Baun was the next to go.

One thing that got a lot of publicity out of that draft meeting was the business of me and Red Kelly. It was set that Red Kelly was going to be the Los Angeles coach. Still, as far as the rest of the world was concerned, including me, Kelly was one of the best hockey players who hadn't been protected by anybody. And he wouldn't be until Los Angeles claimed him.

I don't know what kind of a deal Jack Cooke, the Los Angeles owner, had with the other owners, but I guess it was an unofficial thing that they would respect his plans to have Kelly as his coach. I hadn't made any such agreement. And I was the one that stood to lose most, because in Red I was losing a hockey player. Los Angeles seemed to have the idea that they didn't have to use up one of their early picks to get him. They figured they already had him and it was just a matter of using about their eighteenth pick to make it official.

When I saw that this was the way things were going, I had already pulled in a few of the guys that I wanted, like Allan Stanley and Murray Oliver, filling for players I lost. So I sent Clancy over to tell Red that if Los Angeles didn't take him pretty soon, I'd take him myself.

Clancy came back and said Red had told him, 'Don't take me.'

But I'd warned them. Then there was a break and when we came back, Los Angeles had another pick and still didn't take

Kelly. So the next player I lost I took him. Then, of course, all hell broke loose. Kelly was sore and Cooke was sore. Real pandemonium. But I stuck to my guns. Eventually we made an agreement and I accepted Ken Block for him – a guy that Los Angeles had picked before.

Anyway, considering everything, we came out of the draft not too badly. We hadn't lost anybody we didn't figure on losing, and I was fairly satisfied with the way things had gone. For one thing, I had back together the same defence that had won the Stanley Cup the previous spring – Horton, Stanley, Pronovost, and Hillman. The thing I couldn't have foreseen was that in the fall two of the guys I'd protected, Conacher and Walton, would be holdouts. And Hillman – I can't blame him after the great Stanley Cup he'd played – wanted a lot more money and was a holdout even after the season started. When he did start playing he was so far behind in training that he never did play again for me the way he had played the previous spring, which is why I'd protected him.

The Year the Team Died

In the season of 1967-68, coming right off winning the Stanley Cup and sitting right on top of the hockey world, I finished out of the playoffs for the first time in my life. I realized why eventually, but I didn't correct it in time. I've had teams lose their sense of aggressiveness on me before but I'd always been able to see it coming. This time I didn't. I've done a lot of thinking about it since. I go right back to training camp in the fall of 1967 to one incident that should have shown me what kind of team I had, and should have told me to do something about it right then, before the season even started.

This was an exhibition game with New York Rangers in Peterborough, on a Tuesday night, September 26, 1967. And while we had lost a lot of guys in the expansion draft, the real core of the team that had won my fourth Stanley Cup had been saved. For instance, a lot of the reason we'd won the Stanley Cup was Pete Stemkowski. He had been centre on our best line for the whole playoffs, with Bob Pulford and Jim Pappin on the wings. I remember Gordie Howe talking about that line the previous spring — nearly six hundred pounds of them, and 'they use every ounce when they're checking,' he said. Anybody who saw that series in the flesh or on television knows how good Stemkowski was. He stood there in the other guy's end with his arms and stick out and

157

dared them to try to get by him. They stop looking at him and bash, they're down. He is six feet and two hundred pounds and when he was cruising everybody on the other team kept his head up. He'd had a pretty good season with us, thirteen goals, but in the playoffs he'd been even better: five goals and seven assists, eating up the heavy going and the pressure as if he revelled in it.

All right. This game in Peterborough was only an exhibition and some people have the attitude that exhibition games don't mean anything. They mean something, don't fool yourself. They can mean a hell of a lot.

Right then Stemkowski was playing the same way as he'd been playing to help win the Stanley Cup. He wasn't picking any soft spots. He nailed Vic Hadfield in our own zone and Hadfield nailed him right back. Then down in the Ranger end Stemkowski really reefed Rod Seiling. The play came out of there fast and went down to our end but in the meantime two or three Rangers ganged up on Stemkowski to retaliate for him hitting Seiling. They got him on the ice. They're kicking the living so-and-so out of him. Of course, the play had gone to our end and at first our guys couldn't see what was happening. But when they did come back, Boom-Boom Geoffrion, Hadfield, Seiling, Orland Kurtenbach, and Arnie Brown are all taking turns whaling hell out of Stemkowski, sometimes two or three at a time, and our guys are there as peace-makers! Not doing any damn fighting at all! Finally Pete fell to the ice with a couple on top of him, and in the melee somebody stepped on his hand. Blood started pouring out of a cut in his finger, which later needed seven stitches. And still our other guys are standing around saying, 'Now, now, boys . . .' or some damn thing.

Red Burnett in the *Star* later wrote that the fight was the blowup after Stemkowski had had a 'vendetta with four Rangers'.

Any time four guys from one team have enough free time to have a vendetta with one guy from another, that second team is in trouble, and I should have seen it. I should have known right then. I should have taken them straight into the dressing room at the end of that period and said, okay, we'll straighten this out right now. I should have just pointed out to them that there were too many guys backing up. When there was trouble, like that night, and one of their own guys got clipped, the next guy wasn't doing anything about it. We won that game 4–3, but it was like winning the battle and losing the war.

So what happened with that 1967-68 hockey club I should have seen in the Stemkowski incident in training camp. And it should have been clinched by something that happened six weeks later, in Boston, on a Sunday night, November 5.

Some of you will remember the Boston team in the fall of 1967. They were just coming up to being the kind of team they are today. They were really tough. They fought for each other. There were five big brawls in the first two months of that season, and Boston was in four of the five. There was nearly $6,000 in league fines for fighting, players jumping onto the ice to get into fights, and all that stuff – and Boston players paid more than half those fines.

So okay, early in this second period in Boston – 5.28 it was – we were short-handed and Brian Conacher was out there killing off a penalty. Now here was a guy who had played good hockey for us when we won the Stanley Cup too. He had that Conacher name and size and he was getting one of the best salaries I remember for any relatively untried player, better than $20,000, because he was tough, a good bargainer. He'd been a holdout for it and he'd got it.

Anyway he was carrying the puck into the Boston end, killing this penalty, when Bobby Orr came out to check him. Conacher dumped the puck past him, to get it out of there. Seeing Orr taking a run at him, he got his stick up to defend himself. The stick hit Orr between the eyes. Orr went down to the ice bleeding. The fans were screaming for a penalty. I don't remember whether the whistle blew right then or not, but Johnny McKenzie took a run at Conacher from behind and jumped on his back and knocked him to the ice. Then Orr got to his feet and skated over, as if he'd gone nuts, and flung himself on Conacher and started flailing away at Conacher's head, shoulders, kidneys, and everything he could reach – all the time with two Boston players holding Conacher down. All Conacher was doing at that time was covering up. What had happened was that, either when McKenzie hit him or when Orr started to pound him, one of his contact lenses had slipped sideways and cut his eye. His vision was blurred and he knew the eye was hurt, so he just covered up.

And meanwhile, you might ask, how come three Boston players

were all over Conacher? Where were our guys? Well, us being short-handed to start with, there were more of their players there than ours. The ones out there paired off. But also, Johnny Bower stayed in our goal, which is where a goalie is supposed to stay during a fight or he gets fined. But Gerry Cheevers came out of the Boston goal to fight, so that really gave them a six on four man-power advantage. That meant three pairs and three left over to hammer Conacher.

This happened a lot faster than it takes to tell it, but George Armstrong, our captain (he'd come out of retirement, all right), led the rest of the Leafs off our bench. There was a general free-for-all. In the mix-up Conacher did manage to get up. Ken Hodge jumped him and knocked him down again. Conacher's eye was hemorrhaging and he wasn't retaliating to anyone, in any way. It took twenty or twenty-five minutes to get things straightened away. By then Orr had got some attention to the cut on his forehead but was back on the ice skating around trying to get at Conacher.

When they handed out the penalties, it pretty well told the story of what had happened. Conacher got a five-minute major for highsticking. Orr got a fighting major. Allan Stanley got a two-minute penalty for roughing, and McKenzie and Hodge both got twos for roughing. In other words, there wasn't a fighting penalty given to anybody on our team, although you could give Stanley at least an honourable mention. Of course, both our guys and the Bruins who had emptied both benches were fined later. I would have fined our guys if they hadn't left the bench under those circumstances.

When people were interviewing Conacher after, he said one thing that stuck in my mind. He said his vision was blurred and he thought his eye was cut. 'So,' he said, 'I just covered up. There was no sense trying to fight fifteen Bruins.'

No sense trying to fight fifteen Bruins! That tells you something. He knew that nobody was out there helping him. After that Conacher never did come back to play the kind of hockey he was capable of. I think it was because he had learned right then and there that night in Boston that, when he was in trouble on that team, he was pretty well on his own.

Those two incidents come pretty close to illustrating one of my basic beliefs about hockey — that it's an aggressive game, that aggressiveness is the most important thing on any team, that any team that loses its aggressiveness is dead. A guy doesn't play and coach in the game all his life, as I have, without noticing a few things. As a coach, I have stood behind benches at hockey games in rinks everywhere from Chicoutimi to Los Angeles for more than twenty years; nearly two thousand hockey games, counting them all. I see what other people see, but I also think a coach has a chance to see a little deeper, right into the soul of the game. And what I see as the soul of a hockey game is a tough man who never backs up. You have to have enough of them on every team to give that team its aggressive character, because you're always going to have some players who show their aggressiveness in goal-scoring or checking, and have to be helped out a little when tough guys on another team challenge them with fists and other forms of belting around.

It isn't that fighting, as such, is essential. It is just that you need guys who will fight when they are challenged. There were one or two fights I'd seen in other years that I'd rather forget, because they told me things I didn't want to know. One fight that Carl Brewer had with Murray Balfour falls into that category. I understand that Brewer is going to return to the NHL. You can be sure that he is going to be challenged early and often. Other fights prove something one way or another, no matter who wins. One between Kurtenbach and Terry Harper of Canadiens – when Kurtenbach was with us – is a case in point. That was no contest of course. Kurtenbach cleaned Harper's clock plenty. But you had to hand it to Harper. He took as bad a beating as I've ever seen in a fair fight in hockey, but the next game he was right back playing his kind of game. He challenged Kurtenbach again the following night. Olmstead and Fleming had a pretty tough fight one night. But I also remember the time that Lou Fontinato and Olmstead were fighting – fought twice in one night, when Fontinato was with Canadiens – and on the second one Fontinato jumped Olmstead from behind and had him down, and Tim Horton came off our bench and took on Fontinato and anybody else who wanted a fight. That was the kind of support I like to see for anybody on one of my teams who gets into trouble. It isn't a personal thing in hockey at all. Horton had fought Olmstead one night when Olmstead was with Montreal, but Horton was helping out one of his own players then too.

Do players get hurt in fights? I remember a young fellow who played for me in Quebec – Dan Poliziani. One night he got a fist in the eye, really a bad one. I called him over to the bench and said, 'Do you want to come off because of the eye?' 'No,' he said. 'It just hurts for a little while.' I think that goes for what happens in most hockey fights.

In a good team, the players support one another. You get hit and you're half stunned and for a few seconds you can't defend yourself, but one of your teammates comes from somewhere and reefs the guy who gave it to you. The first guy then knows, 'Hell, the team is behind me.' That gives him the steam to go out and play harder for the other guys, knowing they'll stand behind him.

Or maybe it's one of those plays where a guy gets clobbered and nobody can do anything about it right then without getting a useless penalty, but you go up to the guy that got clobbered and you say, 'I'll get that bastard for you,' and the first time he gets the puck you take a run at him. Or you take a run at somebody else. That's what counts. The guy that got clobbered then knows that you're behind him and that you're going to help him.

But when he knows that you don't care if he gets clobbered, his attitude is the exact opposite. He gets clobbered. Nobody helps. He gets up looking around at the guys who didn't support him and says to himself, why the hell should I get clobbered for you? When this happens to a team, first thing you know nobody is helping anybody else.

I've had people listen to me talk this way and ask me, well, how are you supposed to play it? Are you supposed to forget the puck altogether? It's not that at all. But when they challenge you, you've got to challenge them right back. Or even better, you challenge them first and make them react. You must be the aggressive type, not the other way. If your team isn't aggressive, you haven't got a hockey team – you haven't got any kind of a team.

The feeling that their teammates didn't care was the main reason for some guys on our team that year losing their aggressiveness, but it wasn't the only one. Usually when I get a guy in young, he is single to start with, and hungry as well. He makes the team. That takes away some of the hunger. He gets married, and maybe that takes away some of his fight too. I mean, it's no longer only *him*. I know one player who got into a hell of a fight one night in the penalty box and got told off by his wife for acting like a barroom brawler. He lost an awful lot of his aggression right from that one incident. I tell them sometimes, geez, when you and I met life was simple. We didn't have all these family responsibilities to worry about.

I'm not naming any names. All through that season, trying to get their aggressiveness back, I spoke to the team, not to individuals. I'd say to the team, 'I saw you challenged out there and you didn't go back at them. What's the matter, didn't you like it?'

And maybe I'd say that if I saw somebody refusing a challenge I was going to fine him, or something like that. But I was talking to the team. And everybody on the team would know who I was talking about, without me ever mentioning the guy's name. Especially the ones sitting on the bench, you know. Maybe the guys on the ice don't see it but the ones on the bench do – and that's one of the worst things that can happen, for one guy to be sitting on the bench and seeing that his team is not going to the defence of a player under attack. It makes the guy leery of provoking anybody when he gets out there himself, in case he winds up all alone too.

This is not so much a rap against the guys concerned as it is an explanation of a kind of sickness that can come to a team. A guy who turned into a real bunny rabbit with me might go to another team and be a tiger again, like I wanted him to be. But as long as he feels he's playing with a lot of bunny rabbits, he'll be one, right? And if he feels he's with a bunch of tigers again, well, he knows how to play that way, too – because that's the game, and all these players know it, deep down, and have been playing it that way all their lives.

That year, with the lack of aggressiveness, it was a very bad road team. We just couldn't win on the road. I suffered. It was disgusting at times. They played like a bunch of dogs with their tails between their legs. We played that way even against expansion teams – guys we should have beaten but didn't beat, because they were simply more aggressive than we were.

As a contrast I look back to some of the teams we had back in the early sixties, even before we won the Stanley Cup. Those teams were great on Sunday nights away. Like in the 1960-61 season when we challenged Canadiens for first place all year long, we didn't have a bad weekend in the whole season. Even if we lost at home on Saturday, more often than not we'd win on the road Sunday. That kept us up there. Now a lot of those guys from those teams were still with us when the club started to lose its edge. But it's the old story, you're coming down a little, getting old, losing your grip. You've stopped going looking for trouble and then you run into some other team that really is aggressive and they push you around. Once this sets in, you can't seem to get it out without changing the team some, giving it something new to go on.

I knew pretty well in January of that year that I was going to have to shake up the team. But we had a road trip of about sixteen days, including a lot of games against expansion teams. I thought if I could get the Leafs going on that trip we just might squeak through into the playoffs. But we'd goofed around too long. I scathed them, hit them with two practices a day, told them that if they weren't going to work in the games they could work in the practice – but nothing seemed to stir them. The road trip was disastrous.

In the middle of February I decided that one way to snap Brian Conacher and Jim Pappin out of their difficulties was to send them to Rochester. Sometimes a player will go to a minor league team and will start to score and get his drive back. It had happened with Eddie Shack and many others before. The idea was to send them down for two weeks and then, if they were playing well, bring them back. But Pappin refused to report and had to be suspended. And sending Conacher down brought on a very nasty incident. I had asked Clancy to tell Conacher to report to Rochester. In a column Dick Beddoes wrote about it in the *Globe and Mail* he quoted Conacher as calling Clancy my 'errand boy'.

I was furious. For one thing, nobody – Beddoes or Conacher – was going to talk about Clancy that way and get away with it. Secondly, I didn't think Conacher actually had said it. After all, his uncle, Charlie Conacher, had played with Clancy on the old Leafs and they had been great buddies – and I just didn't think the kid would talk about Clancy that way. So I phoned Rochester and told Joe Crozier to show Conacher a copy of Beddoes' column, especially that one remark, and ask: 'Did you say that?' I told Joe, 'If he didn't say it, get a lawyer to draw up an affidavit to that effect and get Conacher to sign it.'

Conacher denied using that phrase about Clancy and signed the paper. Joe sent it to me. I wanted to take it to court on the grounds of – well, some damn grounds. But a lot of people I respect thought I shouldn't press it. One of these was Jim Vipond, sports editor of the *Globe and Mail.* I have a lot of respect for Vipond, so I dropped the idea. But I didn't forget it, and I won't.

Meanwhile, we were still going nowhere. I'd been trying to make deals here and there all along but nobody would deal with us. They had us down and they wanted to keep us there. The only thing was that as the last weeks of February wore on, Detroit was in worse shape than we were. We were fifth, but Detroit was behind us. By then there was just barely a mathematical chance that we could make the playoffs, but to do that somebody in the first four had to go into a real tailspin. By then I was prepared to deal big. I knew the team had to be shaken to its very foundation. I wasn't going to do us any good at all by moving out two or three relatively minor guys on our team. If I was going to get something really good, I had to give up something good. Something much bigger. And that meant Frank Mahovlich.

Nobody knew about it, but I'd been talking seriously for more than a year about dealing Mahovlich. I had tried to deal him even up for Stan Mikita of Chicago. I'd tried to deal him even up for Jean Beliveau of Montreal. I wanted to get a new big guy on our team, and I knew I'd have to give up Frank to get him.

But nobody would give me what I wanted and then finally, in the last days of February, with us fifth and Detroit sixth, we started talking turkey with Detroit – and Mahovlich was going to be the key man in the deal from our side, with Norm Ullman the key man from their side.

My Life with the Big M

I guess a million words have been written about how wrong I was in the way I treated Frank Mahovlich in the ten hockey seasons we spent together. I've already outlined my case: that my way of doing things was almost always to say 'You guys' when I went into a dressing room, instead of saying 'You' and picking out one of them instead of the team as a whole. But I do remember twice in particular when I did single out Frank.

November 1, 1967, was a Wednesday. We were in Toronto that night against Montreal. Frank had been playing great hockey for us but that week there had been something wrong. He had missed practices on Monday and Tuesday. I gave it out that he had hurt his back in our Sunday night game with New York which we lost 3–2, but I knew there was more than that to it. On the Wednesday, I had a talk with him privately, and what he told me made me as mad as I've ever been in my life.

He said he was upset about the Players' Association. They all knew I didn't like the idea of anybody from outside having anything to do with my hockey club, but whether a player joined I guess was his own business, his own decision. Being the easygoing team man he was, it must have been a hard one for Frank to make when most of the other players on the team were members. But this day he told me that the Players' Association was bothering him.

He was the big man on the team. The members on the Leafs felt it hurt them not to have him in. He said he had had letters asking him to pay his dues, and other guys on the team soliciting him, and it was bothering him very much.

I was mad. Alan Eagleson, then a recently defeated politician and executive for the Players' Association, had been one of the mouthiest guys around in telling me what I was doing wrong in the way I treated players. Even then he was practically carrying on a vendetta against me, through a few mouthpieces in the press, on the score that I rode them, interfered with their lives, etc., etc. And here the oufit that he ran, the Players' Association, was bothering Frank. And in a way I never would. One thing sure – if I bothered Frank or anybody else, any time, it was about hockey, not about his private life and whether or not he joined a union.

When Frank left me that day I went into the dressing room. I was flaming mad. I said, 'If I ever find a son-of-a-bitch in here soliciting for that union – look out, you're gone. I don't give a damn who it is because none of you is as good a hockey player as Mahovlich is.' I said, 'If that goddam thing there, the union, is gonna put me out a good hockey player, there is no way I can be in favour of it. So,' I said, 'now you know which sides we're on.'

That night we beat Canadiens 5–0. Johnny Bower was named the first star of the game by Foster Hewitt, and Frank was named the second star. He had played a magnificent game. He was on the ice when we got four of our five goals. He scored one himself and assisted on two others. He went up and down that wing, came back to back-check, and the line he was playing on that night, with Dave Keon and George Armstrong, was far ahead of any other on the ice. Yet when his name was announced as the second star, there were some boos mixed in with the cheers. So there is no doubt about it, that week he had two blows to his peace of mind. He had the matter of the Players' Association bugging him. Maybe it wouldn't have bugged another player but that is not the point – individuals are supposed to be treated as individuals, remember? That's what they say. And once again he had heard boos from the Toronto fans after he had played as good a game of hockey as they'd ever see from him or anybody else.

We had a game to play in Detroit the next night. We had a special sleeping car set aside in Union Station all night that would be hitched to a train leaving for Detroit at 8.30 a.m. Some players liked this arrangement and some didn't, but I thought it was a good one because no player finds it easy to sleep after a game. At least this way, they didn't have to get up early in the morning to get the train to Detroit. Some don't like to fly, either, and so when we could take a train, we did.

Frank got on the train when the others did, around midnight or so. His berth was across the aisle from Bob Pulford's. I don't know whether Frank slept at all that night. But about four or five in the morning Pulford heard him say to somebody that he couldn't sleep and was going home, and to let me know that he'd left because he wasn't feeling well. Then he went straight to the home of a doctor and from there was admitted to Toronto General Hospital. A diagnosis of deep depression and tension was announced in the afternoon by Dr. Hugh Smythe. Dr. Smythe estimated at the time that he would be out of the lineup for a couple of weeks, but it was four.

We beat Detroit 9–3 that night, but the matter of Frank being sick again was the top thing in my mind. In ten years I'd got to know him pretty well even though we never talked much. I mean, he knew me, right? Because I talked a lot. And I knew him because he'd been a constant concern of mine for ten years. He didn't have to do much talking; he's got, a damn good head on his shoulders and he's a pretty level-headed guy. He just wanted to be left alone; at least, that's the way it seemed to me. He is one of the most high-class individuals, one of the finest guys, you'd ever want to meet. When we had contract talks, naturally he would want to do the best he could and we would want to do the best we could. But when we negotiated, it was polite. We'd make our point and he'd make his, but never would he raise his voice or swear or get rough. Clancy used to do a lot of the talking with him, as he did with most of the other guys. I would arrive at a figure that I thought we could go to, then Clancy would do the talking. Once Clancy told me about another player who, hearing our offer, had said, 'You're insulting me.' As Clancy said, if we were insulting that guy we were insulting Frank a hell of a lot more. That year, 1967, he had signed a contract that really pleased him, I heard indirectly. We gave him a raise and bonus arrangement that was better than he'd expected, considering that the year before his goal-scoring had fallen off to eighteen, the lowest he'd ever had in the league.

Things that happened to him often hurt me to hear them. Like boos in the game, sometimes, when he was playing great hockey. In 1963 when we finished first and won our second Stanley Cup and were being introduced at City Hall, everybody on the team got cheered – but not Frank. Some dough-heads booed him.

Well, stretch that over the years and it's got to affect his hockey. In my theory, physically and mentally you have to be ready. You can be in the best physical shape in the world but mentally you don't want to play. If that is so, you can't play or you're not going to play well anyway. Some other player can have the best outlook, wanting to be the best damned hockey player that there is ever going to be, but if he's fifteen pounds overweight the outlook doesn't count. It's a balance deal. You have to have both going, both the physical and the mental – and then you've got a perfect athlete. But who the hell gets up the same way every day? Nobody. You can get your body keyed to your goal, but then human nature and everything else plays a part. You have a fight with your wife before you go to work, or before the bloody game. Or your kid does something, upsets you. All these things are the human factor.

With Frank the way he was, penning everything up inside him all the time, the fact that he was always in perfect physical shape sometimes just wasn't enough, as we learned the first time he had one of those breakdowns, in 1964. That was early in the season too – November 11. Also right after he'd played a good game where he'd been booed. The first thing I knew about it that time the doctor wanted to talk to me.

'We would like you to talk to Frank,' the doctor said, 'to tell him to go to the hospital.' I was really shocked when they told me what they thought was wrong.

I said, 'Of course I'll talk to him. If there is something wrong with him, it should be looked after.' He'd got in worse shape that time because he didn't know what the hell was happening to him. I think anyone can sympathize with a man trying his utmost to concentrate, but having his concentration destroyed in a way he wasn't equipped at that time to understand or cope with at all. He was in a depression. And it's a bad one when it gets to that stage.

That time he missed eleven games, out from November 11 to about a month later, but for some reason it was never announced what was the matter with him. That made it a mystery, so that all the amateur headshrinkers who work on the sports pages and do broadcasts could put their psychological training to work and come up with the answer that what was wrong was the way I treated him. Anybody else in the world can have a nervous breakdown and it's a nervous breakdown, made up of a variety of pressures. But in the pressure cooker of hockey and what it means to millions of fans, the public has to find a goat – some other goat than themselves, of course – and I naturally took some of the rap.

In the meantime there in 1964 Frank was fighting his own battle. After a couple of weeks of rest and medical attention he started leaving the hospital from time to time to skate alone at the Tam O'Shanter rink. His wife, Marie, would drive him up and drive him back. He started to practise with us again on December 1 and played his first game back on December 9, against Montreal. I didn't put him out until about halfway through the first period. He got a standing ovation. There must have been some of those people standing cheering him who had booed him other nights. He didn't get any scoring points that night but in the first few seconds he was on the ice he body-checked Terry Harper hard, and a couple of times later dumped Claude Provost on the seat of his pants. He was okay, again.

I mentioned earlier that I could recall twice when I had singled out Frank in the dressing room. Maybe there were more times – at least times when I said 'You guys' and Frank had a pretty good idea he was the guy, or one of them, that I was referring to. But the other time I have in mind was the final game of the Stanley Cup in the spring of 1967. That season he'd got only eighteen goals, which was about half of his lifetime average up to that point. And in the playoffs he'd scored I think three goals and hadn't been doing much against Canadiens in the final. We had come back into Toronto for the sixth game, leading the series three games to two, and I had a feeling that if we didn't win this one we might be in trouble. I mean, even though we were leading the series, Canadiens had outscored us at that time over the series and with Bower badly hurt and Sawchuk getting pretty used up, the longer the series went the worse our chances were. I looked over the team. The one guy I figured wasn't playing up to his full potential was Mahovlich I told Clancy that I was going to tee off on him in the dressing room Clancy pleaded with me not to. It would be a hell of a risk, because there was the matter of his breakdown two and a half years before I'd been especially careful with him since. If I landed on him hard didn't know which way he was going to go – either go out and pla as he could, or play worse than he had. But this day I took the chance. In other words, I talked to him as if he were any other good player I thought was letting us down. I remember I looked at him once at the height of it and said, 'I don't know where you are from, Chicoutimi or some place, but you should have stayed there and then I wouldn't have to be bothered with you!' I don't know how Chicoutimi got in there at all. That was one time I teed off on Frank – trying that, for a change, to get him up to play the kind of hockey I knew he could. I knew if he played his game, we would win. Nobody could stop us. If he didn't play his game, we might not win.

So we went out and won it 3–1. Frank didn't get any of the goals but he played a very strong game. I talked to one of the players later about what had happened in the dressing room before they went out for the game. Frank hardly ever talked in the dressing room, you know. Never assumed the role of leader. But this time he was first on his feet. Everybody was watching him to see how he would react after my bawling-out. 'Okay, fellows!' he said. 'Let's go get 'em!'

The player who was telling me about it, I think it was George Armstrong, told me, 'When Frank said that, everybody in the goddam room knew we were going to win.'

During Frank's four weeks away from the team six months later, in November of 1967, we still wound up looking like a respectable hockey team. When he came back on November 29 for a game against the Canadiens, we were only two points behind Boston Bruins, who were in first place. Frank had been working out by himself at Tam O'Shanter and Maple Leaf Gardens with just a nurse and his wife watching, and then he'd rejoined the regular team practices, usually going back to the hospital after. I knew he was in pretty good shape. Once again (like in 1964) when he stepped on the ice for the first time there was a great ovation. I'm no psychologist myself, but is there some kind of a guilt reaction in a crowd like that because of the bad times they've given him?

Again, this game was against Canadiens. Keon had been hurt while Mahovlich was out, so I'd put Mike Walton at centre with George Armstrong and Wayne Carlton. Carlton didn't do a thing on the first shift. On the second one I left him on the bench and sent Frank out. Well, it was electrifying. There was first the ovation, while Frank skated out for a face-off in the Leaf zone. When the puck was dropped it was knocked to Armstrong who bounced it off the boards into the centre zone. Walton tried for it there, but missed. The puck drifted in over the Canadiens blueline. All of a sudden, there was Frank, bashing in. He beat Jacques Laperriere to the puck, and when Terry Harper was rushing over from the other side to cover up, Mahovlich slipped a perfect pass over to Walton. Mike lined it up and, bingo, it was in from about fifteen feet out. It was exactly nineteen seconds from when Frank had stepped on the ice and he'd set up as nice a goal as anyone could hope to see; set it up aggressively, by beating a Montreal defence-man to the puck in his own zone.

We beat Canadiens 2–1 that night but it was in the next few weeks that I began to recognize what was wrong with the team and to work towards the trade we eventually made, that took Mahovlich from Toronto.

I had tried before for Mikita, for Beliveau, but we couldn't make any headway. So that died. But now another thing came up – Brewer. Sid Abel of Detroit came after me for Brewer, whose pro rights we owned, although he'd been reinstated as an amateur after he quit Leafs. Detroit had tried for him before. I knew Brewer wouldn't play for us again so in him we had nothing, but still, hell, to trade him we had to get someone good.

Then suddenly after talking on and off with these people for a couple of years, we were both ready and we did start to get some-where, on a Friday, March 1, 1968. At the time we were fifth, thirteen points or so out of fourth. Detroit was sixth. Both of us had to do something.

We wanted to have Norm Ullman and Paul Henderson and they'd throw in Floyd Smith. We were going to give them Mahovlich and Brewer, and they wanted Walton and somebody else. I think it was Pappin at that stage. We said no, we weren't going to give them Walton because that was too much. Mahovlich and Walton were the two biggest scorers we had. Walton was our leading scorer at that particular time.

So when we were talking about it, they changed a little and said they wanted Gary Unger. Unger was a good junior who'd played with my son, Brent, for London Nationals. He'd played for Toronto a bit and who the hell was at one game but Bruce Norris, the Detroit owner, and he liked him. 'So we want Unger,' they said. 'You get Ullman, Henderson, and Smith and we get Mahovlich, Brewer Walton, and Unger.'

I said, 'No, not Walton.'

Then they said how about Stemkowski? They'd take Stemkowski ahead of Walton anyway. When they said Stemkowski I knew we had a deal.

We did do a bit of refining on it from there. They were getting the rights to negotiate with Brewer but there was a time limit on that. They had until the end of the following season, the spring of 1969, to try to sign him. Then if Brewer wouldn't sign his rights would revert to us and for this we would have to pay Detroit $15,000.

This was all on Friday. We were playing Saturday and they were playing Sunday, but we don't play on the Sunday. So I said, 'All right. But there is no sense in shipping hockey players after Saturday night. So we'll make the deal after your game on Sunday. I'll call you back.'

So I had to get a hold of Stafford. I got him in the office and I said, 'I got a deal. I'm recommending very strongly that you take it.' Of course, they didn't want to get rid of Unger, who'd looked pretty good lately, and they didn't want to get rid of Mahovlich. I explained my feelings as strongly as I could: Ullman was a star, a checker, a scorer; Henderson was one of the best young kids in the league; Smith was better than some we had.

Stafford and Harold were the ones I told. So now Stafford phoned the hockey committee, to see if they wanted to make the deal or not. I was thinking, Lord, can you imagine? Here they have to go and ask the hockey committee. I would say half of the people they are going to ask haven't seen thirty games that year. And yet they have a say in whether we are gonna make a deal, for Christ's sake, that is going to be vital to the hockey club. This was a little ridiculous, that's all.

In the end, they okayed it. I called Abel back on Saturday at noon and said, 'Okay, we're gonna make the deal. I'll come over to your game on Sunday. After the game we'll sign the papers.' Then Abel brought the question up, 'If the big guy doesn't report what is gonna happen?'

'Well,' I said, 'if Frank doesn't report then I guess the deal will be off.'

Clancy and I took the plane over to Detroit on the Sunday. We went into the hotel and stayed there until game time. Then we watched Canadiens and Detroit, a hell of a game. One thing that made me feel good was that Henderson challenged John Ferguson, the Montreal tough guy. It had been a long time since one of my guys had done that. After the game we went into the room, the hockey office. Of course, by this time newspapermen were running around, asking what the hell am I doing in there? I didn't tell them a thing, because we had agreed that we'd announce in both places at eleven a.m. on the Monday. We signed the papers, sent a wire to the league's Central Registry outlining the deal, and that was it. We went out the back door and missed the reporters.

But what the hell had happened in the meantime was that someone who was no damn good at keeping a secret, even when secrecy was part of an agreement, had told somebody. I think he told one sports editor, Milt Dunnell of the *Star,* and then got worried that the others would be sore at him if they weren't tipped off, too. So he called the others and told them. So we wake up on the Monday morning with a press conference scheduled for eleven a.m. to make the announcement, and the *Globe and Mail* has published the full story of the deal. A whole page, with pictures. I don't know a thing they were wrong on. They had to get it from somebody in the know among the Toronto executives because they didn't get it from me or Clancy or Abel. I was sore. For one thing, this meant that instead of us having a chance to notify the players before the publicity came out, they'd get it the way they did – by phone from other papers asking if it was true. That's how Frank got it, by a telephone call at eight in the morning or something. It was just one more thing in a long string of leaks about private club business that used to drive me batty.

The deal Abel and I had was that we would be in touch just before the eleven a.m. press conferences in Toronto and Detroit. The *Globe and Mail* story with all the details was all over the radio and so on in Detroit. When I called Abel about quarter to eleven the secrecy that I had promised Abel was gone, and it wasn't my fault, so I was mad.

Ballard was standing right beside me when I phoned Abel.

'Okay, Sid,' I said. 'You've got your chance to call it off right now. I'm sick and tired of the goddam leaks all over the place. If you want to, we'll call it off. Right now.'

Abel didn't say anything for about half a minute. I must say that whoever had leaked to the newspapers must have been breathing uneasily. Because he'd told those sports editors and now if Abe decides he doesn't want to make the deal, all hell would break loose. Right then the other two Toronto papers, the *Star* and the *Telegram,* were carrying the story as gospel. If Abel had backed out then I would have just walked into the press conference and said that Pappin had reported or whatever the hell it was he'd done right then. And somebody would say, 'What about the Mahovlich deal?' And I'd say, 'What Mahovlich deal? I never said that we were trading Mahovlich, did I?'

But Abel said, 'No, it's a deal. It goes.' There was no more talk about whether Mahovlich was going to report or anybody else was going to report, that was it. And a thing like that, a player hearing about a deal from a newspaper, could be the thing that could have made him mad enough *not* to report, you know.

So when I got off the phone I said to Clancy and John Andersen, my assistant, 'Okay, phone 'em.' John called Unger and Stemkowski. King called Frank. You can't call everybody at the same time. So somebody has got to know later than the others. As it turned out Frank was the last to know. But if the deal had been kept secret like it should have, he'd have been first to know. Instead of everybody telling him before we did. This was the unfortunate end of all this, and there was nothing I could do about it.

There were some things I didn't like about the deal, of course. But losing Frank wasn't the worst of them. I knew that it might be the best thing that ever happened to Frank, to get out of Toronto. To get down to Detroit. I knew it just might be the answer for him, and if it was he'd play hockey god-damned well and he'd be a greater asset than ever to the game. I mean, he'd be something big and I'd be the stupidest bastard that ever walked for letting him go. But it isn't going to hurt hockey. I mean, if it's good for him, it's good for hockey.

Same with Stemkowski. He had died on us. Maybe the change would help him.

I hated to let Unger go untried. He might be a great one but we never had a chance to find out. That is something you hate to lose, an untried kid who might be great. I tried to get Detroit off him but they kept coming back until he became a big name in the trade. He's a fine kid. I got to know him in his last two years in junior when I went up to London to watch him play along with our son Brent, and sometimes drove him back to Toronto. I talked to him about the deal. He understands that it is no reflection on what I thought of him as a hockey player. I told him before he left if he ever needs advice on hockey, not to go to strangers – just give me a call. That's how I feel about that kid. But also I feel that, over all, we got three fine hockey players: a proved big one in Ullman; a good young one in Henderson, who we'll get the benefit of; and Smith, a guy I've always admired. He'll go into the corners as well as anybody in the league.

Harold Ballard told me when I first told him about the deal for Frank that all hell would break loose when it was announced. They didn't let me down. That night I was coming downstairs at home about midnight and I hear this open-line show going at me hammer and tongs, calling me every name in the book for trading Frank. Of course, the open-line guy was having the time of his life. He doesn't have to win hockey games. He can have a hell of a time, any time. One radio station put out the question, Should Punch Imlach be fired for trading Mahovlich? If you wanted to answer yes, you dialled one number, and if you said no, dialled another.

I said, 'Well, this is great.'

Especially when the yeses, that I should be fired, beat the noes.

But it was still the same old Mahovlich split, really, without much to do with me at all. The people in his fan club would answer yes, and the people who usually booed him would answer no. That's the way it goes, the way it always went with him.

When Detroit came into Toronto the next Saturday night, Frank was really flying. He scored practically the first time he touched the puck. They had us down 4–0 before we even scored a goal. I wanted to get underneath the bench. After Detroit's fourth goal the crowd was calling me everything you could lay a stick to. But we beat them 7–5 in the end and the ones who'd been booing were cheering. That's hockey. And for the last three weeks of the season we went out and beat everybody in sight. We did fall a few points short of making the playoffs that year. But when the deal was made, Chicago was fourth with 73 points and we were fifth with 59. Fourteen points back. In the end, they just barely nosed us out. If I could have made that deal for Frank Mahovlich two weeks earlier, we would have made the playoffs that year, and they would have had a hell of a time beating us for the Stanley Cup.

Of course, I don't pretend to be the last word on what Frank feels inside himself. He had a great year in 1968-69, with 49 goals, the most he'd ever scored. The Toronto pressure was off him, and whether that pressure was mostly public, or the hockey club, or me, or whatever, only he can say. After the trade, when he might have felt like sounding off, he was asked a lot of leading questions. But he wouldn't criticize either the Leafs or me. He said he'd been treated well in Toronto and didn't feel that he'd been a failure at all; he thought he'd done okay. As to whether he'd be happier in Detroit, he said, 'I'll just have to wait and see. Maybe I'm just not a happy guy.'

15

Getting Ready for a Comeback

When I went to the hockey meetings in Montreal in June of 1968, I was beginning to get the feeling that I had a hockey club again that would move the way I wanted it to. One more move I had made was to trade Jim Pappin to Chicago for Pierre Pilote. When Pappin had refused to go to Rochester the previous February, that had pretty well sealed it for him with Leafs as far as I was concerned. He did eventually report to Rochester and then was brought back to the Leafs because we needed him. He was a better hockey player than the way he was playing showed, I was convinced of that. But that was no good to me if he wasn't producing for me. Meanwhile Pilote had gone sour with the Chicago fans despite his great record as an all-star there. I was sure he could help us. I had in my mind that if my defence settled away all right I might even experiment with Pilote at right wing or at centre, give him a new life the way Red Kelly had got it years before. Pilote was a good playmaker and I was happy to have him.

At the meetings I would have made deals for either Pulford or Walton, if I could have. I'd run into general managers from other clubs and I'd ask, 'By the way, are you interested in Pulford? Or Walton?' Then I'd listen to the names they fired back at me. They weren't exactly sensational. It didn't take me long to find out that wasn't going to be able to make a deal for either of them, simpl because nobody would offer me what they were worth. I tried to get Vic Hadfield for Pulford from New York. But they wouldn't.

Los Angeles offered me Sawchuk for Pulford, but Sawchuk wasn't what I needed, with Bower and Gamble playing the way they had the year before – nearly winning the Vezina even with a bad team in front of them.

Tommy Ivan wanted Pulford for Chicago but he wouldn't give me what I wanted. I mean, Pulford, year in and year out, was one of my better hockey players. He didn't always do everything I wanted him to do but I certainly couldn't afford to get rid of him unless I got something good in return. The best offer I had was Doug Mohns, even up. That was not a bad deal. But I didn't take it and didn't regret that decision.

Walton was a different matter. The year before he'd run into a hot streak. Everything he was doing went in. But I really felt he'd maybe be better at left wing than at centre, because he didn't utilize his wing men to the best advantage – didn't set them up enough, or use them enough at all. And he'd loaf coming back when he should have been digging. But he was just a kid and I figured with another year under his belt he was going to be better. After all, that had been his first full year in the league.

He had teed me off a little on another matter. His contract for 1967-68 called for a bonus on goals after the first 15. He'd get $500 for 20 goals, $1,000 for 25, $1,500 for 30. His contract called for $100 a goal for everything after 30 goals. But there was something in the way the contract was worded that gave him an opening, and when he did get the 30 goals he claimed he had $3,000 coming to him – $500 for the 20, another $1,000 for the 25, and another $1,500 for the 30. That meant in effect $100 a goal between 15 and 20, $200 a goal between 20 and 25, and $300 a goal between 25 and 30. But then the contract did say specifically $100 a goal for anything over 30. Now you know bloody well that there is no hockey player who is going to sign a contract that calls for $300 for his thirtieth goal and $100 for his thirty-first goal.

Tell him that and he'd just look at me. I said, 'You can't tell me that in your mind you believed you had accepted a contract that gave you $300 for the thirtieth goal and $100 for the thirty-first.'

He just looked at me.

I would have respected him if he'd said, 'Okay, I do understand that – but you guys wrote the contract wrong, you made the mistake in the wording, and you should pay.'

If he'd said that I would have said, 'All right, you're right. The next time we'll make sure that we don't make that mistake, but this time we'll pay.' I might call him everything under the sun, but I'd pay.

But when I knew damned well a guy was trying to give it to me, that's another story. Anyway, we paid but I didn't like the way he did it.

I didn't make any more deals. I left Conacher and Stanley unprotected in the draft and lost Conacher to Detroit and Stanley to Philadelphia. Then Conacher decided to quit hockey and that was that.

One little thing happened in training camp in September of 1968 that got a lot of publicity. This was me making a ruling against sideburns. I had an early camp with Bruce Gamble and George Armstrong and a few others, besides a lot of the younger guys. It was more or less a voluntary camp.

Gamble was the guy I landed on about the sideburns. I went into the dressing room one day and said to him, 'You! Get those sideburns off, have them off before you come on the ice tomorrow, or you don't come.'

I said to all the other guys in the room too, 'That goes for all of you. Get the sideburns off.'

I'll let you in on a little secret. I had that one cooked with Gamble. I don't like long sideburns, and I figured if guys were going around representing the Toronto Maple Leafs I should have some say as to their appearance. After all, it was my club they were representing.

In August I had Gamble in to talk about his contract. We were talking away and he wanted a certain amount of money and we weren't getting together. And finally I looked at him. He had sideburns down to his chin. I said to him, 'All right, I'll give you the money. But on two conditions. One, you get those sideburns off.'

'Okay,' he said. 'They'll be off tomorrow.'

'And second,' I said, 'you come into camp about 207 or 209 pounds.'

I don't remember exactly what the figure was I gave him but I told him, 'I don't want you coming into camp at any 217 pounds, because that won't be good for you.' And he agreed to that too.

Suddenly I had an idea. 'Okay,' I said, 'you got the money you want. We're not gonna fight about that. But look, you keep the sideburns on. You come to camp. The first day I walk into the room I'm gonna look at you and I'm gonna say, "Gamble, you get your damned sideburns off!" And then you're gonna take 'em off!'

He said, 'Right away!'

I said, 'Good. When you do that, you're gonna straighten the rest of the team around. They're gonna say, "That son-of-a-bitch!" about me. But when you take them off, a veteran player, they'll realize I mean business and everything will go just like nothing.'

I knew that when that happened, Walton would be sitting down in Toronto with his long sideburns on, and he'd be reading the paper. And I knew that Eagleson would be having a say to the papers. And all the hippies would be going crazy and writing letters to the papers. And that amount of fuss would look after our first week of training camp, as far as publicity was concerned. Reporters would be telling me what the papers said and what Eagleson said and what other guys with sideburns said, like Rod Gilbert and Derek Sanderson, but all I'd say was, 'I'm paying those guys to represent this club and it's with sideburns off. If they can find somebody who wants to hire them with sideburns, let them go ahead.'

I knew we could milk that, and it would give the newspapermen something to write about for a few days instead of being around all the time asking who was signed and who wasn't signed, and all that kind of thing that sometimes makes trouble for the club.

And that, of course, is exactly what happened. The sideburns issue looked after the first week of camp. And in the second week the main part of the team came in to be confronted with the two Army physical-training instructors I'd brought in from Royal Military College. That gave the newspapermen something more to write about without getting too much into the signing and contract end of things. A lot of people thought Gamble should have defied me on the sideburns, for gosh sake. They didn't know we had it all cooked weeks before. Two newspapermen even bet me that Gamble would refuse to take them off. I collected and split the two bucks with Gamble.

By then, of course, much more serious things were happening. In early September I had the meeting with the hockey committee where we set December 1 as my deadline to be in contention for a playoff position, or bring in Johnny McLellan from Tulsa to coach. (See Chapter 1.) Armstrong decided he couldn't help the team and quit – although, as it turned out, he came back to the team early in December.

I moved in a lot of new young guys, especially on defence. I knew I was going to give Mike Pelyk a lot more work. Jim Dorey was a real tough egg from Tulsa and he was going to get a shot at it. Another tough guy was Pat Quinn from Tulsa. A real surprise in camp was Rickey Ley, a junior with Niagara Falls, with no pro experience. So we had all those and Marcel Pronovost, Pilote, and Horton. We had the same goalkeepers, Gamble and Bower. And among the forwards I'd picked up Larry Mickey and Bill Sutherland in the draft, and we were going to give Gerry Meehan a real shot at making the team, as well as Terry Clancy, King's son, and Mike Byers.

I knew that with all these young guys there were going to be mistakes. They were going to cost us goals. But I was going to have a team that would try and would play entertaining hockey. I thought we could make the playoffs, if the young guys came along and the old guys held up. But I also knew that we were going to be life and death to make the playoffs, all season long. That there would never be time to relax.

16

Four Bottles of Champagne

On Wednesday, February 19, 1969, we were in fifth place, two points behind Detroit in fourth, and a little up on Chicago in sixth. Montreal was in Toronto for a game that night and we were to play them again in Montreal the next night. It was getting to be critical for us. We had to catch either Detroit or New York to make the fourth playoff spot. I thought we could do it and the team felt that way too. We'd played well on the road all season; never setting the world on fire but never being humiliated. I thought a lot of this team. The kids on defence had played well. I don't know anybody, any time, in the NHL who has ever used three rookies consistently through a season on defence. They had cost us goals some nights through inexperience, but they were learning and we were coming.

That night we showed how far we had come. There were 16,485 paying customers in Maple Leaf Gardens and they loved to see the way we manhandled the Canadiens. Gamble played great goal for us. He'd had to more and more all season because Johnny Bower seemed once again to be coming pretty well to the end of the road, although he had fooled people before. Norm Ullman got his twenty-eighth goal of the season in the first period, on a power play from Walton and Ron Ellis. I was using Walton mostly on the power play, not as a regular centre, because in my opinion he wasn't playing as dependably as the other centres. We were short-handed in the second period when Dave Keon scored his twenty-first of the season while he and Murray Oliver were killing a penalty. A short-handed goal against anybody, let alone Canadiens, is something that lifts a team. Sutherland scored his seventh from Pilote and Pulford, and Ellis got his seventeenth from Ullman, before the second period ended with us leading the best team in hockey 4–0. They got one by Bobby Rousseau in the third before Paul Henderson scored his twenty-first of the season from Ellis and Pilote. We won it 5–1. We hadn't handled the Canadiens that way since back in our strong years of the early sixties.

With the game in Montreal the next night, we went down to catch the overnight train. A few minutes before it was supposed to pull out, trainer Joe Sgro and the CN man came to me. Mike Walton wasn't on the train, they said. 'How about holding the train?'

I said, 'Well, we could hold it for a couple of minutes. But he's had over an hour and a half since the end of the game. It's his responsibility to be on it. What the hell's the use of holding the train, with all the other people that are on it, if he isn't going to show anyway?'

Knowing the way Walton was, I mean his attitude towards lots of rules, I thought it was entirely possible that, if he wasn't on by now, he wouldn't be on.

However, I did tell them to hold it for five minutes. Then I went to the players' car and I said to somebody, 'Where's Walton?'

One kid tried to cover for him and said, 'His coat's here.'

I said, 'Well, maybe he's on another car.' I went and said to the conductor, 'Let's go,' and we pulled out. But he wasn't on and I knew it soon after we left.

The next morning when I registered the rooms I left the list the way it was, Walton registered as being in with Pulford. The reason was that some people do miss trains and planes and buses. He could turn up. But there was no message from him or anything.

Certainly it was a story but no reporter was going to get it from me. If I have to discipline a player I don't care to do it in the papers. If he showed up before the game I'd fine him for missing the train and raise a little hell with him, but that was all. The game was the important thing.

Well, I waited and waited and waited. All day. I tried to get Stafford in Toronto to let him know what was happening, so that if he did hear about it elsewhere, he wouldn't make things worse by sounding off, saying we're going to do this or that, without knowing what I wanted to do.

I also waited for one of the hockey writers to come up and ask, 'Where's Walton?' But nobody did. I mean, the players weren't telling, and the fact that he wasn't seen all day didn't necessarily mean anything to the writers – he could have been sleeping or out shopping or walking.

Right at four o'clock there came a pounding on the door of my suite in the hotel. It was Lou Cauz, the hockey writer for the *Globe and Mail*. 'Would you care to comment on Mike Walton quitting the team?' he said.

'I don't know that. Who told you?'

'My office informed me.'

I told him I had no comment.

Well, then it turned out that Smythe had been in Ottawa all day at a meeting with the Health Minister, John Munro, over Toronto and Montreal maybe helping out the national hockey team. Eagleson was along with him, and Eagleson's friend Dick Beddoes, the sports columnist for the *Globe and Mail*. Eagleson being the Players' Association lawyer, Walton apparently had gone to him and told him he was jumping the club. Then of course Eagleson tells Beddoes, and some time that day they tell Smythe. Anyway, the situation is that Eagleson and Beddoes seem to know a hell of a lot more about my hockey player than I or any of his teammates do. Beddoes had been phoning and had given Cauz all he knew, apparently, because then Cauz asked, 'Have you got a telegram from Walton?'

'I haven't got a telegram from Walton or anybody else,' I said.

'Well,' he said, 'what have you got to say about it?'

'Nothing,' I said. And I closed the door.

You'll notice that all this happened right at four p.m., too late for getting it into the afternoon papers. I mean, Eagleson let Beddoes know but he didn't bother to let the afternoon papers in on the same news, which is something you'd think the afternoon papers and other sports reporters would remember from time to time when they're dealing with Eagleson on other things.

So now I call in the two other newspapermen from Toronto. George Gross, from the *Telegram*, and Red Burnett, from the *Star*. I told them Walton was missing. 'I just want to let you know,' I said. I know you can't do anything about it, but I know you're probably going to be in deep water over it if this guy doesn't show, because the other paper is gonna have it.'

They were sore at me for not letting them know before, but I told them, 'There is no possible way I can tell you that the guy isn't here. No possible way. If he shows up, everything is forgotten. But I gotta cover for my hockey player as long as I possible can.'

Gross and Burnett were mad as hell. They were mad at the players, they were mad at everybody. I said, 'Lookit, at least put the blame where the blame is. Don't be blaming everybody else. There are only two people involved. Walton and Eagleson. They're the guys that did you in. If you think you got screwed on the deal, well you had to get screwed there. You can't blame the trainer for not telling you, or some other hockey player for not coming up and telling you that Walton didn't make the trip.'

They could guess that the *Globe* guys had known about it for at least a couple of hours, but naturally hadn't tipped their hand, while the afternoon papers could still get on it. The *Globe* people were only looking after themselves.

Gross and Burnett said, 'What are you going to do?'

I said, 'I'll tell you just before game time.'

So I walked into the dressing room at the Forum later, about seven o'clock, and said to Pulford, 'Is Walton here?'

He just looked at me.

I said, 'Did he show at all?'

He said, 'No.'

I said, 'Okay, that's all I want to know.' I walked out of the room and told the newspapermen, 'I'm suspending Walton for missing the game.'

That was it.

We lost that game 2–1. The team played well, but the matter of Walton being missing had to bother them.

When I got on the train pulling out, Pulford came in to see me.

He said, 'If I can get Walton back, is it going to be all right with you?'

I said, 'Look, if he comes back and he can help the hockey club, it will be all right. He's got to come back with the right attitude. That's all there is to it. But I won't be adamant and say I won't take him back.'

He said, 'I'll talk to him first thing in the morning. Could he come and see you?'

I said, 'Just pick up the phone and we'll talk it over.'

I didn't hear any more. When we got home I heard Walton had gone with Eagleson to Oklahoma City in the Central League or some place. Anyway he was out of town.

I also read in Beddoes' story, from Eagleson of course, that a telegram Walton was supposed to have sent me said he was unhappy with the team and wanted to buy up his contract. I never got that telegram, then or later. If it was sent, maybe it's still hanging around in the Mount Royal Hotel, for all I know. And the matter of buying up his contract – of course, that's pure malarkey. It didn't take me to make that clear; Brian O'Neill, director of administration for the National Hockey League, was asked about that before we left Montreal that Thursday night. His answer was, 'He sure as hell can't.'

The newspapers were full of the story for the next few days. One more thing we learned was that the night Walton had jumped the club he had sat up until four a.m. telling his troubles to Eagleson. I would have thought that Eagleson, one of whose jobs is to make sure that clubs live up to their contracts, might have pointed out to Walton that one of his responsibilities was to live up to his end too.

We lost 4–2 to Chicago that Saturday night in Toronto and dropped into last place. Then we got clobbered 7–2 by Minnesota Sunday in their rink. We were one point behind Chicago, five behind New York, and six behind Detroit. New York and Detroit were the ones we had to catch, one of them anyway, to make the playoffs. Some of the Leaf players were quoted as feeling that Walton had let down the team, just at the time when they should have been making a drive to get into the playoffs. That was right enough. When one guy, through preoccupation with his own real or imagined troubles, lets down his teammates in a way that takes playoff money out of their pockets, he can't expect them exactly to form a cheering section for him.

This brings up another thing. When I talked to Pulford on the train on the way from Montreal, I told him I would take Walton back if everybody on the team wanted him back. I asked him to go around and sound out the players on that matter. Then I heard on the Monday, when we got back from Minnesota, that Eagleson had phoned Smythe and told him that Walton had been thinking of coming back to the team until he read what some of the other players said about him. Now he wouldn't come back because he felt he wasn't wanted.

With us going down in the standings now and all the fuss

about Walton, the hockey committee had a meeting on the Tuesday. That meeting was specifically about Walton and of course I was there. The matter of my job was brought up by Smythe again. 'Why don't you step down and let someone else coach the hockey club?' he asked. He said this a couple of times.

I said, 'Look, let's get one thing straight. Are you suggesting to me that if I don't coach the hockey club, Walton's gonna come back? In other words, I'm gonna lose my job as coach because he walked out on the hockey club? If this is what you're saying, let me know.'

Well, they can't very well admit that. So I got them to back off it again. Then we talked about what to do about it. The best player at Rochester right then was a kid named Ron Ward. But we didn't own him. Rochester did. They suggested I try to buy him and I said I would but that the price probably would be high. (Later in the spring, after the playoffs were over, Toronto did make a trade to get Ward.)

Also, at that meeting it was brought up about the attitude of the players to having Walton come back.

So the next morning, Wednesday, I got to Pulford again. He came up to my office. 'Look,' I said, 'I want to find out how the players feel about him coming back.' I suggested he call Armstrong, Horton, you know – those guys and the other senior ones are the guys to call.

Well, I'll be damned if it didn't turn out that Eagleson called some of the players with this question. I'm pretty sure that he didn't call them all. Anyway he called enough that later they could put out a little story saying that everybody on the team wanted Mike back. I don't know if that was entirely true.

I had an idea about Wednesday noon that something was about to break. Obviously Eagleson and Smythe were communicating because the previous day, Tuesday, Walton first had called a press conference to speak to the sports editors. As Eagleson said it, Walton was still convinced he could no longer play for me. But then this had been called off because of the hockey committee meeting coming up to discuss the Walton case. Maybe Walton and Eagleson thought I'd be fired right then and solve the problem. We had a game with St. Louis that night. I even made a bet privately that I would get a telephone call from Walton at exactly four p.m., too late for the afternoon papers but just in time for the *Globe and Mail*, again because of the mutual aid society between Beddoes of the *Globe* and Eagleson.

He did call, right at four p.m.

He said, 'I'd like to talk to you. I want to play tonight.'

I said, 'Well, I'm not sure if I'm going to play you tonight or not.' My thinking was, he hadn't been on skates for a while and maybe it wouldn't be fair to put him in right away, especially at home. I told him maybe it would be better to wait until the next night on the road, to get out of the pressure. But he said he wanted to play that night.

I said, 'You'd better come down and talk to me.'

So down he came about five and we talked things over. It was rather a loose kind of talk.

'It's partly your fault,' he said, 'and partly mine.'

Well, if a guy is going to play for me that night I'm not going to start arguing whose fault it is. I just said that we had to get a few things straightened out, such as that he would have to obey the rules, the same as the other players on the team, that he couldn't be an exception, had to be part of the whole thing. He accepted that. I think he'd been a bit surprised by the public attitude to the thing. On the Mahovlich deal, the public had wanted to hang me. But when Walton walked out, some guy on the radio asked for opinions on whether I should be fired for the way I'd handled Walton. The calls were about twenty to one in my favour.

It wasn't quite all over. We beat St. Louis 3–2 that night to get back on the beam again. But when Clancy came into the rink before the game I hadn't had a chance to tell him that Walton was back. When he found out Walton was actually going to play, it caused the only serious rift we ever had. After the game he challenged me. 'Why did you take him back?' he demanded. And when I said a few words, he said, 'I've got no use for a quitter! If I was on your bloody team tonight I wouldn't play if he was going to play, and that's all there is to it!'

I tried to cool him down but nothing would. 'That's it,' he said. 'I'm finished, after we make this trip tonight.' We were due in Philadelphia for a game the next night. I saw there was no use talking to him any more that night, but in Philadelphia in the morning I brought it up again. 'If I listen to you,' I said, 'you are going to quit. You are going to do the very thing he did. How can you do that?'

He thought it over and then said, 'Yeah, I guess so.' So he stayed. But he didn't bother keeping his feelings to himself on the matter at all. Even a few days later he was still hostile enough to say that if Walton was with the team next year, he wouldn't be.

Walton scored the tying goal in a 1–1 game that night in Philadelphia. On the Friday morning I get home to read the papers and find that Beddoes was saying, in effect, that I didn't take Walton back of my own accord, but was ordered to by Smythe. This was altogether false. I thought Smythe would correct Beddoes on that. But the next day, when there was no correction, I went on the radio program I had on Saturday nights and said that this thing about me being ordered to take Walton back was an unmitigated lie. Of course, if Beddoes takes as gospel what Eagleson tells him about me, or what Smythe tells him about me, not all of it is going to be true.

Beddoes got very hot about that. He came into the rink that night for our game with Pittsburgh and said he was going to sue me. He said to somebody, 'You tell Imlach that when he fools around with me, he's not fooling around with those other hacks that cover the beat.'

Well, when I hear that, at least I'm starting to have some fun. I get Gross and Burnett in from the other papers and tell them about Beddoes saying they are hacks. They get mad. And then I thought I really should get somebody to tell Beddoes that what happened at that Tuesday meeting was not as he had printed it – was not a matter of the hockey committee ordering me to take Walton back. I mean, I thought he'd got it from Eagleson, that being the kind of wishful thinking that I thought led in that direction.

Paul McNamara, one of the hockey committee who had been at the meeting, was around for that night's game. I said, 'I don't care if he sues me or doesn't sue me, but go and tell him what the hell happened at the meeting, you were there.'

I would have asked Smythe to do it, but Smythe wasn't around – he'd flown to Florida that day.

McNamara went out and told Beddoes what had happened at the meeting; that I had not been ordered to take Walton back. Beddoes, defending himself, said, 'Well, my information came right from your president.' Meaning Smythe. So you can imagine where Beddoes got one of his other lines that he was repeating at that time, that it was a hundred per cent sure that I was going to be fired after the season was over. (In fact, he made a bet on that and I'm sorry to say, he won.)

At this time I had other things on my mind, as if all this wasn't enough. The trading deadline was Sunday midnight. I had talked to Bud Poile, the general manager in Philadelphia, about a deal for Brit Selby and Forbes Kennedy. We were going to give them Gerry Meehan and Bill Sutherland, and Poile had agreed to that. But the Selby-Kennedy deal was only part of what I wanted to do. Nobody ever knew it at the time, but that Saturday I also made a deal to send Walton to Boston.

All this gets fairly complicated when you're trying to get a deal through in a hurry, but I had got through the most of it. Selby was one guy the club badly needed. And I wanted more. The week before, when we were having trouble with Walton, Boston had got in touch with me, and were interested in him. Now I called Milt Schmidt in Boston. They agreed to give me Eddie Shack and a kid named Jim Lorentz who I think is pretty good. The new line I wanted was Shack, Selby, and Lorentz, and I think it would have been a good one. I thought it would give the team the shot it needed to make the playoffs.

I had everything arranged late on the Saturday afternoon, before the little blowup with Beddoes – arranged except for one thing. When I made the deal with Milt Schmidt, I told him, 'Nobody knows I'm going to trade Walton. I've got to tell the owners sooner or later about it and if they tell me I'm going to be fired if I make this deal, I might want a chance to reconsider. Okay?'

Now he had been the one initiating this deal all along. He said okay. Then Poile in Philadelphia phoned me back on the other deal. Suddenly he wanted a little more for Selby and Kennedy so I threw in Mike Byers. I might have backed out of that deal then if I hadn't been so sure that the Boston one was all set.

Between then and the game I did a lot of thinking. I got thinking to myself, 'Look, the way I've always operated, I do what I think is right for the hockey club. This Walton deal is right for the hockey club. If they want to fire me, let them fire me – I'm going to make the deal.'

In fact, when I was talking to Paul McNamara that night I told him about the Kennedy-Selby deal and also that I was going to trade Walton, but I didn't tell him who to, or who for.

That weekend in our two Toronto games, we tied Pittsburgh

3–3 Saturday night and beat Chicago 2–1 on Sunday afternoon. Doing all right. In the meantime Clancy had gone to Florida to help raise money for the Charlie Conacher cancer research fund. When I got home from the Sunday afternoon game against Chicago, Clancy phoned me from Florida.

'I just got a call from Boston,' he said. 'They don't want to make the deal.'

I went back to the office and I called Schmidt.

'Now look,' I said, 'we had a deal!'

He said, 'Well, you were hesitant about the deal and we didn't want you to lose your job or anything.'

I said, 'I've thought it all out. I've decided I'm going to run this the way I've always run it. This is a deal as far as I'm concerned. I don't expect you to back off. I expect you to call me after your game tonight. I'll be sitting here in this office at 10.30 waiting for your call.'

He called me at 10.30, all right. 'We still think it's not a deal,' he said.

I said, 'You can say any damned thing you like – you started the deal and you're backing out.'

He said, 'Do you want to talk to Mulcahy? He's right here.' Charlie Mulcahy is a Boston club vice-president.

I said, 'No, I don't want to talk to Mulcahy. As far as I'm concerned if that's the way you want to operate that's the way it has to be.'

I've had it suggested to me since that somehow Stafford heard about the Walton deal and killed it directly. I don't know. If so, he had to hear it from Boston. Milt had to tell his superiors and it is possible that one of them mentioned it to Stafford, or called him in Florida. I suppose this could have been a situation where Stafford told them, 'We won't honour this deal,' and they backed off for that reason. It's not impossible.

Anyway, we made the one deal. And we played some damned good hockey in the next few weeks. We got up to fourth place and when we had a chance to cinch it, we did – in mid-week, the last week of the season. We were down 3–0 to Montreal one night and we came back and won. The next night we went into Detroit and beat Detroit, the only team with a chance to catch us by then. That game put us in and them out. Our whole effort had been geared to making the playoffs and we were there. Earlier, I had seriously considered quitting the job the night we made the playoffs. I'd been fighting all year to prove one point, that I could coach this team into the playoffs. I was still hearing all the rumours that I was sure to be fired. It would be nice to beat them to it. But then I thought – what the hell. I had a contract. I also had a lot of players who had done this for me – how could I walk out on them? The only point I'm making is that quitting did enter my mind.

When Stafford had left for Florida four weeks before, we had been in last place. Now, surprise, we were in the playoffs against Boston, a tough team. Before that East division semi-final opened we could have used a little morale booster – no more than we deserved, but just a little. Well, Stafford had a chance to give it to us. He arrived back from Florida for the playoffs and we had the usual team picture lined up.

We were all there ready, and he was late. This is his normal procedure, of course, to let everybody know who he is.

He walked out there. This team had been playing its guts out to fill his rink. He could have said, 'You did a hell of a job, fellows, getting into the playoffs.'

Instead of that, he didn't say a thing to them. He just ignored them, as well as me. The newspaper people were watching. Some of them said to me, 'Why the hell didn't he shake your hand?'

'Well, he hadn't seen Mr. Bassett for a while,' I said. 'They got talking.' John Bassett was there for the team picture too.

The newspaper guy said, 'Well, you were only one step farther than Bassett.'

'Hell,' I said, 'I didn't think of it.'

So that was one thing, a sort of slap by refusing to compliment the team on what they had done. And the next damn thing, Lou Cauz grabbed Stafford right after the picture-taking was over, and rubbed it in a little about us making the playoffs.

Away back the previous autumn Stafford had knocked the team, talking about a fifty-year-old goalie, and saying Pulford was over the hill, and – about Gamble – that 'one good season didn't make. him a major-leaguer.'

Lou asked him about these things. Stafford still maintained that he was right about Bower. 'And how many goals did Pulford get? Eleven.'

Really the kind of stuff to get a team up for a Stanley Cup series, eh?

I told him later, 'You're the worst son-of-a-bitch I ever came across, for morale. You just kick the living daylights out of everybody.'

He also told Lou Cauz in that interview that getting Leafs into the playoffs was 'a tribute to Imlach's coaching', a compliment that would have done the team more good if it somehow had been made to apply to the team. Also he said that he had nothing new to report on my future with the club.

I don't think that was right, if he'd been levelling. I think he had made up his mind a month before that he was going to fire me as soon as the season was over. Now it had to be postponed a bit because of the playoffs. I can't be sure, but I feel Mike Walton might have been told back then, 'You go back with the team now. Imlach won't be coaching next year.' I think Beddoes and Eagleson also were told I would be fired. I kept getting it from everywhere.

Anyway, we were bombed in Boston two games in a row, 10–0 and 7–0. It just happened that way. Breaks, some bad plays, and a morale knock from the club president. And he was still at it. After one of the games in Boston he came to me and said, 'Well, you didn't deserve to be here anyway.' I teed off on him plenty. If we didn't deserve to be here, who did? Detroit, who we'd beaten when we had to beat them? Chicago, who'd finished sixth? But it made me feel sick. It was like the time we made the playoffs in 1959 on the last night of the season, and were down 2–0 at the end of the first period, and he said, 'Well, you gave it a good try,' as if the bloody game was played in twenty minutes instead of sixty. But after those two bombings in Boston, we lost the next two in Toronto too. But it was only by one goal a time. The Leafs played well.

When the last game was over and we were through for the season I did like I do any year that I finally lose. I don't try to go into the visitors' dressing room. I go stand where the opposition team comes in from the ice and I shake their hands as they are going by me and wish them luck, and that's the end of it.

I was standing there when Stafford came along. The Boston players hadn't all been by yet. He got out his key and opened the door to a little room there. He was going in. Lou Cauz happened to be standing around at the time too. 'I want to see you,' Stafford said. 'I want to talk to you.'

I wasn't going in – I was going to wait until I'd shaken hands with or spoken to all the Boston players.

I said, 'I'll be with you in a minute.' So in a few minutes I went into the room. Cauz was right behind me. 'Can I come in?' he said.

Stafford said, 'No, I want to talk to him alone.'

When the door was shut, Stafford stuck out his hand. I took it. Hell, I didn't know why he wanted to shake my hand. He shook my hand and said, 'Well, that's it.'

I looked at him. It took me a few seconds to get it. Then I said, 'You're telling me that I'm fired. Is that what you're saying?' If I hadn't been expecting it, I don't think it would have been possible for me to deduce it from 'Well, that's it.'

'Yes,' he said, 'you're through. I want to run the club now.'

I said, 'Well, that's your privilege.'

And he said, 'How would you like to handle it?'

'What do you mean, how would I like to handle it?'

'Well, you can retire, you can quit, anything you want.' He said he would make it easy for me.

I said, 'Look, you just fired me. There is no way I walk out of here and say I just fired myself.' I said, 'You walk out and tell them, for Christ's sake. You fired me.'

'You don't have to worry, you are going to get paid,' he said.

Of course, I had a contract so I would expect that.

With that out he went. I understand he went to tell Clancy.

I stayed in the room for a while. You know, I half expected it but still . . . When it happens, you know it is going to happen and everything else, but I didn't expect it to happen at that particular time. I mean I wouldn't have done it like that. I would have shaken hands with the guy and said, 'Well, you got in the playoffs. I didn't expect you to get in. You did a pretty good job.' The next day, maybe, you take the guy and tell him he's through.

I was still in the room when Lou Cauz did come in. But I didn't say anything to him. I had some things I wanted to do, fast, and then get out of there before my wife heard about it some way, out in the corridor.

The toughest thing for me was that I had to go into the dressing room and walk around to all the players. I do it every year after the last game. Now there is no reason I won't do it. I mean, after all, these guys had played pretty well. We all accomplished the main thing that we wanted to accomplish, which was getting into the playoffs. And we played well enough in Toronto. We were not ashamed of the way we played in Toronto. We got beat with the goal tender out. We were trying. What I'm getting at is that for the players' sake, some of them being pretty disappointed, I wanted to go around and talk to them. Some of them I wanted to say something to, because I may never see them again you know.

So I went around. 'You did well,' I'd say. And to another, 'Thanks for the way you played for me.' And I kept on going.

I went to Pully and shook his hand and said, 'You did all right.' Keon is right next to him. I shook Keon's hand and I said, 'Davy, thanks for the way you played for me.'

I kept going to Oliver and said, 'You had a pretty good series.' I said the same things to everybody. But, well, Keon picked it up somehow. He followed down the line behind me. When I got down to the end by the door, he said, 'What do you mean?'

I said, 'What do you mean, what do I mean?'

He said, 'Well, the way you thanked me for the way I played for you . . .' He wasn't sure but he sensed something.

I said, 'Come on in the little room here.' We went in and I said to him, 'I'm finished.'

He said, 'What do you have to do, win a Stanley Cup every year?'

I said, 'Look Davy, the day I took the stand last December first it was just a matter of time. If they'd have had the guts to do it then, they would have done it. Don't worry about me.'

He was rather upset. He went back in to the dressing room and then I went over and talked to Clancy for a minute. Then I wanted to get my wife and get out of there.

I got a little boot out of the people as I went by looking for her. 'Don't worry, Punch, we'll get them next year,' they'd call. 'We'll see you next year.'

I said, 'I don't think so.'

You know how they go on. I just kept on saying, 'Ah, I don't think so.' And then I picked up my wife and our daughter, Marlene, and suddenly I saw Lou Cauz of the *Globe and Mail* coming. He was looking for my wife, you know, to get a quote from her. I caught his eye and got behind her and shook my head at him, saying silently, don't tell her. He may have thought that I had already told her, you see. If I had told her, then there would have been no question about it, about him talking to her. But he respected the situation, which I thank him for.

So we left. I wanted to get my wife home before I told her. She had her own car. We were going along the street. First it was north on Church. Traffic was bad. Then we're going east along Bloor Street, my wife in one car, Marlene and I in the other, keeping the cars close together, when here it comes.

'Imlach has been fired,' said the radio.

My wife's car was right beside me. We stopped at the Castle Frank light. I pulled up opposite her and put down the window.

'Fired!' I said.

She looked around. Traffic was heavy and noisy. 'Fire?' she said. 'Where is the fire?'

'I mean, I've been fired!' I yelled. She still didn't get it. I didn't want her hearing it on the radio but I wasn't getting through.

'Aren't you listening to the radio?' I yelled.

She said, 'I'm listening to the Canadiens game.'

'What's the score?'

'Four-two for Canadiens.'

I said to myself, well, it looks as though somebody else might get fired tonight. But I kept yelling and she finally understood me. By the time we got to the Don Valley Parkway the game was over, and they had the news about me in New York by then. Red Fisher of the Montreal *Star* got on the radio and he was pretty good on the subject of Stafford. That made her feel a little better about it.

So we drove home, the two cars fairly close together all the way. She was either in front of me or behind me depending on how the traffic was. It wasn't a bad evening. Spring. Our big old collie dog who stays outside all the time opened his eyes and wagged his tail.

When we went into the house my wife was talking about it, all upset. This was why I'd wanted to get her out of the Gardens before she heard. I said, 'Let's go downstairs.' The TV is down there. Also, I'd been saving champagne down there. One bottle from each of our four Stanley Cups. 'We'd better go down and get out the Stanley Cup champagne,' I said.

So we went down. Later a few people arrived. Clancy came first. Then Tommy O'Neill and George Gross. And we drank the four bottles of champagne.

Epilogue

An epilogue, I understand, is a short speech addressed to the audience at the end of a play. If so, that makes it a proper description of a few words I said at noon on April 23, 1969, which was a miserable day in Toronto – raining, with the temperature in the mid-forties, and with other teams still playing for the Stanley Cup.

But the day was exceptional in at least one respect: it can't have happened often, a city giving a testimonial luncheon for a fired coach.

A few days after my last night with the Leafs, there was an end-of-the-season party at Davy Keon's house. Most of the players and their wives were there. Davy drove to my house and invited my wife and me. He had to come in person, because I'd stopped answering the phone for a while.

At the Keons', the players asked us to another party they were throwing a few days later – the annual Giveaway Party, the one they had every year with the five-dollar fines I took from them every time they gave away the puck in a game. I'd always stayed away from them before but this seemed a bit different. It wasn't exactly the coach drinking with the players any more.

When we arrived at the Giveaway Party at a downtown restaurant, Gord Walker of the *Globe and Mail* came up to me.

'What do you think about the city deciding to give you a banquet?' he asked.

I just stared at him.

He said this had been suggested that day at City Hall by Controller Allan Lamport.

'I'm speechless,' I said.

It takes a man a while to get used to being fired. There'd been some bitterness, especially when Stafford tried to justify the way he'd done it by suggesting that I'd let the player strength be depleted (which really he had caused by selling whole hockey clubs), and by saying I had a conflict of interest through owning part of the Vancouver club. There wasn't a Vancouver share in my name, but some people had assumed that my longtime friend Joe Crozier was fronting for me. I'd been tempted to retort that the three NHL clubs that had offered me jobs didn't seem bothered by any possible conflict of interest, but I hadn't. I'd decided to let him talk and let the public judge – which it usually will do.

Anyway, I was speechless. It didn't matter so much to me right then whether the city thing really came off or not. Just the idea that they'd think I'd done something for Toronto was enough for me.

But a day or two later I was approached more officially by the city. And on that rainy noon of April 23 I stepped off the elevator on the thirty-third floor of a hotel called Sutton Place. Six players from my 1967 Stanley Cup team were there, and Clancy, and some other friends, as well as the official representatives of the city where I'd been born and raised.

The Mayor, Bill Dennison, made a speech about me being a famous citizen of Toronto, up from the playgrounds. Coaches and mayors have something in common, he said – it's sometimes a little lonely at the top. But there were consolations, one being that we never lacked for free advice. Then he gave me, on behalf of the city, a silver pitcher engraved with what they thought of me, which seemed to be quite a bit.

Then I had to speak. It wasn't easy at all, but there were things I wanted to say. I said that, when they honoured me, they honoured not only me, but Clancy, and all the old guard of players, the ones who won the games. I said that if I ever took another hockey job I hoped I would be fortunate enough to have men like them playing for me. I said I wouldn't have missed for all the world the years I'd spent managing and coaching the Leafs, especially the four years we'd won the Stanley Cup. It might be the end of an era, I said, but one thing about that era – it had never been dull.

Index

Plante, Jacques, 74
Players' Association, 166-7
Prentice, Dean, 64
Price, Noel, 58
Primeau, Joe, 13, 78
Pronovost, Marcel, 68, 69, 116,
    121, 144, 156
Pulford, Bob, 58, 61, 65, 67, 81,
    90, 92, 93, 105, 106, 135, 144,
    145, 179, 186-7

Quebec Aces, 29-36, 56

Reaume, Marc, 58, 76-7
Reay, Bill, 2, 53-5, 57, 59, 60-1
Regan, Larry, 43, 65, 68, 69
Richard, Henri (Pocket Rocket),
    74, 87
Richard, Maurice (Rocket), 74,
    137
Robert, Claude, 43-4

St. Laurent, Dollard, 91
Sawchuk, Terry, 121, 134, 136,
    142, 144-6, 155
Schmidt, Milt, 27, 51, 151-3, 191-2
Selby, Brit, 137, 191
Selke, Frank, Sr., 23-4, 32, 33
Shack, Eddie, 85, 90, 106, 121-5,
    128, 134-5, 151-2, 164
Shore, Eddie, 47-50, 51, 95
'Silver Seven', 3, 9, 104, 174
Simmons, Don, 85, 86, 89, 91,
    92, 106, 136
Simons, Dorothy. See Imlach,
    Dorothy

Smythe, Conn, 1-6, 53, 54, 60,
    103, 134
Smythe, Stafford, 1-10, 53, 68,
    103, 108, 134, 153-5, 173,
    184-95, 199
Smythe Trophy, 146
Stanley, Allan, 57, 58, 67, 90,
    122, 156
Stanley Cup, 1, 2, 63, 74, 83-98,
    104, 149
Stasiuk, Vic, 84
Stemkowski, Pete, 134, 137, 142,
    157-8, 175
Stewart, Gaye, 43
Stewart, Ron, 58, 65, 93, 105, 133
Storey, Red, 67

Toronto Goodyears, 21, 22
Toronto Marlboros, 7, 14, 16, 22

Ullman, Norm, 69, 165, 183

Vezina Trophy, 85, 136
Vipond, Jim, 164-5

Walker, Gordon, 10, 198
Walton, Mike, 134, 137, 154-5,
    179-80, 183, 184-92
Watson, Phil, 33, 67
Wildey, Ed, 12-21, 53
Wilson, Johnny, 85
Worsley, Lorne (Gump), 87,
    90, 145

Young, Howie, 83-4, 130
Young, Scott, 71-3
Young Rangers, 11-18